MORE ADVANCE PRAISE FOR
Shaping the Adaptive Organization:

"In *Shaping the Adaptive Organization,* Fulmer demonstrates his acute understanding of the changing landscape and what is required for organizations to succeed. He definitely gets an 'A+' for mapping the key success factors of ambiguity, acceleration, adaptation, and alignment. Read it, and you will learn something to help you more successfully lead your organization."

—Dr. William K. Harper, President,
Arthur D. Little School of Management

"Professor Fulmer has accomplished a great feat in making a very complex subject both understandable and focused. In the current business and economic environment, *Shaping the Adaptive Organization* is a 'must-read.' "

—E. Joseph West, Chartered Financial Analyst,
Salomon Smith Barney

"Whatever your company size or industry, William Fulmer has written an easy-to-follow road map for survival and adaptation in today's rapidly changing marketplace. This will be a required reading for my key managers and board members. I hope my competitors don't adopt the concepts Fulmer has so vividly described."

—Dr. Richard W. Elder, President and CEO,
Plastic Fabricating Company, Inc.

"In the midst of major change fueled by the Internet, this is the best book to prepare a company to adapt to the challenges. It's not only theoretical, it's practical."

—Tally C. Liu, Vice President,
Finance & Advanced Technologies, Knight Ridder

Shaping the Adaptive Organization

Landscapes, Learning, and Leadership in Volatile Times

William E. Fulmer

AMACOM

American Management Association

New York • Atlanta • Boston • Chicago • Kansas City • San Francisco • Washington, D. C.
Brussels • Mexico City • Tokyo • Toronto

This publication is designed to provide accurate and authoritative information in regard to the subject matter covered. It is sold with the understanding that the publisher is not engaged in rendering legal, accounting, or other professional service. If legal advice or other expert assistance is required, the services of a competent professional person should be sought.

Library of Congress Cataloging-in-Publication Data

Fulmer, William E.
    Shaping the adaptive organization / William E. Fulmer.
       p.   cm.
    Includes bibliographical references and index.
    ISBN 0-8144-0546-0
    1. Organizational change. 2. Organizational learning. 3. Technological innovations—Management. I. Title.
    HD58.8.F85 2000
    658.4'063—dc21   99-047659

Printing number

10 9 8 7 6 5 4 3 2 1

Contents

Preface

I n 1997, *Business Week* published an article about the Internet that contained a quote from an entrepreneur that has stayed with me ever since. He observed that the Internet is "a little like taking a farm boy from the Midwest, putting him in the middle of Manhattan, and telling him to go have the time of his life."[1] I think his observation could apply to many business leaders today. Many companies, including large, well-established firms, are facing a very challenging world.

At almost every company with which I have worked in recent years, whether as a researcher, consultant, or executive education instructor, the pressures and changes their people are confronting seem to be increasing. They certainly seem far greater than when I began my career in the late 1960s. They also seem to be greater than what I witnessed in the 1970s and 1980s. Most of the businesspeople with whom I have dealt in recent years say the same thing. Unfortunately, most do not think their companies are very good at dealing with rapid change.

This book reflects my personal effort to try to understand this phenomenon. In 1997, after almost twenty-five years as a professor of business and several years of serving in various administrative positions at university-based business schools, I asked for a one-year leave of absence to try to better understand what I was seeing around me. I was especially intrigued by the numerous Internet start-ups that seemingly were springing up everywhere. It was an interest that had begun a few years earlier while serving on the board of a technology incubator and then sponsoring several students who also wanted to study these new companies. I had begun to suspect that these companies and what they represented were something unique in our history and that they were changing the way we do business more than any development in my lifetime.

After my year's leave, I decided not to return to the academic world but to continue my research and begin to try out some of the ideas and materials that I was developing with a few of my personal clients. The responses that I received plus the continued encouragement of some friends and colleagues convinced me to try to write a book about what I was seeing. This is that book.

It is not a book about technology, technology companies, or even Internet companies. It is a book about how people in business and especially business leaders and managers will need to think about their organizations with a new mindset. It is a book that attempts to help people in business organizations better respond to the new world of rapid and constant change. As such it draws lessons from technology companies since, in my experience, they are operating in the most rapidly changing and uncertain environment in today's global marketplace.

This book is aimed at the audience of business professionals and managers who are looking for ways to make better sense of the changes going on around them and who are looking for ways to help their people adapt to those changes. Hopefully it will help the reader to think about his or her organization in a different way.

I have concluded that we are in the midst of the greatest change in the way businesses operate since the Industrial Revolution. These changes will make many traditional industries look more and more like the world of high tech looks today. As the quote at the beginning of this book suggests, at one moment such a world can be very exhilarating and the next moment be very frightening.

To push the Manhattan analogy a little further, it seems increasingly obvious that the street maps of Manhattan are hopelessly out of date. Not only that, but it is as if the major streets and landmarks are constantly changing around us. Before we can begin to enjoy the best of what Manhattan has to offer, we have to begin to learn our way around the city. If the old maps no longer help and no new maps are yet available, are there some basic ideas that will help us? Perhaps if we remember such things as: Manhattan is an island that runs north and south, the Atlantic Ocean is at the southern tip, New Jersey is on the western edge, we can begin to make some progress in our visit.

This book is an effort to give the reader a few ideas that might make his or her visit to Manhattan more successful. Although it draws on some of the work being done in the field of complex systems and from the insights I have gained from people who are operating in the various technology sectors, in the final analysis this book is my interpretation of those ideas. Even so, the book has greatly benefited from specific contributions of several people whom I would like to acknowledge.

First and foremost are two great friends, Richard Elder (Dick) and Dianne Houghton. Dick is president and CEO of Plastic Fabricating Company and a former colleague. Without Dick's encouragement this book never would have been started. Dianne Houghton is the former president and COO of Jaffe Associates and a former student. She reviewed several drafts of this manuscript and made numerous suggestions that greatly improved the final product.

Nick Unger, another former student and friend, now President and CEO of Audiopoint, reviewed an early draft and offered valuable suggestions. I also want to acknowledge two friends at Arthur Andersen who reviewed some portions of the book and offered valuable suggestions: Ed Hess, a partner in the Washington, DC office and Kirsten Hirt, also in the Washington, DC office. In addition, both of my brothers made contributions to the final product: Joseph Fulmer, Manager of Interactive Distance Education at Western Kentucky University and Robert Fulmer, Brooks Professor of Management at the College of William & Mary. I also would like to thank the businesspeople who allowed me access to their companies in the course of my studies.

Finally, I would like to thank the Harvard Business School and especially Associate Dean for Executive Education, Earl Sasser, for allowing me the opportunity to return to the school, after a ten-year absence, to work with the newly created Executive Development Center. For the past year it has allowed me an up-close look at several non-U.S. companies that also are operating in the midst of rapid change. This experience has convinced me that adaptable organizations are not just needed in the United States but are needed wherever businesspeople are facing a turbulent landscape.

Part I

INTRODUCTION

The art of prophecy is difficult, especially with respect to the future.

—Mark Twain

Mark Twain was one of the clearest observers of the world around him during the latter half of the 19th century. Reading almost any of his books, it becomes clear that many of his views are just as relevant 100 years later as they were at the time they were written. In particular, his view of predicting the future is especially appropriate for the world of business and economics we face today. Our ability to predict the future in specific ways has never been very good but is going to be even more challenging in the 21st century—a time that is likely to see even more uncertain economic conditions than the 20th century.

So what can we do? At a minimum, those of us who are interested in the success of businesses must develop a better understanding of how successful organizations adapt to rapid and unpredictable changes. In this book I try to address both the issue of *how* to make better sense of the business developments going on around us and *what* managers and leaders will need to do to increase the chances for business success in this environment. My focus is on adaptability, not prediction and control.

After a brief introduction I explore the concept of adaptability first by using biology as an analogy for economic activity. I have found that for many of us, thinking about the parallels of these two very different but similar systems—biology and economics—can free us to see today's world of business in a very different way from the way most of us were trained. We begin to see the world of business as a complex adaptive system in which the future cannot be predicted and certainly cannot be controlled with a high degree of precision. Such a realization challenges the validity of many of our management concepts and practices. In the chapters that follow, I try to address the questions of *how* to make sense of what is happening around us and *what* we can do to increase the chances for success by exploring The Three Ls of Adaptability—Landscapes, Learning, and Leadership.

CHAPTER ONE

A New Race

At a time when the world land speed record was 394 miles per hour (mph), the Federation Internationale de l'Automobile (FIA), which regulated the land speed record, required that a car have four wheels and that at least 60 percent of the power be delivered through them. Craig Breedlove, a former U.S. fireman, ignored the FIA and on August 5, 1963, in a dart-shaped jet car, averaged 407.447 mph and unofficially broke the old record that had stood for more than fifteen years. In doing so, Breedlove came close to becoming airborne.

A year later Donald Campbell of England, who had been working since 1956 on a car that met FIA requirements, broke the official world record but not Breedlove's unofficial one. When the two friends met, Campbell congratulated Breedlove for not only reaching 407 mph but also forcing the FIA to introduce an unlimited class for the record. According to Campbell, it had never occurred to him to ignore the rules. He never again attempted a land speed record, and Breedlove went on to become the first man to travel 500 and then 600 mph on land.[1]

After he broke the land speed record in 1963, Breedlove described his record-breaking six seconds as "cold blooded." He said there was no time to think.

I was concentrating so hard, I could only make two 600-mph runs in a day. I was driving the car to within an accuracy of ten inches at that speed. You could see every detail passing underneath.

When his parachute opened, deceleration at 130 mph-a-second upset his middle ear and displaced the horizon. "You're certain you're driving vertically down a mine shaft. Get scared, and from then on you are in dead trouble. It's not fun." He said that there was a cycle of triumph and disaster every few hours and that in forty days on the desert, the team members came to know one another almost telepathically.[2]

He was then asked, "What if things go wrong?" His response was equally insightful:

There's always the moment of shock. Thereafter I'm busy looking at the options and making decisions. The difference between the successful high-risk athlete and the majority of us is that one will continue to choose options, no matter how rapidly they are presented or how unpleasant, while the other will freeze up and hit the brakes.[3]

Breedlove recently was asked, "What is it like to drive this fast?" His response was very revealing:

The biggest fight you have is to keep your emotions calm. The only way to do the job is to get in the car and get the belts done up and the engine started. And course clearance. And you're on your own. If ever there's a moment you're alone with God, this is it. There's a lot of noise. It's rough. . . . All business.[4]

ALL BUSINESS

Breedlove's example illustrates the mindset that I believe will be required of people who will succeed in the complex business environment of the 21st century.

Successful business leaders throughout much of the 20th century were more like Donald Campbell. They played by the rules and if they executed well, they succeeded. Much of the emphasis in the latter part of the 20th century on reengineering and best practices has been a reflection of playing by the rules. How can we do better those things that we currently are doing? Who is doing a better job of playing by today's rules?

As we enter the business world of the 21st century, I am convinced that the leaders who will succeed in a big way are those who have Breedlove's mindset. They have a clear objective in mind and are willing to challenge the old ways of doing things to achieve that objective. They often not only win the race but change the very rules of the game in doing so. Jack Welch, Andy Grove, Bill Gates, John Chambers, Jim Clark, Michael Nell, and Jeff Bezos are just a few of the names that come to mind when we think of business leaders who are challenging the rules and have become front-runners in winning their respective races.

Like Breedlove, these business leaders have confronted a very challenging world. They face a tremendous amount of noise and distractions, and have had to make lots of decisions very rapidly. But they have been able to focus on the important issues at hand and have shown a willingness to make tough decisions. They seem at times to be engaged in a delicate balancing act of pushing an organization toward the limits of what is possible but not allowing it to fly apart.

A NEW WINNER

As impressive as Craig Breedlove's racing career has been, he lost the land speed record in 1983 to Richard Noble of England. On October 4, 1983, almost six years after his first car crashed, Noble, a former industrial products salesman, covered a mile measured on the Black Rock Desert in Nevada in his jet car, *Thrust 2*, at 650 mph. When combined with an earlier round, it gave him an average of 633—a new land speed record.

Interestingly, one of his most difficult moments came after he had achieved the record. According to Noble, "We were on the back side of the mountain. What next?" Ultimately, his new challenge became to break the sound barrier on land—a goal that both he and Craig Breedlove would seek.

On October 13, 1997, Richard Noble's team achieved the goal of driving through Mach 1 on land and two days later became the first to achieve a supersonic two-way FIA record. His *Thrust SSC* (SuperSonic Car) had succeeded where Breedlove's *Spirit of America* car had failed.

In reading accounts of his six-year effort, I was struck by how little attention is focused on the man Richard Noble. All through the descriptions that I have read of his success, the emphasis was on "the team," and "the organisation." Even the headline of his November 1997 Web site update was entitled, "We Did It—And We Did It Together!"

Perhaps most significantly, he chose a younger man, Andy Green, to be the actual driver, a man he called the "immediate hero." According to Noble, "It was a painful decision but I'm not as young as I was, nor as fit, and I realized someone was going to have to go through the nightmare of raising the money."

The team also consisted of a group of experts employed by Noble. In addition, he signed up more than 180 corporations to be part of the team and developed a club (the Mach 1 Club) that approximately 5,000 people joined so that they could feel some sense of membership in the project. He also made extensive use of the Internet to communicate to that community (as well as the world beyond) about both "the good news and the bad."

Richard Nobel began the final update on his web site with the exclamation: "What a tremendous experience!" Then he went on to speak of his impressions of the supersonic runs as a "mixture of awe and downright fear." This is a very human way of speaking of an uncertain world that confronts more and more businesspeople each day. On one hand, there is the awe of the unknown—the volatile, chaotic world that may be full of opportunities. On the other hand, there is the fear of what could happen and the impulse to stay in a safer, more controlled environment. It is keeping an organization balanced between the two emotions—near the edge—that seems to me to be the true organizational and leadership challenge of the 21st century. It will require the mindset of Craig Breedlove and the organizational skills of Richard Noble.

ORGANIZATIONS ON THE EDGE

Through my consulting and executive education work in the 1990s, I became increasingly convinced that all companies face an increasingly uncertain and chaotic world. To try to make some sense of this world, I initially chose to focus my research around the sector that appeared to me to be the most volatile of all—the technology sector, broadly defined. I was able to spend a few years working with and around a variety of small technology companies. In doing so I became especially interested in how organizations succeed in a high-speed and very uncertain environment —not unlike the environment faced by Richard Noble and his team. I paid particular attention to the Internet segment, which seems to be especially chaotic and uncertain. I then began to look for larger, well-established companies that seemed to be adapting well to significant change.

This research has been a combination of fieldwork and library hours in which I have focused on two broad types of organizations—companies in the technology sector and relatively diversified companies that compete in a variety of sectors, including technology. In the former category I have examined Intel, Microsoft, Sun Microsystems, Hewlett Packard, Cisco, America Online, Intuit, SAS, AGCS, Compaq, and Dell. In addition, I have included a collection of pure Internet companies—Netscape, Yahoo!, Cybercash, Amazon, Virtual Radio, Intelligent Interaction, College Town, Auto-by-Tel, Proxicom, Virtual Vineyard, and CDnow. Among highly diversified companies, I have included 3M, General Electric, Disney, Sony, Philips, Bertelsmann, Emerson Electric, and Mercedes Benz. Although most have been exlempars of success, most have experienced an occasional setback as well, including some that are struggling now and even one internet company that has gone out of business. Nevertheless, I believe it is these companies that have the most to teach us about managing in the chaotic and uncertain world of the 21st century.

I want to stress to the reader that this book is not a book about technology. Rather, the thesis of the book is that all organizations are facing greater volatility and uncertainty, and that there is much to be learned about coping with such a world from those companies that are already operating in it. Those companies have already begun a new race—the race for the future.

CHAPTER TWO

Watching the Horizon

Too many business leaders are having trouble seeing their horizons clearly. Like Craig Breedlove, their horizon is "displaced" and they have "no time to think" as they and their organizations move at faster and faster speeds. This can easily lead to disaster—what Breedlove called "dead trouble."

During the early years of European exploration of the Americas, some native South Americans misread the threat they faced. The first time they saw the sails of the Spanish invaders on their horizon, they concluded that what they were seeing was a freak occurrence of the weather. It proved to be a disastrous interpretation for individuals and nations. To a 20th century person that may seem like a strange interpretation, but Native Americans had never seen sailing ships and had no concept of sailing. They, like all people, interpreted what they saw in light of their past experiences.

Like the Native Americans of old, too many business leaders are misinterpreting what they see on the horizon in light of their past experiences. When I ask business executives and professionals to describe their world today, the most common words that I hear are volatility, turbulence, rapid change, uncertainty, and increased risk. When asked why they are so challenged today, their responses usually cluster around such topics as global competition, new technology, government policies, and a changing and scarce workforce. I am convinced they are seeing real problems and challenges but are not seeing the full picture of what is on the horizon. They are interpreting the new developments in light of their experiences in the 1970s and 1980s.

Fortunately, as we prepare to enter the 21st century, a small but growing number of business leaders are recognizing that what they are seeing may be different from what they have seen in the past and are building what I call adaptive organizations. Yet many leaders still are having trouble comprehending and coming to grips with the significance of the sails on their horizon.

This book suggests a different way of viewing that horizon—a way that draws on the new science of complexity. It not only can help us better understand the significance of what we all face as we prepare to enter the world of the 21st century, but also better prepare our organizations to adapt to that increasingly chaotic and uncertain future.

WHAT IS HAPPENING?

Virtually all managers, executives, and business professionals I encounter think they have to deal with much more change today than even two decades ago, and that their organizations generally are not very good at it. They especially see the risks and uncertainty they face as being greater than in recent years. Apparently, my experience is not unique.

A 1993 *Business Week* survey of 400 American executives found that executives see their environment changing faster but they are not sure their companies can keep up. In fact, 79 percent described the rate of change in their companies as "rapid" or "extremely rapid" and 61 percent believed the rate of change would accelerate. Yet, only 47 percent thought their companies were very capable of coping with change.[1]

A 1995 study by Arthur Andersen and *The Economist* found that only 19.8 percent of the several thousand executives surveyed were "very satisfied" with their "management control systems" for alerting senior management to "potential business risks or performance gaps in critical areas." Other attributes of management control systems scored even worse.[2]

Hugh L. McColl, chairman of BankAmerica Corp., the megabank created by the merger of Nations Bank Corp. and BankAmerica Corp., speaks for many business leaders today when he describes the situation facing many companies and their leaders: "Change is coming at us not like a freight train but like a speeding bullet."[3]

Consider the changes that recently overtook two historically very successful U.S. technology businesses—Intel and Compaq.

Two Examples

On November 22, 1994, while on the Stanford University campus, Andrew Grove, CEO of Intel, received an urgent phone call from his office. Cable News Network (CNN) had learned of the floating-point flaw in the new Pentium Processor and was sending a crew to Intel headquarters. After a math professor had discovered the problem, comments about the flaw began appearing on the Internet. Then the trade press picked up the story and soon CNN became interested. Its piece was quickly followed by articles in most major U.S. newspapers, including the *The New York Times* and *The Wall Street Journal,* and was reported on by various television stations.

Although millions of chips had been shipped, Intel considered the flaw a minor problem since it resulted in a rounding error in division only once every nine billion times. Yet customers began calling asking for a new chip to replace their defective one. For most customers, Intel staff tried to explain the minor nature of the problem and most seemed satisfied. Then, on December 12,

1994, IBM, a company that had helped to make Intel the leading chip company, announced that it was stopping shipment of Pentium-based computers. Andy Grove described Intel's situation in 1994: "All hell broke loose again."[4]

In April 1999 Compaq's CEO, Eckhard Pfeiffer, announced that first-quarter profits would be half of what investors had been expecting. It was clear that Compaq's four-year effort to build personal computers (PCs) to order, like Dell Computer, was still not on track. For example, Dell could go from order to delivery in 3.1 days, whereas Compaq was taking at least twelve days. In addition, Compaq's integration of recently purchased Digital Equipment was bogged down by what one publication called "troubles melding the two organizations, product delays, and an incoherent strategy."[5] The stock price, which was already significantly off its fifty-two-week high of 49¼, dropped another 22 percent on April 12 to 24¹/₁₆. On April 13 Pfeiffer let it be known that Compaq would not give out any more details about its business until an April 21 meeting with analysts. Pfeiffer indicated that the recent development "doesn't throw us off" the prediction to reach $50 billion in revenues by 2000.[6] However, one analyst was describing Compaq as probably being "in the most perilous position in its history."[7]

▲ ▲ ▲ ▲ ▲

Although seemingly unrelated, I believe these two developments, at two very well-known companies—companies for many years considered two of the best managed in their respective industries—are related. Furthermore, they should be seen as early warning signals to business leaders throughout the world. The message is: "Your world has fundamentally changed."

Historically, Intel and Compaq have been among the fittest players in one of today's most fiercely competitive and volatile business arenas—technology. Their histories reveal them to have overcome frequent challenges by adapting themselves to new realities and ways of doing business. Yet, they seemed unprepared for what hit them in the mid- and late 1990s.

Intel

Intel has been described as one of the best models for the world of business as we enter the 21ˢᵗ century. According to *Time* magazine, "Intel has ceased being just a Silicon Valley wonder. It has become a weather vane for an entire digital economy, a complete ecosystem of drive manufacturers, software houses, and Web programmers whose businesses depend on escalating PC growth."[8]

Founded in 1968 by Gordon Moore and Robert Noyce, two unhappy executives from Fairchild Semiconductor, Intel focused initially on selling memory chips. It introduced the first functional 64-bit memory chip, which was followed by more advanced chips. In the early 1970s new U.S. competitors entered the market. By the early 1980s Japanese producers had also entered, often with lower prices and higher quality.

In 1981, Intel's microprocessor was designed into IBM's new PC and demand for Intel's product expanded dramatically. Although the company still thought of itself as a semiconductor memory company, it was losing money with this product. It was not until 1985 that the leadership of Intel decided to shift from being a semiconductor memory company to a microprocessor company—a "microcomputer company." It was a bet-the-company decision that succeeded. Although it took until mid-1986 to exit from the memory business, by 1992, primarily because of its success in microprocessors, Intel had become the world's largest semiconductor company. It also had become such a driving force in the computer business that it could insist that PC hardware companies include Intel's name on the outside of its computers—"Intel Inside."

In 1994, with sales in excess of $10 billion and growing at approximately 30 percent annually, Intel released its much-heralded Pentium chip only to learn that there was a flaw in the design. The problem was an internal routing glitch that caused a mathematical error. But since it would occur so infrequently that most PC users would never have a problem with it, Intel's initial response to customers was not to worry about it.

One week after learning of IBM's decision to stop shipment of Pentium-based computers, Andrew Grove decided Intel should change its response. The company would replace anyone's chip. Ultimately the company took a write-off of $475 million to replace Pentiums.

Compaq

Compaq, founded in 1982, is one of the pioneers in the PC business. It introduced the first IBM-compatible PC in 1983 and achieved first-year sales of $111 million. By 1987, it had shipped one million PCs and sales were more than $1 billion. By the early 1990s, its PCs were under attack from low-cost computer makers like AST Research and Dell Computer.

Eckhard Pfeiffer, who had joined the company in 1983, became CEO in 1991, after the ouster of Compaq's then CEO and its founder, Rod Canion. By aggressively cutting costs and prices and increasing the number of resellers, Compaq's performance began to improve. Perhaps most important, Pfeiffer pushed Compaq aggressively into the more profitable server business and in 1996 shipped its one-millionth server. Soon company performance was improving substantially and its stock price began a dramatic growth.

In 1993, Pfeiffer announced that Compaq now had a goal of becoming the world's leading PC maker by 1996. The company reached that goal by 1995 and then announced that within two years it planned to make all of its PCs to order. In February 1997, Compaq Computer became the first major PC company to begin selling a powerful computer for under $1,000. The same year it acquired Tandem Computers for $3 billion, and Pfeiffer soon was predicting that the company, with sales of $25 billion, would hit $50 billion by 2000. At the time, its profit margins were ahead of its closest competitors—IBM and Dell. In early 1998 Compaq could report that revenues were up 500 percent since 1992.

By this time Dell Computer, a top name in the direct-sales computer business, had begun to seriously consider selling computers over the Internet. It also entered the low-end server business, promising to underprice its bigger rivals. By February 1, 1998, Dell was selling $4 million worth of PCs per day, or 10 percent of total sales, over the Internet. More important, the new system allowed Dell to greatly reduce its costs. Soon Dell was selling to individuals and corporations around the world at a cost lower than its leading competitors'. Other PC makers also were becoming more aggressive. IBM, although losing money with its PCs, was improving its overall position by aggressively selling services with its PCs. Hewlett Packard (HP) was being carried in large part by its very successful printer business. Gateway had begun selling a broad range of products, including software, over the Internet and was opening its own Gateway Country Stores.

Compaq, by contrast, seemed to take its eye off the horizon. In January 1998, Compaq announced an $8.4 billion deal to buy Digital Equipment. This was supposed to allow Compaq to move into higher-margin products and become a full-service supplier of information systems to corporations. It would add 54,000 employees, including 22,000 service and support personnel, to Compaq's 33,000, and bring combined sales up to $38 billion.

Now a major business publication was calling Compaq a "powerhouse" and claiming that its "giant rivals will no more be able to crush Pfeiffer's company in servers than they have in PCs."[9] As late as February 1998, a major business publication was reporting in its cover story that the Compaq-Digital deal would "reshape the entire world of computers." The article stressed that Compaq might now be "on a par with . . . Microsoft Corp. and Intel Corp."[10]

Yet, Compaq was in trouble. It had forecasted demand poorly and shipped distributors too many PCs. When resellers dumped them at low prices, Compaq's operating profits disappeared since it protects resellers from heavy losses. Dell had no such problem since it builds to order.

Soon it was not just PCs that were experiencing a price war but servers too. In early February 1998, IBM had cut prices on high-end servers by as much as 29 percent. This was followed by a move by Dell on the low-end server market. According to a Dell executive, "We saw that they [Compaq] had become very dependent on those profits and were subsidizing other businesses with [them]. We purposely became very aggressive in our pricing."[11] By some estimates, PC-server revenue dropped 22 percent from a year earlier and gross margins were down from 30 percent to 24 percent.[12]

The Rest of the Story

By the late 1990s Intel had recovered from its earlier challenges, and by the time I began writing this book, was doing well. Yet, it soon was facing new threats. Compaq, a major Intel customer, had begun using a Pentium-compatible chip from an Intel rival for its low-priced computers. This segment was estimated to account for 25 percent of U.S. retail PC sales in 1997, up from 7 percent in 1996. For Intel to respond effectively might require a significant change in the company's long-standing practice of introducing more advanced and high-priced chips every few years. More powerful chips were already in the pipeline, but the company had to respond to what it once called Segment Zero, meaning zero profits. In addition, by early 1998 Intel was lagging behind others in the market for non-PC devices. According to *The Wall Street Journal*, Intel was now an "underdog," and according to an executive with a potential customer, "Intel is running dead last."[13] Even Grove admitted his company was "slow to react to the sub-$1000 PC," attributing the lateness to "internal disagreements over the size of the market."[14] In 1999, for the first time, more PCs sold in retail stores that were powered by Advanced Micro Device Processors than by Intel chips. Intel was also being challenged by the Internet. According to *Forbes*, Intel was standing at an "inflection point of technology" since the driver of its spectacular growth, the PC industry, was losing momentum to the Internet.[15]

Compaq was in even more trouble. *Fortune* reported that in early April 1998, Eckhard Pfeiffer, Compaq's CEO, was honored at a University of Houston gala to celebrate the endowment of a new chair in his name. A portrait of Pfeiffer was auctioned off and guests received MCI thirty-minute calling cards decorated with his photo. The chair of the event hailed him as "one of the world's boldest thinkers." This was not surprising since during Pfeiffer's approximately seven-and-one-half-year tenure the company's stock price had gone up 1,072 percent versus 243 percent for the S&P 500.[16] (Dell stock had increased 13,375 percent.)[17] Yet a week later, Compaq's board of directors met without Pfeiffer and unanimously voted him out. Within days, the company's CFO had resigned, and soon several other senior executives had left the company.

Although Pfeiffer attributed Compaq's problems to "a very targeted action"[18] by IBM and claimed that he was a "scapegoat for Wall Street,"[19] others thought the problem was a crisis at Compaq. According to a recent business publication, "the colossus he built does now seem unable to move nimbly enough to thrive in the fast-changing computer industry."[20] Apparently Compaq's board of directors agreed. According to one of the directors, "We are absolutely committed to speeding up the decision-making process in the company."[21] Although it is too early to say whether Compaq can weather its current storm, the company apparently was unable to recruit a strong outside executive to be CEO and chose to promote an internal candidate. This came after being run for several months by a venture capitalist who funded the company in its startup years and serves as its chairman of the board. The company also announced plans in July 1999 to cut between 6,000 and 8,000 jobs as part of a $2 billion cost-reduction effort.

A CHAOTIC NEW WORLD

If crises of this magnitude can happen to such successful companies as Intel and Compaq, they can happen to any company. Dramatic changes are inevitable in today's economic environment and I believe they will come faster and more often. Change is the key feature of the current global economic system.

Both Intel and Compaq were among the very best—in fact it could be argued that they were *the* best—at what they did just before a major crisis hit them in the 1990s. They were both large, successful companies with very strong global brand names and a strong financial base. Yet neither foresaw what was about to happen to them. Almost overnight, they seemed to be fighting for their survival in industries that they once had seemingly controlled or at least been one of the dominate players in.

It is easy to say that the leaders of these companies, like many others, were blinded by past successes and suffered from what some would call arrogance. At Intel, e.g., Grove later would observe, "For twenty-six years, every day that we did business, *we* decided what was good and what wasn't when it came to our own products. *We* set our own quality levels and our own specifications, and shipped when *we* decided a product met our own criteria."[22] As of April 20, 1999, Compaq's senior leadership was still claiming "we dominate the consumer-PC business."[23]

No doubt arrogance or at least overconfidence was a factor in both companies. The more interesting question, however, is not, What caused them to be arrogant or overconfident and miss the new threats? but, What was the threat that they missed?

It is too simple to say that Intel misjudged its customers' reaction to a minor design problem or that Compaq's leadership was too slow. I think Intel and Compaq were early examples of big companies facing a new reality. The new reality is a world of increasing complexity, uncertainty, and risk. A significant threshold was crossed in the 1990s, brought on in great part by the digital revolution and the relative free flow of large amounts of capital and information. New information and capital can now move at the speed of light.

WHY CAN'T WE SEE THE NEW REALITY MORE CLEARLY?

As today's business leaders struggle to better understand the world around them, their frustration and stress levels seem very high. Their challenge is made more 'difficult by several human tendencies. There are at least four related reasons for the growing frustration and confusion about what they are seeing on the horizon: a jungle of concepts, a tendency to focus on symptoms, a tendency to see the symptoms in isolation, and the human quality of screening information.

A Jungle of Concepts

In the early 1960s, a well-known business academic of the time referred to the field of management as a "semantics jungle."[24] He was referring to how confusing the growing number of terms and concepts in the field of management had become. As we enter the 21st century, the jungle has spread dramatically and seems in danger of choking out a clear view of the world in which we operate. More and more of us seem to be struggling to make out what it is we are seeing on the horizon.

Over the past few decades, there have been numerous efforts to help managers and executives make sense of the world in which they operate and especially to respond more effectively to new competitive challenges. The explosive growth in management consulting and in publishing business books are just two indicators of this development. For example, in fiscal 1997 the top fifty consulting firms increased their total revenue base from the prior year by 22 percent and the entire sector was expected to increase from $73 billion in 1997 to $120 billion by 2000.[25]

Just in the area of strategy alone, since the 1960s academics and consultants have added numerous new tools, concepts, frameworks, and techniques to the strategy tool box to try to help managers and executives better cope with their situation—management by objectives, the five forces, generic strategies, experience curves, portfolio matrixes, the 7-S model, core skills, core competencies, core capabilities, game theory, strategic intent, etc. Numerous books and articles have been published on these topics.

We saw the wide-scale adoption of quality concepts in the 1980s, reengineering in the early 1990s, and in the mid-1990s a growing movement to emphasize revenue growth and innovation. There also has been widespread adoption of such practices as fewer levels of management, the use of teams, and a move away from traditional strategic planning. All of these efforts represent good faith efforts to help companies operate more effectively in what is perceived as an increasingly challenging environment.

In spite of these new concepts and tools, and more executives with graduate degrees in business, executives seem more challenged and frustrated than ever before. They simply cannot keep up with the expanding number of tools and concepts being introduced in the business literature. As companies race to embrace the newest concepts, employees within the organization often see them as programs of the month.

Seeing Symptoms

Once a problem starts to register with business practitioners, in too many cases people in leadership positions attack symptoms with simple "solutions" rather than trying to get at the root or underlying problem.

One of my earliest business experiences illustrated this tendency for me. At a food-processing plant I was visiting as part of a research program in the 1970s, there seemed to be a serious capacity problem at one stage of the process. Just before approving a major capital investment to expand that stage of the process, a corporate executive who was visiting the plant had the foresight to ask the first-line supervisor responsible for that work area what he thought about the planned investment. His response was "It'll probably work but all I really need is another forklift." Too many people had seen the symptom—lack of production capacity—without understanding the real problem—too few forklifts.

We often see this tendency reflected in the behaviors of politicians and other public officials. If the problem is inflation we attack it with wage and price controls. If the problem is deficit spending we propose a balanced budget amendment. If the problem is violence in the schools we focus on prayer in schools.

One of my favorite examples comes from Hong Kong. In early 1998, Hong Kong's tourist association was concerned about a dramatic drop-off in tourism. This was after Asian countries had begun experiencing serious economic problems. In addition, Hong Kong had experienced the outbreak of avian flu that forced the killing of local poultry. There also was a scare that some hospital patients had been injected with a fluid that might have been contaminated with the human variant of mad cow disease, and there had been an official warning of the risks of poison from eating certain coral reef fish. According to the Hong Kong tourist association chief, "Our research tells us a strong impediment to visitor growth is the perception that we sometimes treat visitors rudely, cheat them and are unfriendly and unhelpful."[26] She unveiled a new campaign to persuade locals to be more courteous. No doubt the lack of courteous behavior toward visitors, perhaps brought on in part by multiple crisis, was a factor in declining tourism but friendlier hotel clerks were unlikely to offset health and economic concerns by visitors and service employees.

Before introducing a new concept that may very well address a specific problem, it is important for corporate leaders to try to understand why there is this continual need for new concepts and tools. What is going on? Is it just the work of consultants and academics trying to justify their jobs or is there something more fundamental at work?

As I discuss in the following chapters, there is something very fundamental at work here. It is just beginning to be recognized by a few observers, but still is widely ignored by most business leaders and business academics.

Seeing Things in Isolation

Unfortunately, in the rush to introduce and embrace new concepts and practices that address new problems, we have too rarely stepped back to think about the bigger picture. Consequently, too many of us fail to see the big picture and instead focus our energies on only a part of the problem. We frequently see symptoms or problems in isolation.

The tendency is to develop a program for dealing with a specific problem—total quality management to improve product quality, information technology to eliminate jobs, or a cost-reduction program to lower prices. Government officials and politicians often develop legislation and/or regulations for dealing with pollution or job safety without looking at the broader implications. Again, it is not always bad that these programs are developed, and in many cases they dramatically improve the performance of the company or the community for a time, but they often run the risk of unintended consequences. In many cases they attack a problem in isolation without understanding that it is connected to other problems and concerns.

In business we often see the phenomenon of attacking a problem in isolation—even among well-run companies. For example, in the mid-1980s executives at Emerson Electric, after learning from customers that competitors from so-called developing countries were producing competing products that were just as good and considerably cheaper than those produced by Emerson, initially doubted the truthfulness of the reports. They did, however, have the wisdom to check out the reports by visiting places like Brazil and Korea and found the reports to be true. Then they developed an aggressive strategy of being the low-cost producer. According to Charles Knight, CEO of Emerson, they then heard complaints that Emerson was just cheapening its products. It was then that the company began emphasizing best cost, recognizing that it was not enough to develop a program to drive cost down. Customers wanted both high quality and low cost. They wanted value.

Likewise, many companies in the midst of the quality movement also found out that just by improving product quality they did not necessarily improve their overall financial performance since consumers wanted quality, low prices, and innovation. For example, Florida Power and Light became the first non-Japanese company to win Japan's prestigious Deming award for quality only to see its performance in the marketplace decline shortly thereafter. Motorola was one of the first companies to win the U.S. Baldridge award for quality. Yet, by the mid-1990s it had become so locked into improving its analog technology that it was very late responding to customer demands for digital cellular phones.

In the 1970s, American Cyanamid found itself caught by conflicting government regulations. In an effort to protect the lives of unborn children of pregnant employees and satisfy what it thought the Occupational Safety and Health Administration wanted, it restricted the jobs open to women employees and came into conflict with the Equal Employment Opportunity Commission over job discrimination. It "solved" one problem but created another.

Hewlett Packard provides another example of a successful company that attacked one problem without recognizing its relationship to other issues. In the late 1990s, in an effort to make quotas on PCs, it offered discounts of up to 50 percent to keep business from competitors such as Compaq. Then its financial performance deteriorated. According to an HP executive, "We chased deals we shouldn't have chased. You get so into the battle that you can lose perspective."[27]

The Importance and Dangers of Screening Information

Seeing only a part of the picture is not necessarily bad. For us to function, especially in leadership and managerial roles where we are bombarded with information, we have to screen out information and focus on those things we think are most important. One of the reasons successful people are successful is that they generally have learned to do a better job than their peers of screening out those things that are less important and focusing on those things that are more important. The danger, however, is that if we are confronting an increasingly changing world, chances are that we will eventually screen out the wrong things—what we thought was unimportant may become very important very quickly.

We see it all the time in successful businesses—their leaders miss the next big development in their industry and someone from out of nowhere emerges to gain significant market share or even redefine that industry. The watch industry is a classic example of where this pattern has been repeated again and again. Although the Swiss developed the tuning fork and quartz technology, they did not exploit the potential of these technologies. They remained focused on their traditional concept of a watch. It remained for companies like Bulova to exploit the tuning fork and Seiko to exploit quartz and Timex to change the very nature of a watch, from a piece of jewelry owned by a relatively few high-income individuals to a utilitarian timepiece for the masses. It also remained for an outside consultant to see the opportunities for the Swiss in an inexpensive, fashion timepiece that became Swatch.

This phenomenon is not limited to watches. In the computer industry, it was neither Xerox nor IBM that recognized the potential of PCs but two young men in a garage. With motorcycles it was not the established European and U.S. firms that recognized the potential for a small fun bike or for off-road bikes, but relatively unknown Japanese firms. It wasn't CBS, ABC, or NBC that recognized the market for twenty-four-hour television news but a small cable company—CNN. For the most part, the driving forces behind the Internet have not been well-established players in the computer or telecommunications businesses but startups like Netscape, Amazon, America Online, and Yahoo!

Too often the price paid by established companies is not just lost market share but company survival. Jim Utterback, in his study of innovation, observed:

> A pattern emphasized in the cases in this study is the degree to which powerful competitors not only resist innovative threats, but actually resist all efforts to understand them, preferring to further entrench their positions in the older products. This results in the surge of productivity and performance that may take the old technology to unheard-of heights. But in most cases this is a sign of impending death.[28]

I am convinced that as we enter the 21st century, too many companies and their leaders are still pushing productivity and neglecting the new developments that will shape their world.

THE RESULT CAN BE A FEAR OF TAKING ACTION

The Bible tells of twelve spies of the Children of Israel who spent forty days developing an understanding of their future foes in Canaan. In their final report to the people, they acknowledged that the Promised Land was indeed a magnificent place "flowing with milk and honey." On the negative side, they also reported that the people living there were "powerful, and their cities are fortified and very large" and that there were giants there. Ten of the spies concluded, "They would crush us." Two, however, responded differently—"Let us go up at once and possess it for we are well able to conquer it." The masses supported the do-nothing option with some even preferring to return to the past—Egypt—where they had been slaves. Of course, they also considered killing the two action-oriented spies. The result was forty years of wandering in the wilderness before a new generation of leaders would lead the people into the Promised Land.

I have found that even when executives see the sails on the

horizon and begin to recognize that the situation is serious, like the majority of the spies, there is reluctance, if not fear, to take action. Consider the comments of three of the most successful and decisive executives in the world:

▲ Jack Welch, CEO of General Electric: "I've made my share of mistakes—plenty of them—but my biggest mistake by far was not moving faster." He added, "Everything should have been done in half the time." "I was too cautious and too timid. I wanted too many constituencies on board."[29]
▲ Chuck Knight, CEO of Emerson: "We . . . believe that companies fail primarily for nonanalytical reasons: Management knows what to do but, for some reason, doesn't do it."[30]
▲ Andy Grove, CEO of Intel: ". . . [I]n times of change, managers almost always know which direction they should go in, but usually act too late and do too little."[31]

Donald Valentine, founder of Sequoia Capital, a successful Silicon Valley venture capital firm, explains why this situation is all too common:

> Every company, eventually, accumulates legacy customers and applications. They are run by silver-haired guys who are very protective of the past. They are historically oriented. They just do not believe in the abandonment of the past. For a bunch of reasons, they are locked into it. Most recognize what's going on. They just can't decide what to do about it. Remember how late it was when Microsoft discovered the Internet? 1995. They must have been on a trip to Mars. When Gates finally discovered the Internet, he did something about it. But his case is extremely rare.[32]

Like the spies of old, too many corporate leaders, once they see the situation, place too much emphasis on the risks inherent in the new situation rather than the potential rewards to be found in the promised land. Increasingly I hear younger leaders, such as Jeff Bezos of Amazon, speak of being driven by regret minimization rather than risk minimization.

In today's world, no organization can wait for a generation or two in hopes that new leaders will emerge who can help their people embrace the future. The time frame for decisions is being dramatically reduced.

No Easy Answers

In recent years there has been a growing sense that the world of business is becoming more complex, with higher and higher risks to the people and organizations that inhabit that world. Global competition, the digital revolution, and other forces have challenged the skills and abilities of business executives in ways we could not have imagined a few years back.

Many academics, authors, and consultants have tried to help executives make some sense of these changes and offered tools, concepts, and programs to improve their chances of succeeding in this increasingly chaotic environment. Many have helped but none have given us the silver bullet. There always seem to be new problems, opportunities, challenges, and risks to be encountered.

This is neither a temporary nor a new phenomenon but a fundamental characteristic of the market economy. In recent years, the pace of change has increased. A few academics are beginning to recognize this and acknowledge that the life of a new concept or program is shrinking. For example, Richard A. D'Aveni, of Dartmouth College, in his book *Hypercompetition,* stresses that markets everywhere in the world are heating up. By hypercompetition he means an environment of intense change where "advantages are rapidly created and eroded." He believes a "stable equilibria" is

> impossible because constantly shifting technology, global competitors, and strategic positioning will result

in frequent or almost constant disequilibrium in which
new entrants and established competitors disrupt the
balance of power and gain temporary superiority.[33]

D'Aveni argues that this new environment is not just limited
to high-tech industries but is to be found in virtually every industry. In other words, there are no sustainable competitive advantages in a hypercompetitive marketplace.

I think he is right. However, as I discuss in this book, I think
that the rate of change and the level of risks and rewards will
only increase over time. Consequently, there never will be a silver
bullet, only, hopefully, a better understanding of the rapidly
changing horizon and organizations that can adapt.

CONCLUSION

To better understand this environment, I will try to challenge the
reader to think differently about his or her world. The first step in
preparing to embrace the new world is to see the world as it really
is. For many of us this is aided if we can see it from a different—
broader—perspective. Ed McVaney, CEO of J. D. Edwards, an enterprise software company, attributes some of his success to the
fact that he is dyslexic. "Dyslexics see the world as a spatial puz-
zle. I think that helped me to better see the big picture."[34] We
need to find different ways of looking at the picture if we are to
understand the ships on the horizon.

A more conventional solution is to do what Emerson management did—begin to travel outside of our normal routes to see
what others are doing. Some executives attend seminars with executives from other companies to gain different perspectives. Others read extensively outside of their business focus. Whatever the
approach, the objective should be the same—to see the world in
as realistic a light as possible. Once we have that fuller picture in
mind the key is to act decisively.

How can the leaders of today's organizations more quickly

understand and begin to shape their organizations for the kind of changes that are on the horizon? The remainder of this book offers some guidance.

What follows in Part Two is a discussion of how some of us may be able to better understand what is happening around us. It explores a different framework for thinking about business. Drawing from the science of biology, it proposes the concept of a fitness landscape. At a minimum, this new metaphor for today's world of business could be very helpful—especially if it could challenge all executives and leaders to think about their world in a different but intellectually honest way.

Parts Three and Four examine the two key elements of business success in the 21st century that seem to follow from adopting the landscape perspective—learning and leadership (Figure 2-1). I call these three concepts the foundations of an adaptive organization.

Figure 2-1 Foundations of an Adaptive Organization

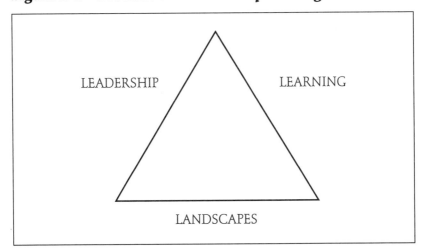

Part II

LANDSCAPES: UNDERSTANDING THE NEED TO ADAPT

No land with an unvarying climate can be very beautiful. . . . . Change is the handmaiden Nature requires to do her miracles with.

—Mark Twain

As Mark Twain understood, change is essential if life is to improve. The same can be said for the world of business. But when things are changing so much, we need new ways of making sense of and responding to the developments confronting us—if we are to make good decisions. Only then can the business equivalent of miracles occur.

In Chapter Three I describe a different world picture that I hope puts some of the developments around us in perspective. Chapter Four explores some fundamental conclusions that I have drawn from this new perspective—each of which has significant implications for the way we create and lead organizations. In the final chapter of this section, I present a framework for making sense of the competitive landscape on which companies operate.

CHAPTER THREE

Making Sense of a Complex World

Sigmund Freud observed, "Analogies prove nothing . . . but they can make one feel more at home."[1] Increasingly, writers about business are introducing new analogies to try to help executives understand various business issues. Perhaps the oldest business analogy is warfare. In fact, the very word "strategy" is taken from a Greek word referring to the role of the general.

Over the past decade a number of business writers have used the worlds of sports and entertainment, especially music, as analogies. Most recently the new analogies are coming from the world of science—chaos theory, complexity, quantum physics, and biology. I believe science can be especially useful in helping business leaders develop a better appreciation for what is happening around them. After all, science is, in Albert Einstein's words, merely a "refinement of everyday thinking."[2]

From my experience, this refinement seems more easily grasped by most nonscientists when it is focused on the world of biological science as opposed to physics. In fact, there seems to be a growing recognition among businesspeople that the worlds of biology and business have some interesting parallels. It is not surprising that biology and ecosystems in particular have drawn recent attention; witness the recent publication of such books as *The Death of Competition* and *The Living Company*.

Although this book is about business, I think it is important to provide a brief overview of some aspects of biological life as an analogy to economic life. This should give the reader a somewhat different way of thinking about the world of business.

A BRIEF OVERVIEW OF BIOLOGY

Author's note: The next few pages are my interpretation of some of the writings of biologist Stuart Kauffman, a member of the Santa Fe Institute and a MacAuthur Fellowship recipient, and Murray Gell-Mann, a theoretical physicist at California Institute of Technology, Nobel laureate, and also a member of the Santa Fe Institute. Because I have tried to distill some of their ideas into a few pages, I hope I have not done their works an injustice. Much of this section is based on Stuart Kauffman, *At Home in the Universe,* New York: Oxford University Press, 1995. Anyone wishing to know more about these ideas should also read Stuart A. Kauffman, *The Origins of Order: Self Organization and Selection in Evolution,* New York: Oxford University Press, 1993; and Murray Gell-Mann, *The Quark and the Jaguar,* New York: W. H. Freeman & Co., 1994.

Scientists are familiar with two major forms by which *order* arises: (1) a low-energy equilibrium system and (2) a nonequilibrium ordered system. The former can be visualized as a ball in a bowl that rolls to the bottom and stops, thereby minimizing its potential energy since no further energy is needed to maintain order. The latter, such as a whirlpool in a bathtub, is called a dissipative structure, in that the system is sustained by the persistent dissipation of matter and energy. A nonequilibrium system requires a constant source of mass or energy to sustain the order, such as the water and the pull of gravity of the whirlpool.

Scientists now view biological life as a nonequilibrium ordered system; an emergent phenomenon that arises as the molecular diversity of a prelife chemical system increases beyond a threshold of complexity. In other words, at some point, although scientists do not know how, gases, molecules, etc.—all the chemical components from which life somehow organized itself—produced a life form, and dead chemistry became living biology.

By emergent these scientists mean that it has no singular cause, like a life force, but rather is an overall trait of the collective system. A good analogy can be found with water. When you get a collection of water molecules together, you have something that has the property of being wet. Any single molecule itself, however, is not even damp. Likewise, no single molecule that we have discovered is alive. It takes teamwork from a collection of molecules to produce life.[3]

The current view of most biologists is that life is structural in nature and structures have properties. If enough of these properties are in place, there is life. This means that when the ingredients of life, such as carbon, hydrogen, and oxygen, are coordinated in an organized system, there is life. Thus, a description of biological life is a description of a certain kind of highly organized chemistry.

In biological life systems, the rate at which chemical reactions occur depends on how rapidly the reaction partners collide with one another. Catalysts can be used to speed up reactions, and controlling interactions to a single-dimensional, thin surface, as opposed to three-dimensional, can do the same.

What Does This Have to Do with Business?

It is useful to view the economic world today as an ordered system. A business organization is also an organized, ordered system. They clearly are not random occurrences.

A traditional view of economics often seemed to suggest that the economic system is a low-energy equilibrium system. If we pull the right levers we could have a system in equilibrium and optimize the benefits to society. Most of the economics courses I took in the mid-1960s stressed the objective of reaching equilibrium and hopefully staying there. It is not surprising that one of my instructors would claim, "With what we know about economics today we may never have another recession." It was as if the U.S. economy had found equilibrium, and with occasional fine tuning, it was believed we could stay there.

In those economics courses we never discussed, e.g., Austrian economist Joseph Schumpeter's idea of creative destruction. Writing in the first half of the 20th century, Schumpeter argued that technological innovation was a driver of long industry cycles. Consequently, an economy was constantly being disturbed and rarely if ever was in equilibrium.

I find it much more realistic to view the market economy we are a part of today, especially the global economy, as a nonequilibrium system—one sustained by the dissipation of business equivalents of mass and energy. It is an emergent phenomenon that arises as human skill or knowledge diversity within a social system increases beyond a threshold of complexity—a collective property of systems of interacting human skills and abilities with a rapid exchange of information and capital.

Just as biological life is a natural property of a complex chemical system, economic and organizational life can be thought of as being natural properties of a complex information- and capital-intensive social system. In other words, the economy (and a business) is an information- and capital-intensive social system that can never be in equilibrium.

In the economy and in business organizations, catalysts also speed up interactions. Here the interactions are between individuals (organisms), each with different skills/abilities (genes), and organizations (species). Leadership can play the role of a catalyst, as can various organizational processes that stimulate and facilitate the rapid exchange of information and capital. In addition, leaner organizations can facilitate reactions, i.e., create the equivalent of a thinner surface on which the interactions take place.

Evolution as a Key to Understanding Biological Life

The National Aeronautics and Space Administration (NASA) adds a key characteristic to the idea of life as organized chemistry by defining life as "a self-sustaining chemical system capable of undergoing Darwinian evolution."[4]

According to *The New York Public Library's Science Desk Reference*, "Evolution is usually defined either as the adaptation of species to their surrounding environment(s) over time or as the theory that life on Earth gradually developed from simple to more complex organisms."[5] It goes on to observe that

> over time, living organisms have adapted to physical and chemical processes in their environment to increase their potential for survival and reproduction. As certain traits are passed on from parent to offspring, some organisms prove to be ill-adapted to the environment and disappear, while others increase in number.[6]

Thus, the fitter the population the more the population grows.

In general, evolution is a two-part process: mutation and natural selection. It begins with random genetic change (mutation) in an offspring. Then, as proposed by Charles Darwin in his *On the Origin of Species*, the process of natural selection takes over. In natural selection the unfit organisms are eliminated as a result of selective pressures in the environment.

Evolution occurs whenever there is reproduction and competition for finite resources. A reproducing system might intend to produce exact copies of itself but no copying process works perfectly. Usually mistakes will impair the copy's ability to reproduce successfully. The mutant will probably perish, or at least its genes will become less numerous than those of its parent. Sometimes, however, the mutant will be superior, in which case its genes may be more successful than its parent's and as a result become more common. Thus, selection is a filter that determines by competition which individuals within a population survive to reproduce. In other words, reproduction permits innovation through the alteration of genetic traits and thereby provides a route for the evolution of increasingly successful individuals.[7]

Biological evolution does not usually proceed at a uniform rate. Instead, it often exhibits the phenomenon of punctuated equilibrium, in which species stay mostly unchanged for long periods of time and then undergo comparatively rapid change over a brief period. These changes can come from a variety of sources, including the external environment and from internal developments, all of which ultimately are reflected in a mutation. There are, in Murray Gell-Mann's words, "breakthrough events" that open up new realms of possibilities and the "opening of a critical gateway results in an explosion of ecological niches."[8]

Evolution is a process that continues every day, although its results are not always apparent. A classic example of evolution within a short span of time involves the Biston betularia moth of England. Before the Industrial Revolution in the 1700s, the moth was mottled with white and brown and easily blended in with the lichen found on trees. As coal came into widespread use in houses and factories, trees were covered with dark gray soot, making the light-colored moth easy prey for birds. By about 1860, dark gray Biston betularia moths were appearing in increasing numbers as the result of natural selection. These better-camouflaged individuals were no longer easy prey for the birds. By the early 1900s the dark moths outnumbered the mottled moths. Now England's air is less sooty and since the 1950s the mottled moths have been making a comeback.[9]

Some scientists now think that natural selection works on many levels—even at the level of DNA or a single gene.[10] Thus, mutation and natural selection may be the key processes of evolution at all levels of biological life.

EVOLUTION IN AN ECONOMIC CONTEXT

Anyone who has read Fernand Braudel's three-volume study of civilization and capitalism from the 15th to the 18th century cannot help but be impressed by the parallels between biological evolution and the evolution of capitalism. The traditional view has been that the development of preindustrial Europe consisted of gradual progress toward "the rational world of the market, the firm, and capitalist investment, until the coming of the Industrial Revolution. . . ." Braudel's extensive research suggests that the process is much more complicated than the traditional view and that it is possible to "trace a pattern of evolution, or rather several kinds of evolution" to explain the "material civilization" that emerged.[11]

Braudel even uses the word adaptation in much the same way that biologists do. For example, he emphasizes the quality that seems to be an essential feature of the general history of capitalism: "its unlimited flexibility, its capacity for change and *adaptation*." (The italics are his.) He adds, "The essential characteristic of capitalism was its capacity to slip at a moment's notice from one form or sector to another, in times of crisis or of pronounced decline in profit rates."[12]

Charles Darwin wrote of "different places in the economy of nature."[13] These places give us, in MacAuthur award recipient Stuart Kauffman's words, a world where "each organism, the fitter and the less fit, would wedge itself into the filled nooks and crannies of the tangled bank of life, struggling against all others to jam itself onto the wedge-filled surface of possibilities."[14]

It is not too hard to think of individuals (organisms) and organizations (species) "wedging" themselves into the nooks and crannies of our economic system—what we call niches. Individuals and companies are looking for spaces where they can add value to the overall system and consequently be rewarded—at least allowed to live and hopefully prosper. Potential competitors are always looking for ways to enter the system, for other niches to fill.

As in biological life, all economic systems eat; i.e., they take in matter and energy to grow and reproduce. Energy and matter are consumed to produce goods and services that hopefully are valued by other organisms and species.

Organizations and the people within them produce goods and services that other people and organizations need or want for their own advancement. If other members of the system do not value the outputs, the organizations and people will not survive in the long run. Another organization (or person) likely will emerge that is more beneficial to the entire system. Its output, relative to its consumption of matter and energy, will be more beneficial to the system than that of the less efficient, less effective organisms or species.

Most individuals look for niches within an organization where they can trade their contributions (skills, knowledge, labor, etc.) for resources they value (money, power, recognition, prestige, etc.). According to Kauffman, "We swap our stuff." A unique individual we call an entrepreneur, however, recognizes a niche or an unmet need, i.e., a space, to fill among the other organizations.

Entrepreneurs see opportunities to add value to the system with a product or service. But unlike individuals who become part of an existing organization, they must both recognize a niche and create a new organization (a new species) to produce the product or service.

Consider Sun Microsystems and Netscape. They were founded by very capable individuals who recognized the benefit of forming organizations that could exploit niches where they could survive and, at least for a while, prosper. Sun's founders recognized the importance of networking before any other major computer maker and were able to create an organization that has allowed it to become, in the words of one observer, "a thought leader for the whole [computer] industry."[16] Although Netscape's founders were not the first to recognize the power of Web browsers, they were the first to create an organization that could efficiently and effectively exploit the opportunity.

Evolution and the Environment

There are other factors that contribute to the evolutionary effort. External environments can change, thereby creating new niches and destroying old ones. Actions by individuals and organizations can create opportunities for new individuals and organizations to enter the "tangled bank" of economic life. We clearly see such a process at work with new technologies. Again, quoting from Braudel,

. . . as long as society was content with its material surroundings and felt at ease, there was no economic motive for change. Inventors' blueprints . . . stayed in their drawers. It was only when things went wrong, when society came up against the ceiling of the possible that people turned of necessity to technology, and interest was aroused for the thousand potential inventions, out of which one would be recognized as the best, the one that would break through the obstacle and open the door to a different future. For there are always hundreds of possible innovations lying dormant; sooner or later, it becomes a matter of urgency to call one of them to life.[17]

He adds, technology "changes the world." To use Gell-Mann's words, technologies are the equivalent biological "breakthrough events" of economic life. These words call to mind Schumpeter's "creative destruction."

One only has to look at the Internet to get a sense of evolution in today's business environment. For example, in 1994, three million people, most in the United States, used the Internet. In 1998, one hundred million people across the world were using it and some experts were predicting that one billion people would be connected by 2005.

First, the browsers such as Netscape arose. Then in 1994, two Stanford University graduate students, David Filo and Jerry Yang, were able to survey the Web using primitive software tools. Their product, "David and Jerry's Guide to the Web," was available, free, to anyone with access to the Internet. By July 1994, the service was renamed Yahoo! and was incorporated in April 1995.

After search engines, push products, led by PointCast in 1996, were expected to bring another fundamental way of communicating to the Internet. Yet by 1997, leading players in the Internet world were already predicting that PointCast was "going to get squeezed completely out of existence."[18] In 1998 the hot area on the Internet was portals. It did not surprise me when an Internet

CEO observed, "This industry is like Darwinism on steroids. You either evolve or get eliminated."[19]

Even within organizations we see strong evidence of an evolutionary process at work as they seek to lead or at the very least evolve with the market environment. In 1996 Amazon's CEO described his company as "still feeling our way around." He added, "Amazon.com is evolving."[20] As browsers became a commodity, Netscape had to move upstream to more complex software, such as programs to run servers and Intranets. In 1997 they pursued an opportunity in push technology with a product called Netcaster, but it failed. The company also tried to enter the groupware business by acquiring Collabra Software, but it too failed. In 1998, Netscape's CEO James Barksdale observed that "Netscape intends to survive and prosper by mutating into a company that doesn't compete directly with Microsoft."[21] Yet, by late 1998 the company was laying off employees and had decided to become part of a larger—and perhaps more viable—organization: America Online (AOL). According to Netscape cofounder and later AOL's chief technology officer, "Netscape the company is gone. The DNA survives in a mutated form."[22] James Condom of CyberCash states the challenge facing all Internet companies very well: "If you don't adapt rapidly in this environment, you will not survive."[23]

Improving the Chances for Successful Evolution

Some large organizations try to create an internal environment that encourages successful evolution. For example, a key element in Seiko's early success in the watch industry was the creation of two divisions with separate production, design, and research facilities. In a sense, they competed with each other to sell to the parent company. The survivor was thought to then be ready to compete more successfully in an external market.

In a business like GE Capital, there also are efforts to test the fitness of a species before it is let loose on the external world. According to *Fortune,*

If an idea has potential to generate $50 million in profits within five years, then funding becomes a possibility, and the "tight" phase begins. [Personnel in top management] . . . unleash a merciless interrogation about expected margins, potential customers, regulatory issues, prospects for competitive advantage. Most ideas die under the barrage. But the few that survive have access to Capital's deep pockets and the vast resources of GE.[24]

The idea may still be tested in a small way outside of General Electric (GE) and then, if it is successful, the company becomes aggressive in supporting the business by making acquisitions as well as supporting internal growth.

As well, organizations may evolve not through internal means or opportunities, but by such external means as acquiring other organizations that are in the process of fitting into higher evolutionary niches. These acquisitions then serve to pull the organization up along the evolutionary space to a higher position.

But, whether by internal or external means, an organization's success and survival require it to evolve up this space of niches, climbing to performance peaks—all of which lead us to the idea of business landscapes.

USING LANDSCAPES TO UNDERSTAND EVOLUTION IN BIOLOGY

By the 1940s, biologists had invented the image of an "adaptive landscape," a multidimensional space with hills and valleys, whose peaks represent the spaces filled by highly fit forms. In this context *evolution is the struggle of populations of organisms driven by mutation, recombination, and selection, to climb toward those high peaks.*

Things capable of evolving all live and evolve on landscapes that themselves have a special property: They allow evolution to work. And some landscapes are more nurturing of evolution than others.

Landscapes can be thought of as ranging from smooth to rugged. A smooth landscape is one in which neighboring points in the space have nearly the same "fitness value." In the interior of the smooth landscape, hills are small and functionally isolated—like islands. Local optima, or the high points in the landscape, are few and far between. Complex behavior (leading to evolution) cannot propagate across the system. Here virtually all mutations cause minor changes in behavior. When landscapes are smooth, achieving large changes in behavior is very difficult.

At the other extreme are maximally rugged, random, chaotic landscapes, regimes in which the fitness values of neighboring points are entirely uncorrelated. In rugged landscapes, many local optima, or high points in the terrain, exist. Slight changes in structure almost always cause vast changes in behavior. Complex controllable behavior seems precluded.

To benefit from mutation, recombination, and natural selection, a population must evolve on *rugged* (multipeaked) *but well-correlated* (nearby points have similar heights) *landscapes*—spaces where minor mutations can cause both large and small variations. These rugged, correlated fitness landscapes underlie Darwin's view of the world and set the stage for the "adaptive walk" of evolution.

The first essential feature of adaptive walks by populations of organisms is that they proceed uphill on the landscape until a local peak is reached. On a rugged but well-correlated landscape, an organism is more likely to "view" and so climb to a high peak rather than a low one. It is natural selection—the ability to fill the higher landscape niches that is "pulling" adapting populations toward peaks.

Like a hilltop in a mountainous area, such a local peak is higher than any point in its immediate vicinity, but may be far lower than the highest peak in the landscape, the global maximum. Adaptive walks stop on such local peaks. Consequently, as fitness improves (i.e., the higher the population climbs up the peak), the number of directions uphill dwindles.

Why does this happen? Because, in biological evolution, processes are attempting to optimize a system riddled with conflicting constraints and it is the conflicting constraints that make the landscape rugged and multipeaked. Think of each peak as a different combination of constraints. Once the combination of constraints is "selected," the organism seeks to evolve to the peak of that situation.

Put another way, optimal solutions to one part of the overall design problem conflict with optimal solutions to other parts of the overall design. The system must find compromise solutions to the joint problems that meet the conflicting constraints of the different subproblems. Because so many constraints are in conflict, there are a large number of rather modest compromise solutions rather than an obvious superb solution. Therefore, there are many local peaks with very low altitudes—many local optima exist.

Organisms evolve on rugged landscapes as a result of these constraints. It is as if changing the level of conflicting constraints in the construction of an organism from low to high "tunes" how rugged a landscape such organisms explore. The more conflicting constraints faced by an organism, the more rugged—the more local—peaks there are on the landscape. The more rugged the landscape, the harder it is for adaptation to occur. Therefore, the rate of improvement slows exponentially as the organism goes "uphill." In other words, the number of directions uphill declines. Those conflicting constraints imply that as adaptive searches climb higher toward the peaks, the rate of improvement slows exponentially.

Using Landscapes to Understand Economics

The global economy and most national economies are rugged landscapes and new entities always struggle to increase their fitness. When new entrepreneurial firms enter the landscape, they typically are not very fit. The high incidence of mortality among startup businesses testifies to that. If the new firm can adapt to the ever-changing demands of its landscape and improve, it will survive and prosper. Like biological life, individuals and species have to proceed uphill (i.e., improve their fitness) if they are to survive and prosper.

The more rugged the external landscape, as we go uphill, the slower the rate of improvement for the organizations on that landscape. Adaptation becomes harder and harder. As the organization climbs toward the peaks, the rate of improvement slows exponentially. Kauffman calls this exponential characteristic "an utterly fundamental property of very many rugged fitness landscapes."

Kauffman identifies two features of rugged but correlated landscapes, which best nurture evolution: (1) Fundamental innovation is followed by rapid, dramatic improvements that become less and less dramatic over time; (2) after each improvement the number of directions for further improvement falls by a constant fraction, i.e., a learning curve phenomenon. In other words, when fitness is low, there are many directions uphill; when fitness is high there are few directions uphill.

It is not surprising that Bruce Henderson and the Boston Consulting Group's experience curve was a powerful tool in the 1970s and 1980s for many companies to understand their position relative to their competitors'. Boston Consulting argued that there was an exponential cost curve for an industry and it could help companies better understand their cost position relative to the costs of other companies with whom they competed.

The learning curve phenomenon certainly is found in technological innovations. Clayton Christensen, in his recent book, *The Innovator's Dilemma*, makes the point that there are two types of technology innovation—disruptive and sustaining. Disruptive technologies bring to market a very different value proposition than had been available previously, and sustaining technologies improve the performance of existing products along the dimensions of performance that most customers have historically valued.[25] In the early stages of a disruptive technology the rate of advancement can be very rapid, but ultimately, we see primarily incremental advancements, as it becomes a sustaining technology.

Organizations and economies in general are constantly struggling to find compromise solutions that meet the conflicting constraints of their different subproblems—defining the peaks of the landscape. For example, continuing to achieve a 15 percent growth rate is much harder for an organization the size of General Electric or Walt Disney than for an Internet startup, other things being equal. Again, it is because we are dealing with processes that are attempting to optimize a system riddled with conflicting constraints, and it is the conflicting constraints that make the landscape rugged and multipeaked. Optimal solutions in one part of GE or Disney likely conflict with optimal solutions in other parts of the respective organizations.

Generally the larger the organization, the more complex the organization. In addition, the larger the organization, the more constraints it faces (community responsibilities, stock market pressures, union attention, etc.). Consider Disney's problems in the late 1990s with the Southern Baptist Convention over health care for same-sex partners, the government of China over a movie about Tibet, or Microsoft's problems with the U.S. Justice Department.

How Living Organisms Avoid the Traps of Local Peaks

Since evolution by mutation and selection is limited to searching locally in the landscape, the chances of significant improvements in the organism—reaching much higher peaks—rapidly diminish unless something else is at work. The possibility of recombination of organisms at different locations on the landscape is needed. In other words, evolution by mutation and selection alone is limited to searching locally in the space of possibilities, guided only by the local terrain.

What is needed is for the adapting population to take what Kauffman calls "a God's-eye view and behold the large-scale landscape features"—see where to evolve rather than just climbing blindly uphill from its current position, only to become trapped on poor local peaks. Such a "God's-eye view" is possible if recombination between organisms at different locations on the landscape can occur.

Suppose that an adapting population is spread out over some region of a fitness landscape. Recombination between organisms at different locations on the landscape allows the adapting population to look at the regions between the various members. For example, when an organism with a superior quality mates with an organism with an inferior quality, the latter's offspring that inherits the superior quality has been allowed to "look" at the regions between the inferior and superior qualities.

OVERCOMING LOCAL PEAKS IN BUSINESS

As with the biological world, if evolution by mutation and selection is limited to searching locally, i.e., within our own organization or industry, the chances of significant improvements (reaching much higher peaks) rapidly diminish. The economic world can also benefit from recombination of organisms at different locations on the landscape.

It is not surprising that many organizations often hire key personnel from other successful organizations, such as Hewlett Packard's (HP's) 1999 decision to hire Carleton Fiorina of Lucent Technologies as its first CEO from outside HP. Companies also benchmark against "best in class" rather than just within their own organization or industry. They also merge or make acquisitions of companies that can bring them new technologies or knowledge about new markets. For example, since 1993 Cisco has acquired forty companies and its CEO, John Chambers, has built his leadership team from these acquisitions.

Organizations need to be able to see beyond their own local terrain. That is one of the explanations for the recent merger of Citicorp and Travelers. Their executives hope to create a new type of company that can offer a full range of financial services on a global scale.

An even more dramatic example is WorldCom, Inc. From the fall of 1983 to the fall of 1997, it emerged from an idea into what *Business Week* called "the first, new-era telecom giant." By acquiring MCI, the new company, with combined 1996 revenues of $28 billion, could offer a broader range of telecom assets and services than any other company, including AT&T. In the words of one journalist, the new company "should change the competitive landscape for the U.S. telecom business."[26]

WorldCom saw that a merger with MCI would give it the ability to offer long distance, local, and Internet service. By some estimates, the new company will have 30 percent to 40 percent of the Internet traffic. On the day the merger was announced, the manager of a Telephone Income Fund observed, "I think the world changed today. This changes the dynamics of the industry."[27] According to another industry observer, WorldCom's CEO "has basically pushed WorldCom to the top."[28] Yet, almost immediately, it came under close scrutiny by European regulators. Such scrutiny may mean a possible change in the constraints on WorldCom, which could lead to more changes in the landscape.

COEVOLUTION IN BIOLOGY

Landscapes are shaped not only by external forces but by the very organisms that inhabit them. For example, altering the genes of a single organism can affect the fitness contribution of other genes to which it is connected. The more interconnected the genes are, the more conflicting constraints exist. The same is true for species. As one species' fitness improves, if it is connected to another species, it affects the fitness of others and thereby the landscape itself is changed.

Species evolve primarily through selection at the level of the individual organism. Species navigate the fitness landscape by mutating genes. As they evolve, the community a species is a part of (i.e., an ecosystem) evolves. The community navigates its landscape by adding or deleting species. As the community evolves, all other organisms in the community evolve since their landscape is changing. This is coevolution.

The community is a dynamic system in which each move can affect everyone else in the larger community. For example, if the population of wolves increases on a particular landscape, the population of other animals, especially those that are eaten by wolves, will be affected, which in turn may affect the vegetation of the area. The change in vegetation may also affect the population of other animals, which in turn affects the population of wolves.

The more intercouplings among species, the more moves by one species can strongly deform the landscape for partners. The principle of coevolution is significant, because it means never being sure if the next step results in a modest change or a very significant change for the entire system.

COEVOLUTION IN BUSINESS

Like the biological landscape, economic landscapes are shaped by external forces and by the very individuals and organizations that inhabit them. As organizations evolve or change, they influence the performance of other organizations on the shared landscape. As an individual in an organization who is connected to other individuals improves, i.e., alters his or her skills (genes), the fitness contribution of other individuals is affected. Ultimately, the organization itself is changed, which in turn affects other organizations in its landscape.

For example, there are limited resources that an organization can allocate or that the market will provide to a particular organization. Consequently, if I am an employee with a new product idea and I receive corporate funding, someone else in the organization is unlikely to receive funding for his or her idea. (As discussed in a later chapter, a core element of organizational leadership is making hard resource allocation decisions.) On the positive side, what I achieve may create new opportunities for other employees.

If our company is becoming fitter, i.e., gaining market share or improving its financial position, and is connected to other firms, such as suppliers or customers, others in the industry will be affected by our climbing higher on the fitness landscape. To illustrate, if our position relative to other firms is much better, our suppliers and customers are likely to benefit as well. In addition, our competitors may have a much harder time attracting capital. Thus, as we change, we change the landscape on which we compete. Over time, if our contributions prove valuable enough, we may fundamentally change a very large landscape as Microsoft and Intel have done for the computer landscape and WorldCom may do for the telecommunications landscape.

BIOLOGY AND SELF-ORGANIZATION

Author's note: Many of the ideas in this section are based on M. Mitchell Waldrop, *Complexity,* New York: Touchstone Books, 1992, pp. 304–305.

Some scientists, including Kauffman, now believe that life evolves toward a regime that is poised between order and chaos. They propose that life exists at the "edge of chaos," where "edge" is used metaphorically to indicate a critical condition between order and disorder. Kauffman also believes that systems deep either in the ordered regime, i.e., the smooth part of the landscape, or in too random and chaotic a regime, probably are incapable of complex behavior and are not highly evolvable. It is near the edge that life is best able to coordinate complex activities and evolve. Thus, complexity is just at the edge of chaos.

If Kauffman is correct, life exists near a kind of phase transition. Like water, which can exist in three phases (solid ice, liquid water, and gaseous steam), systems too deep into the frozen ordered regime are too rigid to coordinate the complex sequences of genetic activities necessary for development. If they are too far into the gaseous, chaotic regime, they will not be orderly enough. It is the nearly melted state that corresponds to the edge of chaos. Here it is orderly enough to ensure stability yet full of flexibility and surprise. Living systems seem to exist in the solid regime near the edge of chaos; it is evolution that takes them there.

As we discussed earlier, selection by itself can fail when the landscape is random or when it is smooth. On a random landscape the adapting system is frozen into a tiny region of the available space and does not experience significant evolution; i.e., advances to the highest peaks are virtually impossible and the population will typically be trapped on a relatively poor local optimum.

By contrast, on a smooth landscape the rate of mutation may be too high. When it is so high that many fitter and less-fit variants are found over very short intervals, it causes the population to diffuse away from the peak faster than the selective differences between less-fit and more-fit mutants can return the population to the peak. What is known as an error catastrophe has occurred—the useful genetic information built up in the population is lost as the population diffuses away from the peak.

Stated another way, as the mutation rate increases, at first the population climbs a local hill and hovers in its vicinity. As the mutation rate becomes higher, the population drifts down from the peak and begins to spread along ridges of nearly equal fitness on the fitness landscape. But if the mutation rate increases still further, the population drifts ever lower off the ridges into the lowlands of poor fitness. Thus, this catastrophe implies a limit to the power of natural selection. At a high enough mutation rate, an adapting population cannot assemble useful genetic variants into a working whole; instead, the mutation-induced diffusion over the space overcomes selection.

If this hypothesis is correct then there is a link between the stability of a system and the ruggedness of the landscape. On smooth landscapes, selection faces error catastrophe and can become excessively trapped in small regions of the space of possibilities. On rugged landscapes the rate of improvement of the population decreases, but eventually the population is more likely to climb to a high peak than a low one. Consequently, the mean fitness maintained by a population can be higher on a more rugged landscape than on a smooth landscape.

This suggests to Kauffman that the "source of order" in all the life on Earth includes not only selection but also "self-organization." He believes self-organization—the "incessant attempts" of matter to organize itself into ever more complex systems—may be a "precondition of evolability itself." Only those systems that are able to organize themselves spontaneously may be able to evolve further. Spontaneous self-organization generates the kinds of structures that can evolve gradually and are robust. This means that natural selection is not wrong, but inadequate, in that it fails to incorporate the possibility that simple and complex systems exhibit order spontaneously.

Several researchers from the Brookhaven National Laboratory use a different metaphor for understanding self-organizing and the edge of chaos—one that for some is more easily grasped. Imagine a pile of sand on a table top with a steady drizzle of new sand grains raining down from above. The pile grows higher and higher until it cannot grow any more: The old sand cascades down the sides and off the edge of the table as fast as the new sand dribbles down. Conversely, you could reach the same state by starting with a huge pile of sand: The sides would just collapse until all the excess sand had fallen off. It is self-organized in the sense that it reaches a steady state all by itself without anyone explicitly shaping it. It is in a state of criticality, in the sense that sand grains on the surface are just barely stable. The microscopic surfaces and edges of the grains are interlocked in every conceivable combination and are just ready to give way. When a falling grain hits there is no telling what might happen. Nothing may happen or maybe a few grains will shift. However, if one tiny collision leads to another in just the right chain reaction, a catastrophic landslide may eliminate the entire face of the sand pile. In fact, all of these things happen at one time or another. This state is what is called "self-organizing criticality."

Big avalanches are rare and small ones are frequent. Either way, the resulting sand pile is self-organized in the sense that it reaches the steady state by itself without anyone explicitly shaping it.

As with sand, the biological hypothesis of self-organization suggests that the steady input of energy and matter drive biological systems to organize themselves the same way. They become a mass of intricately interlocking subsystems just barely on the edge of criticality—with breakdowns of all sizes occurring and rearranging things just often enough to keep them poised on the edge. Thus, "survival of the fittest" does not mean evolution to a state where every species is well-off, but rather where "individual species are barely able to hang on—like the grains of sand in the critical sandpile."[29]

BUSINESS AND SELF-ORGANIZATION

Kauffman believes "order for free" arises naturally, and he suspects that the fate of all complex systems in the biosphere—from single cells to economies—is to evolve to a natural state between order and chaos, "a grand compromise between structure and surprise."[30] His ideas about self-organization are similar to Adam Smith's "Invisible Hand."[31] In economics, as in biology, there may be a natural order.

In Braudel's history of civilization and capitalism, he observes such a phenomenon in market economies around the world:

> The market economy . . . was the necessary, spontaneously-developing and in fact normal base of any society over a certain size. Once a critical threshold had been

reached, the proliferation of trading, of markets and merchants, occurred of its own accord.[32]

He stresses that, "Everywhere there was the same sequence of events, the same creative evolution. . . ."[33]

At a national level, Braudel uses the evolution of the British economy as an example of what Kauffman would call self-organization. He describes the "growing sophistication" of the English domestic market by the beginning of the 18th century, as it had "begun to look like a living organism." Yet, for almost 150 years there had been little if any long-term planning to structure it. After Elizabeth I stabilized the pound sterling in 1560–61, it maintained its intrinsic value until the early part of the 20th century—a phenomenal record. Braudel concludes that

> the answer seems to be that there is not one single explanation but a series of explanations; not that the English were privy to some general theory which guided a far-sighted policy, but that they devised a series of pragmatic expedients to solve short-term problems— which regularly turned out in the long run to form the wisest course of action.[34]

Even in the global environment at the end of the 20th century it can be argued that the global economic system will organize itself. It is the creation of numerous agents often acting independent of each other. If the market is left alone it will adapt to all manner of developments. For example, in 1998, as the Asian crisis spread, if the International Monetary Fund and other entities had not agreed to try to help bail various economies and businesses out of their problems, creditors would have taken control of the companies in trouble, or at least their assets, and probably found new individuals or organizations that would have paid for the companies and tried to create value. The political will may not have been patient enough for the markets to work, but market forces would have eventually organized themselves. Some might even argue that in the long run this effect may have been better for the larger system.

We also see elements of self-organization at the organizational level. Kauffman points out how no single person at IBM knows the world of IBM, yet collectively IBM acts.[35] Similarly, companies such as Hewlett Packard and Intel have had several generations of CEOs but each has maintained many of the company's original, distinctive qualities. The same is true for other large business organizations.

Like the biological world, organizations (species) evolve primarily through selection at the level of the individual (organism). If the rate of mutation of genes, i.e., many skills and abilities being added to an organization, is too high, the useful information built up in the organization is lost. It does not have time to be absorbed and put to good use. If, however, it is too slow, the organization may not be able to keep up with its environment and will die off.

The organization (species) navigates the fitness landscape by changing skills and abilities (mutating genes) of the individual (organism). The community they are a part of (the industry and ultimately the economy) navigates its landscape by adding or deleting organizations (species). As the community evolves, all other organisms in the community evolve too since the landscape is changing.

The economic system is a dynamic system in which each move by an organization affects everyone else in the large community. As this coevolution is pushing an organization and its people toward the edge of chaos, the participants never know if the next step results in a small change or a significant change—a trickle or a landslide. This is particularly true in the technology sectors. Consider two recent examples—the PC business and the online brokerage business.

As described in Chapter Two, in 1997 Compaq led the move to PCs priced under $1,000. Seemingly in response, in early 1998 IBM cut prices for its high servers by as much as 29 percent. It did this just after Compaq had announced the acquisition of Digital Equipment and was counting on servers to provide a significant source of revenue for the company. Compaq had to announce that in the first quarter of 1998, it would break even rather than earn an expected profit of $500 million. It was the worst performance for Compaq since the third quarter of 1991, making its original move much more than a trickle.

By the end of 1998 it was beginning to look more like a potential landslide. In the fourth quarter of 1998, eMachines Inc. sold 200,000 sub-$500 PCs. (By the summer of 1999, eMachines had shipped nearly one million PCs, making it number three in home sales for some months.) In early 1999, Microworkz Computer announced that it would sell a full-featured PC for $299 and bundle it with a year of free unlimited Internet service, making the computer virtually free. By early 1999 Onsale, Inc. began selling PCs essentially at cost. A few weeks later, tiny Free-PC, Inc. launched a whole new price category: free. Free-PC promised to hand out at least 10,000 Compaq Presarios to people who would submit personal data and agree to receive direct, targeted advertising.

E*Trade was one of the first companies to secure a brokerage niche on the Internet. It made a significant breakthrough when it formed a partnership with AOL in 1992 and offered rates of $14.95 per trade—far lower than that charged by the leading discount brokers of the time. New online competitors have since entered the landscape and cut their prices to under $10 per trade. Now some of the full-service firms with strong brand names and large marketing budgets have entered the online landscape. Whether the price cuts will lead to a major shakeout—a landslide—or result in little change—a trickle—is unclear now, but everyone involved must be paying close attention to their landscape.

Will Compaq and E*Trade make a comeback, as did the mottled Biston betularia moth in England? Probably, but there are no guarantees on a rugged landscape.

HOW CAN WE TEST THESE IDEAS?

If the reader has accepted the analogy so far, then we are in agreement that both biological life and economic life have many common elements, especially as they relate to a world in constant transition between chaos and order.

Although scientists have made considerable progress in understanding many of the microelements of biology, such as cell structure and DNA, large-scale biological systems, such as the weather or the environment, have been much harder to subject to experimentation with the same rigor. For example, it is much harder to create experiments that allow scientists to study the effects of global warming under varying conditions than to create experiments to study the effects of various factors on genes. That, however, is changing.

With the emergence of powerful computers, a branch of computer science that began in the 1950s and came to be called "artificial life" has taken on new importance in recent years. Among some scientists, a whole new metaphor for computing patterned on biological organisms is taking shape. At the forefront of this movement is Professor John H. Holland of the University of Michigan. A member of the Santa Fe Institute and a MacArthur Fellow, he has led the way in creating models of events in the real world, including the field of economics, and solving problems with mathematics, by looking to the world of biology for inspiration. According to Holland, "The biological metaphor is rich, rich, rich."[36] Kauffman agrees: "Biological metaphors aren't just metaphors. It's how the real world works. . . ."[37]

Now considered by many to be the father of genetic algorithms, Holland came to believe fairly early in his career that the "cut and try of evolution isn't just to build a good animal, but to find good building blocks that can be put together to make many good animals." Using his computer and math skills, he set out to show how that could happen. The first step for him was to develop a computer model, a genetic algorithm, that would illustrate the process and help him better understand the issues involved.

Complex Adaptive Systems

Author's note: Most of this section is based on: John H. Holland, *Hidden Order,* Reading, MA: Helix Books, 1995 and M. Mitchell Waldrop, *Complexity,* New York: Touchstone Books, 1992.

Holland has done considerable work in trying to use the computer to model what has come to be known as complex adaptive systems. In *Hidden Order*, he raises the following question: "What enables cities to retain their coherence despite continual disruptions and a lack of central planning?" To describe a city, he writes: "Like the standing wave in front of a rock in a fast-moving stream, a city is a pattern in time. No single constituent remains in place, but the city persists." He also asks, What is it that allows the human immune system, when faced with an ever-changing and endless variety of invaders, to repel and destroy most of them? Similarly, we could ask, What is it that allows a company like Microsoft or Hewlett Packard to retain its coherence in the midst of rapid change?

Like New York City, HP, and Microsoft, each individual's immune system is coherent and persistent enough to provide a satisfactory scientific definition of his or her personal identity. According to Holland, these systems have energy, matter, and information moving around in complex cycles. The whole is more than the sum of its parts. The same can be said for companies like Intel, Microsoft, and HP, because they continue to respond to new developments, internal and external, and yet maintain some identity. They may change. In fact, they have to adapt. But there is coherence.

Even though complex business systems differ in detail from biological systems, Holland sees the issue of coherence under change as the central enigma for each. At the Santa Fe Institute, this common factor is so important that these systems are collected under a common heading—complex adaptive systems.

Holland believes that the coherence and persistence of each system, whether biological or economic, depends on extensive interactions, the aggregation of diverse elements, and adaptation.

Aggregation and Interaction

As a starting point for understanding complex adaptive systems, Holland stresses the usefulness of thinking of a system as made up of large numbers of active elements that are diverse in form and capability. He refers to them as agents (in biology they would be organisms or species and in business they would be employees or firms).

To understand the interactions of individual agents, Holland finds it useful to be able to describe the capabilities of individual agents. He thinks of an agent's behavior as determined by a collection of rules. Stimulus-response (If/Then) rules are typical. For example, if a competitor raises prices by 10 percent, then we will raise our prices 8 percent. If economic growth slows down, then we will reduce capital spending. Rules are simply a convenient way to describe the various agents' strategies. Consequently, Holland views complex adaptive systems as systems composed of interacting agents described in terms of rules.

Agent Adaptation

These systems must adapt (Latin, "to fit") to new developments as they appear, never settling into a fixed configuration. As we saw earlier in this chapter, adaptation, in biological usage, is the process whereby an organism fits itself to its environment. Roughly, experience guides changes in the organism's structure so that as time passes, the organism makes better use of its environment for its own ends. Holland expands the concept of adaptation to include learning and related processes.

Agents adapt or learn by changing their rules as experiences accumulate. In complex adaptive systems, a major part of the environment of any given adaptive agent consists of other agents. Consequently, a portion of any agent's efforts at adaptation is spent adapting to other agents. This one feature is a major source of the complex patterns that complex adaptive systems, such as the economy, generate. In fact, Holland believes it is this *adaptation* that gives rise to "a kind of complexity that greatly hinders our attempts to solve some of the most important problems posed by our world."

Just as organisms and species must adapt to their environment and thereby affect other organisms and species, so business organizations must adapt and thereby change the very landscape on which they "live." For example, when Intel introduces a new chip, it not only affects other chip makers but it changes things for software and hardware companies. They in turn may develop new products that need more powerful chips from Intel or its competitors. When Microsoft introduced Windows 98, other software and hardware firms were affected. Coevolution was occurring.

Holland believes that for an adaptive agent to survive and prosper, two things have to happen: *prediction* and *feedback*. Prediction is thinking ahead; it is what helps an agent seize an opportunity or avoid getting trapped. He believes that all complex adaptive systems build "models" that allow them to anticipate their world. For human beings we often use the concept of "mental models" to describe the models we have in our head that help us imagine consequences, i.e., risks and rewards. Anything we call a skill or expertise is an implicit model—or more precisely, a huge interlocking set of standard operating procedures that have been inscribed on the nervous system and refined by years of experience.

Feedback from the environment is essential if the agent is to improve its internal models without any paranormal guidance. It has to try out the models, see how well the predictions work in the real world, and—if it survives the experience—adjust the models to do better the next time. In biology the agents are individual organisms and the feedback is provided by natural selection. The steady improvement of the models is called evolution. For cognition, the process is essentially the same: The agents are individual minds; the feedback comes from teachers, broadly defined, and experience. For businesses, the agents may be suppliers, customers, etc., and the feedback also comes from teachers (consultants, academics, etc.) and experience in the marketplace. The improvement is called learning—individual and organizational learning.

As Holland sees it, an adaptive agent has to be able to take advantage of what its world is trying to tell it. It is his view that general principles rule complex adaptive system behaviors, principles that point to ways of solving the attendant problems.

CONCLUSION

In this chapter, I have drawn on the work of Charles Darwin, Stuart Kauffman, and Murray Gell-Mann to help the reader understand how biological life is in many ways analogous to economic life. I have used biology to illustrate a complex system in an effort to help the reader gain a different perspective on economic life and the world of business. In addition, I have introduced the work of Professor John Holland, who has taken the biological analogy and, with the aid of sophisticated computers, begun to apply it to business and economics.

According to a 1996 article by Michael Schrage, "Holland attempts to do for mathematics what Darwin did for the animal kingdom. . . . Don't be surprised if businesses . . . begin to use Holland's techniques as tools to model their own enterprises and initiatives."[38] A year later, *Business Week* reported that his "semirandom evolutionary programs" are in fact being used in industry to address a number of problems.[39] By 1998, several leading consulting firms, including Ernst & Young and Arthur Andersen, were investing in complexity research, and firms such as CitiGroup and Texas Instruments were using complexity to solve network design problems, speeding up the process of product design and improve production schedules in factories.

What we are beginning to see is that the work being done on complex adaptive systems can provide us with some interesting insights into the increasingly chaotic world of business. If economic life evolves toward a regime that is poised between order and chaos, then being near the edge is the best position for an organization to be in to coordinate complex economic activities and evolve. In other words, complex organizations and economies will function best when they are just at "the edge of chaos"—a place that is orderly enough to ensure stability yet full of flexibility and surprise. I believe it is this edge that leading companies and their leaders should aspire to reach.

What follows in this book are conclusions I have drawn about how to increase the chances of getting to and staying on that edge. They are based on my own reading about complexity and chaos, and on my own business research and experiences.

First, however, I want to briefly discuss a fundamental conclusion that I believe follows from viewing the economic world as a complex adaptive system. An acceptance of this conclusion can begin the process of helping business leaders better understand their world as they prepare to lead their organizations into the 21st century.

CHAPTER FOUR

The Uncertainty Principle

For most of the 20th century, our view of business has been almost a mechanistic view of the world, as opposed to an evolutionary view. If we take certain actions predictable things will follow. Certainly the early 20th century writings of Fredrick Taylor, the father of scientific management, could lead one to such a conclusion.

Even today, too many managers and leaders seem to have a sense that there exists a set of basic rules that if understood and practiced could virtually ensure business success. Recently I had a senior executive for a company ask me, with a straight face, to make sure we incorporated the "Harvard Business School Management Principles" into an executive program we were designing for his company. I frequently hear businesspeople talk about the "levers" that they need to pull to make things happen in their organization. This mechanistic view clearly is inappropriate and even dangerous in today's world.

If you accept the premise that economies and business organizations are complex adaptive systems, then your way of thinking about building and leading an organization must change. To that end, consider what I call the uncertainty principle of business.

THE ORIGINAL UNCERTAINTY PRINCIPLE

As most people recall from high school science classes, matter is composed of minute particles called atoms. It has been shown that all subatomic particles, such as electrons, sometimes behave as if they were waves. As a wave, a given particle cannot be precisely located. A graph of the wave can be seen only as a description of the probability that the particle is in a certain place at a certain time. This idea was stated by the German physicist and 1932 Nobel Prize winner Werner Heisenberg as the *uncertainty principle*: It is impossible to determine at the same time exactly where a particle is and how fast it is moving.[1]

The uncertainty principle has been explained in physical terms by saying that any attempt to measure the position and velocity of a particle will disturb it. The uncertainty arises because to detect the particle, radiation must be "bounced" off it; the process itself disrupts the particle's position. This phenomenon is not a consequence of experimental error but represents a fundamental limit to objective scientific observation.

For me the uncertainty principle of business rests on the idea that the economic system is nonlinear. It has two basic but related corollaries, notions that challenge some of today's most widespread management practices. First, you cannot predict the future. Second, the future will be less predictable than it was in the past.

THE ECONOMIC SYSTEM IS NONLINEAR

A function is linear if the variables are simply and directly related. For example, the function $A = 3X + 5Y + Z$ is linear. The variables in the equation appear only to the power of one. A nonlinear equation, such as $A = 3X^2 + 5Y^3 + Z^4$ involves powers other than one.

If there is any lesson that comes through clearly in the work of Holland and others who have worked with complex adaptive systems, it is that these systems are nonlinear. It is one of Holland's basic properties of complex adaptive systems. He concludes that nonlinear interaction almost always makes the behavior of the aggregate more complicated than would be predicted by summarizing or averaging.[2]

Nevertheless, many of the models used by businesspeople today to project the future of the economy, an industry, or the performance of a business are linear models. In the United States of the 1960s, many statistical methods began to be used widely in business circles, especially in the areas of finance and marketing, to predict return on investment, cash flows, market share, industry growth rates, etc. Linear models became and continue to be a core element of virtually every MBA and business Ph.D. program offered today.

If one accepts the premise of coevolution, then it becomes clear that as one organization evolves it affects the landscape, which in turn causes other organizations to evolve, and on and on. It is not just that an organization is changing but that the entire system is changing and usually changing in such a way that the economic landscape becomes more rugged and uncertain.

We saw this phenomenon very clearly on a macro economic level in October 1997. On July 2, Thailand's currency, the baht, dropped more than 12 percent in value against the dollar. Then the Philippines, Malaysia, and Indonesia were forced to devalue their currencies. By late October the effects were felt in Hong Kong and then the United States. At first, the fall on Wall Street was blamed on Asia. Within days, the continued fall in Asian markets was blamed on the fall in the United States. According to a *Washington Post* article written in Hong Kong at the time, "analysts here were at a loss to explain which market was affecting which and in what order. 'There's a lot of mutual infection going on here,' said one local investment fund manager."[3]

We clearly are dealing with a system that cannot be reliably modeled by linear models. The causes and effects cannot be easily distinguished; therefore, we cannot say with certainty "if *X* happens, *Y* will follow." In other words, the results are not proportional to the cause. It is a world where almost everything affects everything else.

To use linear models to predict outcomes in such an environment, according to Holland, is much like trying to play chess by collecting statistics on the way pieces move in the game.[4] Yet many academic and business researchers continue to rely on linear models to try to predict the future.

I believe that the bias toward linearity fundamentally affects our way of thinking and acting. For example, in traditional strategic planning we commonly stress a linear framework. First, we identify the organization's mission and purpose; then we establish goals. Next, we develop a strategy for achieving these goals, followed by operating plans and budgets.

A fundamental problem with thinking too linearly is that in some industries, by the time the strategy is well thought out, the assumptions on which we were operating to establish the goals have changed. Not only may there have been a totally unexpected, unique occurrence that made assumptions obsolete, but the moves themselves may have resulted in responses from others on the same landscape that significantly changed the landscape.

To illustrate, consider the plans of General Motors (GM) in Thailand. In 1996, General Motors' board approved the building of a $500 million factory to build automobiles in Thailand starting in 1999. The plan seemed reasonable in light of recent history. Over a five-year time frame, car sales in Thailand had grown by more than 60 percent, creating what some were calling the Detroit of the East. In June 1997 things still looked good for GM in Asia. Yet, when Thailand devalued its currency and its financial crisis spread to other Asian countries, GM signaled that it was scaling back the plant's capacity to about 40,000 cars a year from the originally planned rate of 100,000 units. Then it indicated that it also was likely to change the product to be built there. In early

1998, GM announced it was delaying plans to open its assembly plant in Thailand. Other automobile companies also began reviewing their Asian strategies. Each corporate move added further uncertainty to the Thailand economy, which, in turn, added uncertainty to each company's plans for the future.

COROLLARY #1:
YOU CANNOT PREDICT THE FUTURE

If I could convince business leaders of one thing, it would be that they cannot predict the future—especially the long-term future—with any degree of accuracy, regardless of the models used. By prediction I mean its common usage of "foretelling" the future, not Holland's "thinking ahead."

According to Peter Schwartz, the former head of strategic planning for Royal Dutch/Shell and a leading practitioner and writer about using scenarios (hypothetical stories used to structure thinking about—not predicting—the future), a mistake most of us make is imagining that the future is predictable. Our common view is, "If we only had the right seers, we could predict the future." He adds, "An enormous amount of effort goes into trying to predict what is unpredictable."[5]

The experts often get it wrong. For example, in May 1997, one month before the wave of financial distress began to break over Asia, *Money* magazine ran an investment story with this headline: "How to Cash In on the Asia Boom; Every Investor Today Ought to Take a Hard, Close Look at the Dazzling Promise of the Pacific Rim. Here Are Four Gateways to Earning Spectacular Profits in the World's Fastest-Growing Economies."[6] Similarly, *The Wall Street Journal* roundup of economists in June 1997 reported that more experts picked Asian stock markets, excluding Japan, to be top performers in the following twelve months than chose the United States, Europe, and Japan.[7]

This is not just a recent phenomenon. Darryl Zanuck predicted in 1946 that people would get tired of watching television. Tom Watson of IBM thought there would be a world market for only about five computers. A Yale economist predicted in 1929 that stock prices had reached what looked like a permanent high plateau. Paul Saffo, a director of the Institute for the Future, predicted in 1996 that the Web would mutate into "something else very quickly and be unrecognizable within twelve months." Nicholas Negroponte, cofounder and director of the MIT Media Lab, predicted that one billion Internet users and a trillion-dollar economy on the Net would exist by the year 2000.[8]

Even short-term developments that largely result from our own actions can be hard to predict. In 1997 one of America's most admired companies, United Parcel Service (UPS), found itself in a strike with the Teamsters and seemed to lose the battle for public sympathy. According to UPS' vice chairman, "We didn't expect a strike. Then we thought it would last only a day or two. And we thought the vast majority of our workers would cross picket lines."[9] Three wrong predictions about something very short term and very close to home.

Research on so-called experts seems to bear this phenomenon out. Studies conducted in the 1970s concluded that a "large number of technical people have little idea of what to do when uncertainty crosses their path. . . . Having no good quantitative idea of uncertainty, there is an almost universal tendency for people to understate it."[10] Almost a quarter of a century later, analysts at a brokerage firm came to a similar conclusion. "[P]rofessionals who tend to forecast a higher-than-average growth rate for a company consistently overestimate the actual results, while pessimists consistently underestimate them. '[O]n average,' the analysts reported, 'expectations are not met.'"[11]

Problems Associated with Predictions

There are at least three major problems with the way most predictions are made: They are based on historical data, they fail to account for unique events, and they ignore coevolution. In addition, there are some psychological challenges implicit in predictions.

Using Historical Data

Many researchers and business planners compound the problem of prediction by using historical data in their linear models to try to predict the future. In the August 1997 issue of *Money*, a large section was devoted to encouraging investors to sell stocks. The argument was that "at today's prices, stocks are overvalued by 15 percent to 20 percent. How do we know? History tells us so."[12]

Even if the historical data were accurate, there is still a problem with the lack of complete information. As Peter L. Bernstein has pointed out in his history of risk,

> The past, or whatever data we choose to analyze, is only a fragment of reality. That fragmentary quality is crucial in going from data to a generalization. We never have all the information we need (or can afford to acquire) to achieve the same confidence with which we know, beyond a shadow of a doubt, that a die has six sides, each with a different number. . . . Reality is a series of connected events, each dependent on another, radically different from games of chance in which the outcome of any single throw has zero influence on the outcome of the next throw.[13]

Too much of business planning places a premium on good financial numbers. What is ignored is that traditional financial numbers are historical in nature. They describe how an organization performed in the past. They say nothing about the future. In addition, most of these models require a variety of assumptions about the future. Even something as simple as discounted cash flow requires the prediction of interest rates. Frequently, the users of such models take the rates from the recent past and project them into the future—an act that can have serious consequences.

I had a discussion in the 1970s with an American steel company executive who was especially concerned with his company's ability to compete with the Japanese. His company's financial analysis of an investment in a new steel mill showed that it would never pay for itself. Of course, his company's analysis was based on using current data about interest rates, which at the time were double digit. Therefore, rather than aggressively fighting for its share of the future steel business, the management of this company was virtually paralyzed and was considering diversifying away from the steel business. I suspect discussions at the emerging mini-mill companies and at Japanese producers were very different.

Unique Events

Another problem with trying to predict the future is that we often are trying to predict unique events that have no probability. Peter Drucker believes this kind of planning—forecasting based on probabilities—not only is what most companies still practice, but in an uncertain environment is "futile, if not counterproductive."[14]

Peter Bernstein agrees and explains why: "The prevalence of surprise in the world of business is evidence that uncertainty is more likely to prevail than mathematical probability."[15] The reason is that any given instance is so unique that there are no others—or not a sufficient number—to make it possible to tabulate a basis for any real probability. He adds,

> Because the economic environment is constantly changing, all economic data are specific to their own time period. Consequently they provide only a frail basis for generalizations. Real time matters more than time in the abstract, and samples drawn from the past have little relevance.[16]

Most executives with whom I come in contact admit that they and their people cannot predict the future but their organizations keep acting as if they can. The traditional approach to strategy has been to think of strategy as a plan for the future. For many organizations this has meant trying to project five or more years into the future. What will revenues be in five years? What will profits be in five years? To make those predictions, some companies spend considerable effort trying to predict specific industry or environmental developments that may affect revenues and profits, e.g., the impact of pending legislation or new regulations, the development of a new technology, and competitor actions. The uncertainty comes from trying to predict not just *whether* such unique events will occur but *when* they will occur, *how significant* the impact will be, and *how others will react*.

All of us recognize that there are unexpected developments external to an industry that can have a dramatic impact on a company's performance. War can break out in the Middle East and not only are oil prices affected, which ripple through the economy, but shipping is disrupted and employees are called to fight halfway around the world. A major hurricane can hit Florida or an earthquake can hit California and the performance of the construction industry may improve over the next year, but the insurance industry likely will be adversely affected. We may be able to predict with some range of probability that such an event will occur—and companies should be doing that—but we cannot predict with much accuracy when it will happen and what its magnitude will be.

It is not just the major, external developments that cannot be predicted. There also are unique industry developments that, although closer to home, cannot be predicted either. Consider Dollar General, a successful discount retail chain with headquarters in Nashville, Tennessee. In 1984, its leadership announced that the company's strategy for the foreseeable future would be to emphasize existing store growth and make no more major acquisitions. Almost immediately after that statement was issued, the CEO of a major competitor informed Dollar General's CEO that he soon would offer to sell all of his company's stores in Florida. Dollar General's CEO and his leadership team, after considerable discussion, decided to reverse their earlier position and make another acquisition. The leadership of Dollar General could not have predicted with a high degree of accuracy that a competitor would take such an action much less that it would occur at that particular time.

Even within a single organization, there are many unique developments that cannot be predicted with any managerially useful degree of accuracy (as anyone knows who has tried to predict when a new software release will be ready). The same is true for much less high-tech businesses. For example, 3M management could not have predicted that scientist Art Fry, or any other employee, in searching for a bookmark to mark the pages of a church hymnal, would develop Post-it® Notes, which would become one of 3M's all-time best-selling products. When asked, "How do executives decide what is or isn't a 3M business?" its vice chairman was very honest in his answer: "That's a good question. None of us is foresightful enough to decide that, because our people might find some way to make whatever they're doing work."[17]

Coevolution: Actions and Responses

Perhaps more important than unique external and internal developments are those developments created by our own actions. The impact of our own actions on the landscape cannot be predicted with a high degree of accuracy—especially over the long term. Although we may be able to say, with some degree of confidence, that the probability of a significant change is small—a trickle—there is always the possibility of a landslide.

Who could have predicted that when Seiko entered the watch industry it would change the nature of the industry? Although it started out as a fairly traditional watchmaker, by taking advantage of quartz technology it not only found a niche for itself but also changed the entire landscape for other watchmakers. With quartz technology, the watch increasingly became an inexpensive, electronic device with a very high degree of accuracy. Not only did Seiko overtake industry leaders such as Timex and Bulova, but it also enabled other firms to find new niches. For example, the Swiss found a new niche with a relatively inexpensive, electronic, fashion timepiece—Swatch. This new niche also created opportunities for companies like Fossil to emerge and become the market leader in the United States.

This is not an unusual example:

▲ When Best Buy decided to sell records below the prevailing price of the traditional retail music stores as a way of attracting buyers into its electronics and appliance stores, who would have expected that it would ultimately influence the pricing structure of the record business?

▲ When two young men in a West Coast garage introduced a PC named Apple, who could have predicted that their idea would change the computer industry and virtually every other industry in the world? It created opportunities not only for Apple but helped create numerous opportunities for many companies, including Microsoft and Intel.

▲ When IBM decided to use Intel's microprocessor for its new PC in the early 1980s, who could have predicted that Intel would become a driving force in the computer business and that IBM would decline in importance?

Psychological Challenges

There can be psychological dangers associated with predictions of the future. For example, a real danger with predictions is that they, and especially the plans on which they are based, can become a straightjacket that restricts management. Too many planning systems do not allow for the unexpected change, some of which may make the goals set six months earlier too conservative or too optimistic. Too often these predictions become little more than the basis for budgetary documents, not true statements of strategy.

Another danger is that an emphasis on predicting the future seems to convince some executives that they have a lot of control over their future. The assumption seems to be that if we can predict where the world will be in five years, corporate leaders can establish goals that are appropriate for that world and develop a plan for getting there. The implicit assumption seems to be that leaders of organizations can control the organization, i.e., pull the right levers to move the "machine" toward their goals.

The leaders of small companies know they cannot control the future of their organizations with any degree of confidence. Many would agree with the Taiwanese executives behind the success of Ting Hsin International Group, a company that dominates the Chinese instant noodle market. In describing the uncertain Chinese market he serves, he commented, "Every day after the sun rises you have no control over what will happen."[18] Such a perspective would benefit the leaders of all businesses.

I have been impressed with the intellectual honesty of a few large companies' CEOs, like Fred Smith of FedEx, Jack Welch of GE, and Bill Gates of Microsoft. Jack Welch has observed that "trying to define what will happen three to five years out, in specific, quantitative terms, is a futile exercise. The world is moving too fast for that."[19] According to *Fortune*, Fred Smith "concedes that he has no idea how current trends will affect his company over the next five years."[20] Bill Gates has stated that "Microsoft is the company that will never make any forecasts."[21] A senior vice president agrees: "We don't kid ourselves that we know what's going to happen."[22]

The U.S. Marines speak of "the fog of war" and stress that

the occurrences of war will not unfold like clockwork. Thus we cannot hope to impose precise, positive control over events. The best we can hope for is to impose a general framework of order on the disorder, to prescribe the general flow of action rather than to try to control each event.[23]

More business leaders would benefit from looking for a general framework rather than trying to control events.

A Caution

I do not want to leave the reader with the impression that the exercise of trying to predict the future always is bad. In fact, it can be very positive. As discussed in a later chapter, trying to predict the future can be very positive if it forces a management team to think about various scenarios and how one's company might respond to take advantage of developments or protect itself from these developments. In Holland's words, if prediction means "think ahead," it can be very helpful.

In fact, two officials at Shell Oil stress that "the more uncertainty, the more there is a need for planning." They point out, however, that they are not using planning in the sense of prediction, but in the sense of being prepared through perceiving a wider view of the business environment and by having a deeper understanding of the forces that shape the future.[24]

It is the same view held by Stuart Kauffman. He acknowledges that failure to predict does not mean failure to understand or to explain. Rather:

> We can still have every hope of predicting kinds of things. The hope here is to characterize classes of properties of systems that . . . are typical or generic and do not depend on the details.[25]

We can and should look for patterns to emerge within the system. In other words, we can hope to explain, understand, and even predict the occurrence of these generic emergent properties. However, we give up the dream of predicting the details.

COROLLARY #2: THE FUTURE IS BECOMING MORE UNPREDICTABLE

Yogi Berra once observed "the future ain't what it used to be." As I indicated in Chapter Two, more and more executives seem to agree with Berra. Specifically, they believe the pace of change and the level of uncertainty they and their organizations face are increasing. Consider the views of executives at three leading companies:

▲ Shortly after Jack Welch took over at General Electric in the early 1980s, he predicted that the decade of the eighties would be a "white-knuckle decade." He went on to say that the 1990s might be worse. In 1992 he commented, "It's going to be brutal. When I said a while back that the 1980s were going to be a white-knuckle decade and the 1990s would be even tougher, I may have understated how hard it's going to get."[26]

▲ Intel's Craig R. Barrett sees that the challenge is not just the speed but the uncertainty of when things will happen. He described Intel's situation in late 1997 as "going down the road at 150 miles per hour, and we know there's a brick wall someplace."[27]

▲ In talking about how Microsoft almost missed the Internet, Bill Gates claims that "[once a technology] achieves a critical mass, it feeds on itself—everything has to be tied into that. When you have critical mass things, then you can be surprised by the timing."[28]

Peter Schwartz, former head of planning for Royal Dutch/ Shell and cofounder of the think tank Global Business Network, thinks it is not just that more things are changing today but that both the nature of change and the rate of change are different.

> It used to be in business that you could count on the near-term future being fairly similar to the present and the rate of change being manageable. What has happened in recent years is the nature of change—how substantial it is—has altered enormously. And the rate of change—how fast it happens—is also different. Change, today, comes much faster. Worse, if you wait for change to occur, it's almost always too late to catch up.[29]

According to a former Sony executive, even in the late 1980s its hardware business was facing just what Schwartz described: "Ten years ago, if we developed a unique, clever device, it would be about two years before anybody copied us. Five years ago, we had a one-year lead. . . . Today, we can see imitations in as little as four months."[30]

Not only does the speed of product introduction indicate an increasingly rugged landscape for businesses, but the stock market does as well. For example, in one recent fifteen-week period, the Dow Jones Index witnessed 2 percent swings up or down on fourteen occasions, or on about 23 percent of its trading days. In the entire post–World War II era up to mid-July 1998, the Dow had moved that sharply only on about 3 percent of the days it traded.[31]

The growth of derivatives is another sign that we are operating on an increasingly rugged landscape. According to Peter Bernstein, in *Against the Gods*, "Derivatives have value only in an environment of volatility; their proliferation is a commentary on our times." He adds, "Derivatives are symptomatic of the state of the economy and of the financial markets, not the cause of the volatility that is the focus of so much concern."[32]

For the first time in my experience, I am hearing successful CEOs say they do not know what will become of their industries or how to plan for their companies' future. The Internet is clearly making the future more unpredictable for many executives. Even Bill Gates acknowledges that "we don't know what the business model looks like in the future—can content providers hold up? With the information highway, maybe no one will make money because everything will become a commodity."[33] In mid-1998 Gates claimed that over the next ten years, "if Microsoft is still a leader, we will have had to weather at least three crises."[34]

Even among very savvy Internet players there is concern. According to Bill Melton, the CEO of CyberCash, "this is harder than a lot of people thought it was." In early 1997, his CFO observed, "This is the most complicated thing I've been involved with. Nobody is sure of whether the Internet was 10 percent or 90 percent different from what we already know."

I do not think we are seeing a more modest breed of corporate executives than we had in the past. Rather, these executives are seeing a reality with which few of their peers have come to grips. The landscape on which they operate has become much more rugged—with more complexity, uncertainty, and change. Perhaps most disturbing to some readers, I think it will become increasingly rugged. There are four related reasons why I think this will be the case.

More Agents to Change

According to Paul Saffo of the Institute for the Future in Menlo Park, California, "There is this funny acceleration effect that comes from the fact that even though the individual components are all changing as slowly as ever, more things are changing at once."[35] Thus, even if individual developments and agents are moving at the same rate as in the past, the overall effect is more rapid change because there are more agents.

Contrast the number of players today with 16th century Genoa or 18th century Amsterdam, where, according to Fernand Braudel, "a few wealthy merchants . . . could throw sectors of the European or even world economy into confusion."[36] In all likelihood, most had dealings with each other and could more easily control what Braudel called the "zones of turbulence." Furthermore, the average person was little affected by the actions of a few merchants.

In the United States alone, approximately four million people start their own businesses each year. When we look at the number of business formations throughout Asia and in the former Soviet Union, it is clear that there are a growing number of "species" on the global landscape. Add to that the growing number of stock market investors and the number directly affected by stock market performance, and it is clear that the number of agents has exploded in recent years. For example, in 1981 approximately 16 percent of American adults owned stock. Today the number is approximately 40 percent.

More Linkages

Both Kauffman's and Holland's work stress that the greater the connectivity in a system, the more constraints there are on the agents; the more constraints on a system, the more moves by one agent can strongly deform the fitness landscapes of its partners. The outcome may be a trickle or a landslide. There is always the possibility of a great evolutionary breakthrough or even the extinction of various species.

In recent years, we have not only seen more agents emerging in the global economic system but also a greater connectedness among these agents, partially as a result of the lowering of trade barriers and the widening of global capital markets.

Consider the fact that in 1980, less than 1 percent of pension-fund assets in the United States was invested abroad. By 1997 that figure had increased to 17 percent. On a typical day in early 1999, the total amount of money changing hands in the world's foreign exchange markets alone was $1.5 trillion—an eightfold increase since 1986 and equivalent to total world trade for four months.[37] Furthermore, the volume of shares traded will likely increase. Whereas in 1987, on "Black Monday," 684 million shares traded on the New York Stock Exchange (NYSE), on September 1, 1998, 1.2 billion shares were traded. The NYSE is gearing up to be able to handle five billion trades a day by the fall of 1999.[38] Equally important, more and more investor wealth is held in liquid form, not in tangible assets, so it can move very quickly, from agent to agent.

When the Asian stock markets began dropping in late 1997, it did not take long before markets in Europe, South America, and North America were affected. In reflecting on the 1997 stock market turmoil, a *Wall Street Journal* editorial stressed the interconnectedness being brought on by globalization:

> The lesson here is that in the highly integrated world economy that is making the modern world rich, exchange rate roulette has the potential for disaster. When

businessmen invest and do deals across many borders, they must cope with an array of currencies—and promises made by the countries that back those currencies. And when it's unclear what those promises might be, or whether they will be kept, it becomes a lot more difficult and expensive to do business.[39]

A good example was the impact of Peregrine Investments Holdings Ltd., Asia's premier homegrown investment bank. On January 13, 1998, its management announced that the company was filing for liquidation. Hong Kong stocks on the key Hang Seng Index dropped 8.7 percent following the news. The company's collapse, triggered by the failure of a single large loan to an Indonesian firm, struck many in the financial community in Hong Kong as emblematic of the crisis that swept across East Asia in the last six months of 1997.

Peregrine had loaned $260 million in cash—in the form of an unsecured bridge loan—to a local taxicab company operator who reportedly enlisted Indonesian President Suharto's eldest daughter as an equity investor. The taxicab company operator planned to create a system of car ferries, linking the islands of Indonesia's sprawling archipelago. The bank planned to recoup the loan, which represented a third of its capital, through underwriting bonds issued by the taxi company. When the value of Asian currencies and stocks began to decline in the summer, Peregrine was stuck with bonds no one wanted to buy. Then in July, the Indonesian government lifted trading curbs on the rupiah—an effective devaluation following a similar move by Thailand—and the bottom immediately fell out of the currency.[40]

Soon, several big international banks were expecting to incur losses on their investments in Peregrine. Furthermore, in early 1998 economists with California's Finance Department were predicting that the Asian slowdown could cost California up to 65,000 new nonagricultural jobs in 1998, or about a sixth of the new jobs expected for the year. Other West Coast states soon would be similarly affected.[41]

Within months the U.S. stock market was adversely affected. According to Paul A. Volcker, former chairman of the Federal Reserve Board, in a speech in October 1998:

> Suddenly, it all seems in jeopardy. All that real-growth— all the trillions in paper wealth creation—is at risk. What started as a blip on the radar screen in Thailand— about as far away from Washington or New York as you can get—has somehow turned into something of a financial contagion.[42]

According to the senior chief economist at Zurich Kemper Investments in Chicago, "Nobody even five years ago could have expected such a scenario."[43]

As trade barriers come down and companies expand globally, they become interconnected—frequently forming alliances—with many more organizations. In addition, companies are much more linked today with suppliers and customers than ever before. This was a key element of many companies' approach to TQM and it has increased with the development of the Internet and Intranets.

In general, the more intercouplings, the more likely a small change is to propagate throughout and cause the system to veer off into significant and unpredictable changes, deforming the fitness landscapes of its partners. With coupled landscapes, it is the interconnectedness between the agents that counts.

Digital Convergence

The technological revolution, often referred to as digital convergence, not only increases connectivity among agents but results in more and more previously disconnected industries becoming much more linked. For example, entertainment, consumer electronics, telecommunications, and computers all seem to be converging into one huge landscape that will impact virtually every other industry. A significant development by Microsoft, e.g., could impact not only computer hardware and software producers but also potentially the television broadcast industry, the consumer electronics business, and telecommunications firms. Companies such as Hewlett Packard, Xerox, Kodak, and Sony increasingly are competitors, customers, and even partners, instead of being in different industries as we once thought. According to a writer for *Fortune,* "Computer hardware and software companies are looking for opportunities in telephony, photography and gas utilities. Understanding where these things are headed is getting harder, not easier."[44]

The worlds of telecommunications and information technology in particular are increasingly interrelated and unpredictable. When World Com purchased part of CompuServe and then made an offer for MCI, it had implications not just for the traditional telecommunications industry but for electronic commerce in general. According to a telecom analyst at Morgan Stanley, who was watching this development, "It's just unpredictable. You don't know what's going to happen next. You work around the clock and you have to switch gears instantly."[45]

Faster Information to More Agents

One of the reasons that in earlier times a "few wealthy merchants" could throw the world economy into confusion was, according to Braudel, that only "certain groups of privileged actors were engaged in circuits and calculations that ordinary people knew nothing of."[46] At the time, the speed of information over great distances could not exceed the speed of sailing ships or horses. Today, with the communication revolution—represented by the Internet, LANs, cellular phones, cable, satellites, twenty-four-hour business television channels, news agencies, etc.—an increasingly larger number of actors or agents are exchanging information instantly.

The impact of global media organizations and the emergence of the Internet are increasing the potential volatility of the business environment. As discussed in Chapter Two, at Intel it was the media that strengthened the hand of its unhappy customer—

IBM. It was not only the traditional media that picked up the story but both CNN and, more important, the Internet, became key players in spreading the story instantaneously throughout the world. It was like a tidal wave. Things were calm one minute and then Intel was in the middle of a major storm. It is not surprising that Andrew Grove has compared this experience to a typhoon and talks about "10X" forces—forces ten times what they were recently.

CONCLUSION

The 1960s was the decade when formal business education began to increase dramatically. It also was the time when the concept of business strategy began to emerge as a field of study. In hindsight, this was a remarkably stable and relatively simple business environment. For most of the 1960s, large U.S. companies faced relatively few strong foreign competitors and were experiencing the effects of a growing economy, fueled in part by baby boomers entering the market as both consumers and employees. There seemed to be a tendency to extrapolate the growth of the sixties into the 1970s and view the economic environment as not only stable but also as nearing equilibrium.

The decades since the 1960s have demonstrated that stability is very hard to attain for any length of time. I believe this is because we are dealing with a complex adaptive system and always have been. Because we are dealing with growing complex adaptive systems, the future will be even less predictable than it is today. In fact, this is the pattern of history.

The uncertainty faced by European merchants who traded with China in the Middle Ages was much greater than that faced by earlier merchants who dealt only with a local market economy. Business leaders during the emergence of the industrial revolution faced much greater uncertainty than that faced by merchants a few hundred years prior, who were relying on animal or human power to produce goods for expanding markets. In the same way, the uncertainty faced by business leaders in today's age of a greatly expanded and connected world economy is much greater than when most markets were primarily national. Future global commerce that is linked via the Internet, I believe, will be even more unpredictable.

Unfortunately, too many business leaders are continuing to rely on a managerial way of thinking that took hold in the 1960s. They fail to recognize that the level of complexity in the system has increased substantially in the decades since.

I believe an understanding of complex adaptive systems will give business leaders what is missing from much of management practice today—a broader perspective on their world. As they come to understand these systems, they will have to accept the uncertainty principle of nonlinearity for the economic system and its corollaries about predicting the future. The acceptance of these ideas can open us up to thinking about how best to cope with the unexpected rather than trying to control the future.

Now we turn to some concepts and practices that business leaders can use to help their organizations adapt to the increasingly turbulent and complex world of the 21st century.

CHAPTER FIVE

Understanding the Business Landscape

S tephen Hawkin, who holds the Isaac Newton Chair as Lucasian Professor of Mathematics at the University of Cambridge, has observed that:

> We find ourselves in a bewildering world. We want to make sense of what we see around us and to ask: What is the nature of the universe? What is our place in it and where did it come from? Why is it the way it is? To try to answer these questions we adopt some "world picture."[1]

Business leaders need a useful "world picture" that can help them and the people with whom they work make more sense of the "bewildering" economic world that surrounds them; otherwise they can easily become confused by developments. Even if the senior leadership of the firm has a world picture, it rarely is easy to convey to others. The current president of Sony reports that it took nearly two years for him to convince Sony management about "the dynamics of our business."[2]

Intuit's founder, Scott Cook, discovered that getting his organization to accept a new strategy in the late 1990s was a much bigger challenge than he expected. "The Internet was such a breakthrough that I thought that people would get it more rapidly. But trying to get people to see the world differently means changing assumptions. And that's hard."[3]

This chapter attempts to help readers better understand the dynamics of their business. Specifically, it explores a framework for applying the concept of a fitness landscape to their own situation. Without employees having an understanding of the relevant landscape, the organization cannot be truly adaptive.

THE IMPORTANCE OF HELPING PEOPLE UNDERSTAND WHAT IS HAPPENING

In recent years, in most of the strategy sessions with which I have been involved as both a practitioner and facilitator, and in many of the seminars that I have given to organizations, I have tried to stress to the participants that strategy should no longer be primarily about planning. Rather it is about trying to see the world as it really is—which may be very different from the conventional viewpoint—and then preparing the organization so that it has a good chance for a successful future.

I sometimes use visual puzzles to illustrate, on a simple level, how easy it is for us to see only part of what we look at and that, even within the same organization, people see different things when looking at the same picture. Some see the sails on the horizon as a freak occurrence of nature whereas others see the sails as a threat to their survival.

The business world is full of examples of successful business leaders who saw their world differently from their competitors. For example, some business leaders view the emergence of the Internet as a threat to their business. Others see it as a great opportunity. In an earlier generation, when most movie studios resisted television, Walt Disney embraced it. In the late 1980s, when

Rupert Murdock purchased *TV Guide*, he, unlike many others in the media business, saw opportunity in the value of user-friendly information.

Few large organizations today face an eminent crisis. Yet more and more corporate leaders recognize that profound changes are under way in their environment and that their organizations are not prepared to respond to the changes that are coming. They are not very adaptive. In an increasingly unpredictable world, business leaders must not only personally understand the competitive environment in which their organizations operate but also help the people in their organizations to understand it as well. Only then can people throughout the organization act appropriately. They cannot respond in a constructive way if they do not know what is happening around them and management may not have time to tell them when the unexpected occurs.

Unfortunately, very few organizations spend much time helping the people in the organization understand their competitive environment. Even if they do make the effort, they often find that the existing frameworks and techniques that are widely used by managers and executives are not very helpful. For example, as a part of most strategic planning processes, executives traditionally explore the current structure of their industry. This has always been a more difficult issue to understand than it would seem at first blush. For example, if Microsoft employs me, do I work in the software industry, computer industry, or information and communications industries? Clearly the answer is all of the above. Yet if I define the industry too narrowly or too broadly, it is largely meaningless and potentially dangerous. I have found that the relevant system almost always is a larger system than the traditional definition of an industry. We need a different way to think about the arena—the competitive space—in which our companies operate.

A New Metaphor

Robert S. Shaw of the Institute for Advanced Study at Princeton, and a leader of the Dynamical Systems Collective at the University of California in Santa Cruz in the late 1970s, has observed, "You don't see something until you have the right metaphor."[4] Although admittedly a crude and oversimplified concept, I have found the biologist's fitness landscape to be a very useful metaphor for beginning to understand how to deal with the uncertainty that surrounds more and more businesses today.

By landscape I mean the managerially relevant system in which the various individuals and organizations operate. People throughout the organization need to have a basic understanding of the nature of the landscape on which their organization operates and how well their organization is functioning on that landscape.

There are three key questions that business leaders must try to answer about their organization, and help the people in their organization to understand, if they are to appreciate the need to adapt to unexpected developments: (1) What is the relevant landscape for our company? (2) How rugged is our landscape? (3) How fit is our organization relative to that landscape? Until there is some consensus in their views, the organization and its people cannot hope to make sense of the changes going on around them, much less position themselves well for the future.

Jeff Bezos of Amazon has observed that "you better recognize the environment you're in, and try not to build an airplane to fly under water."[5] In a colorful way, he has captured the essence of this chapter. Before an organization can perform as it should, the people who make up that organization need to understand their landscape.

WHAT IS THE RELEVANT LANDSCAPE?

Before we can begin to address the question of how rugged is the landscape on which a company competes, its leaders have to know on what landscape the company is a player. As noted above, traditional concepts are not very helpful in today's world.

Traditional Definition of "Industries"

The term "industry" is a common but very imprecise term used throughout government, business, and especially investment literature. For years the term has been used as a basis for reporting statistics and trends. Essentially, an industry included those businesses engaged in similar activities, i.e., paper industry, steel industry, motion picture industry, etc.

The standard reference document for industry classifications in the United States is the *Standard Industrial Classification Manual*, published by the Executive Office of the President, Office of Management and Budget. The Standard Industrial Classification (SIC) was developed for use in the classification of establishments by type of activity in which they are engaged. The primary purpose of this manual is to promote uniformity and comparability in data-collection reporting. Each operating establishment is assigned an industry code on the basis of its primary activity. The two-digit code includes the industry group number, i.e., 08 (Forestry), and the four-digit code identifies the subgroup, i.e., 0811 (Timber Tracts). Although the SIC Code Manual is a useful tool for establishing a base of uniformity of data reporting, it is extremely limited for researching and understanding rapidly emerging markets, businesses, and industries.[6]

Starting with the 1997 Economic Census, the U.S. government began switching to a new way of classifying industries. Called the North American Industry Classification System (NAICS), it includes information on more than 300 new industries, from satellite communications to casinos to nail salons, while grouping new and existing industries into more relevant sectors. For example, "information" would include publishing, software, motion pictures, broadcasting, and telecommunications. The first data did not appear until 1999 and will not be fully integrated into the federal statistics until 2004 at the earliest. By that time many of the new classifications will be out of date.

To further muddy the waters of industry groupings and classifications, a number of private organizations have established their own classification schemes. (Some cross-reference industries using the SIC code and others do not.) For example, Moody's Investor Services, Dun & Bradstreet, Standard & Poor's (S&P), Value Line, *Fortune*, *Business Week*, *Forbes*, Dow Jones, and numerous brokerage firms all have established industry groupings. With the growth of the Internet, various search engines such as Yahoo! and AltaVista have created various classification schemes for assigning companies to particular economic sectors and industries.

The ability to compare and analyze industries and companies is made difficult by the various classification schemes and industry definitions that various data collection organizations use. For example, in some classifications, telecommunications and electric utilities are combined into an overall classification of "utilities," whereas others treat them separately. In some classifications, Nike is not listed as a shoe company but a service company, since it does virtually no manufacturing of its own shoes. Other companies, such as 3M and General Electric, frequently are thrown into a "diversified" or "conglomerate" category.

This confusion was confirmed in a 1996 study. Using approximately 10,000 firms jointly covered by Compustat and the Center for Research in Security Prices (CRSP) from 1973 to 1993, the researchers found "substantial differences in the SIC Codes designated by the two databases."[7] More than 36 percent of the classifications disagreed at the two-digit level and nearly 80 percent disagreed at the four-digit level.

An Expanding View of "Industries"

Historically, if a company's leaders wanted to understand their industry, the key question was, Which companies should we be studying closely? Usually the answer focused on, Who are our competitors? Industry largely came to be defined by competitors.

In the late 1970s, Michael Porter of the Harvard Business School expanded our thinking about the agents that should be considered in analyzing an industry by focusing on the forces that could influence profitability. By including not just competitors but buyers, suppliers, substitutes, and new entrants, he offered a valuable framework for understanding the broader forces at work in an industry.[8]

In recent years, Porter's expanded concept of an industry has become more difficult to apply, especially in some service- and information-intensive industries. It is especially challenging to apply the Porter framework (or almost any framework) in a rapidly changing industry. For example, in what industry does Sony compete? Until the 1980s we could be fairly confident in answering "consumer electronics," although Sony was already broader than that, in that it served a number of business customers as well. After the acquisition of Columbia Pictures, some within the organization talked of being an entertainment company. Yet entertainment is such a broad concept that it is almost meaningless. Does Sony compete with theme parks or live entertainment? Now that the computer companies are interested in television broadcasting, should Sony consider Microsoft and Intel as competitors? As Nabuyuki Idei, Sony's president, sees it: "Convergence is happening not only between audio and video but between computers and communications. There is a fundamental change in society. . . ."[9] He adds, "Everyone is jumping into everyone else's business domain, and all the old rules are broken."[10]

Bill Gates has a similar view of the competitive space he faces. "In twenty-five years in this industry, I have never seen so much competition in every single area, and the competitive landscape and market boundaries are constantly changing."[11]

Precise industry classifications are proving to be difficult to determine even in established industries. For example, IBM and Digital Equipment ignored for a long time the PC threat—perhaps seeing the product as belonging to another industry. As "industries" become increasingly volatile, the definitions will become even more blurred and less meaningful. As they blur, executives can be blinded to serious competitors.

I, like a growing number of people, find the traditional concepts of industry to be increasingly useless and perhaps dangerous.

As Hamel and Prahalad observed in their book *Competing for the Future*, "Traditional industry structure analysis, of the kind that is the subject of strategy textbooks, is of little help to executives competing in unstructured industries."[12]

Drawing from macrobiology, James Moore, the author of "The Death of Competition," has suggested that in place of "industry," a more appropriate term would be "business ecosystem." For example, he sees companies such as Disney and Microsoft as anchors for an ecosystem. In the case of Microsoft, the ecosystem encompasses at least four major "industries": personal computers, consumer electronics, information, and communications. The Microsoft ecosystem also encompasses an extended web of suppliers including Intel and Hewlett Packard and many customers in a variety of "industries."[13]

I have found that the concept of a fitness or adaptive landscape is a richer metaphor than an ecosystem—although they are addressing the same concerns. Whatever the metaphor used, corporate leaders need to be able to think more broadly about the competitive space in which their firms operate. It can be helpful to challenge people to think about three levels of analysis: current players on the landscape, potential entrants onto the landscape, and environmental forces that can change the landscape. The volatility or increased ruggedness of the landscape can and does come from all three levels of the system.

Current Players

Current players are those who already are active participants on the landscape. As can be seen in Figure 5-1, I have identified five key players who are active in any given competitive space: direct competitors, suppliers, customers, substitutors, and complementors. All of these can try to raise barriers to entry to potential entrants.

The direct competitors are those with whom we currently compete for customers—the traditional definition of industry. The suppliers are those from whom we and other direct competi-

Figure 5-1   Current Competitive Space

Barriers to Entry

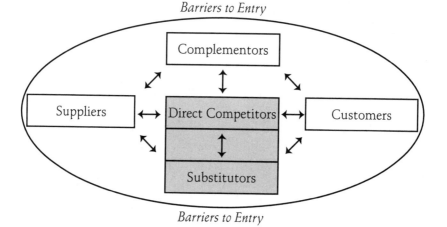

Barriers to Entry

tors acquire key resources. The customers are those to whom we and other direct competitors try to sell our goods and services. I consider the substitutors[14] to be an indirect form of competitor because their goods and services can be used in place of ours, but they are not directly comparable. For example, travelers' checks are a substitute for a credit card. In some countries bicycles and motorcycles are substitutes for an automobile, but hardly comparable. The complementors are those organizations that provide a product or service that is critical to our competitive space but with whom we do not necessarily have a direct exchange of resources. For example, oil companies are an important consideration for automobile manufacturers and software companies are important to technology consulting companies, whose customers use a particular software developer's product.

Potential Entrants

The second level of competitive landscape analysis I call potential entrants (see Figure 5-2). Here attention is focused on two types of organizations that have the greatest chance of overcoming the barriers to entry for the relevant competitive space.

Figure 5-2

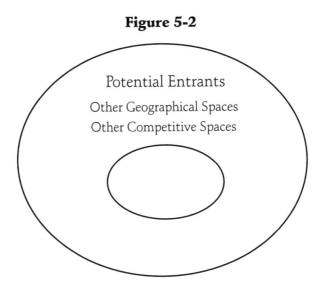

Potential Entrants

Other Geographical Spaces
Other Competitive Spaces

The first potential entrants are those from other geographical spaces—those organizations that are already established players in providing the same basic goods or services, but for whatever reason have to date chosen not to enter our geographical market. For example, in the mid-20th century Japanese automobile companies were already well-established firms but were primarily competing in Japan and other nearby countries, leaving the U.S. market primarily to the big three—General Motors, Ford, and Chrysler—and some European companies. As we enter the 21st century the situation is dramatically different. Not only are Toyota, Honda, and Nissan major players but Korean firms are also becoming significant. In the film business Kodak had a virtual monopoly on the U.S. market until the entry of Fuji. Now Kodak is trying to counter Fuji's moves by entering the Japanese market. On a local level, Ukrops grocery chain, the leader in the Richmond, Virginia, market, has recently moved out of its local market and up Interstate 95 about sixty miles to Fredericksburg, Virginia. For the first time it will compete with Giant, the dominant player in the Washington, DC area, which has moved down Interstate 95 to open a store in Fredericksburg. With the growth of the Internet, more and more firms will compete to some degree in all geographical markets.

The second type of organization to worry about are those that have never been in our space before but, for whatever reason (unusually attractive profits, perceived synergy), could easily move into our space. For example, when Sony purchased Columbia Pictures, it no doubt saw the possibility of synergy between electronic hardware and movies. When Westinghouse acquired CBS, it no doubt saw greater profit potential in broadcast television than in its traditional businesses. When General Electric acquired Utah Mining in the 1970s, it did so in part as a hedge against inflation. Most of these organizations entered a new space by buying someone who was already in the space. But occasionally, a firm will decide to "start from scratch," as did Dreamworks, when it established a new movie studio in the 1990s. These firms usually are started by individuals who have considerable experience in the industry. They either decide to "go for it" on their own and raise the necessary capital or another organization recruits them to start a new business.

For companies in very rugged landscapes, such as technology companies, the unknown competitor is of considerable concern. Often the new competitor can come from out of the blue. According to the founder of Amazon, when asked about competing with the large book retailers, he replied, "Frankly, I'm more concerned about two guys in a garage than Barnes & Noble."[15]

Although most current players on a landscape will continue to try to raise barriers to entry for potential entrants, the barriers will continue to diminish over time. Furthermore, the life of most barriers will become shorter and shorter and in many cases will not be worth the effort to build. This may be especially true for Internet-related commerce. Consequently, the threat of new entrants from other spaces will increasingly be a concern of executives in the 21st century.

The Environment

The third level of landscape analysis is the environment. This is where developments, largely beyond any particular competitive space, can increase the level of uncertainty of such a space and perhaps many more. Sometimes these forces will be specific to a particular competitive space but most often they will affect more than one.

As can be seen in Figure 5-3, there are two primary and inter-related areas of analysis: **fundamental forces** that are at work in the world and **spheres of influence**. The fundamental forces are those forces that cannot be controlled by any organization, at least in the short run, but must be monitored carefully since they can profoundly affect a competitive space. Such forces include geography, the weather, and demographics. Clearly a change in any of these areas can have a major impact on a variety of "industries" and companies. For example, a fundamental shift in weather conditions not only affects agricultural concerns but the travel business, including transportation companies, oil companies, clothing manufacturers, and retailers.

Historically, geography has been a key factor in the location of various businesses and the emergence of various "industries."

Figure 5-3   The Environment

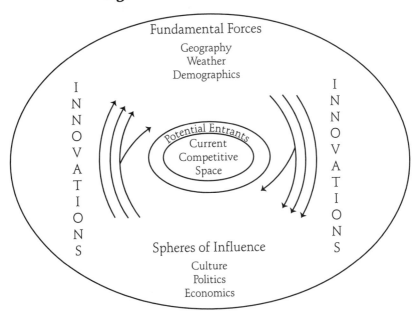

The location of natural resources often determines where many businesses tend to concentrate. On a broader scale, it is not surprising that one of the factors that influenced the emergence of the industrial revolution in England was its easy access to the sea and thereby to distant markets.

Demographic trends certainly shape most landscapes. "Global Trends 2010," a classified study by the CIA's National Intelligence Council, reportedly is being studied closely at the Pentagon to learn what enemy it is likely to have to deal with in the future. The answer reportedly is demographics. Each year an additional 90 million people will inhabit the globe and 95 percent of them will live in the world's poorest nations. The study finds that growing populations, widening gaps between rich and poor, and continuing revolutions in communications will incite new ethnic and civil conflicts, which could demand U.S. military intervention with increased frequency.[16] If the U.S. military is concerned about global demographics, most companies should be too.

These fundamental forces can be reflected in three primary but overlapping spheres of influence that are found in any society: culture, politics, and economics. Consider the number of "industries" affected by baby boomers. The emergence of baby boomers into adulthood not only affected the politics of the 1960s, but also influenced the culture of the Western world as well as the economic performance of various countries.

Especially important to consider is how innovation can come from any one of these spheres and can affect the landscape of its players. These innovations can range from incremental improvements to transforming innovations. For example, in the political arena, the U.S. Declaration of Independence and the English Magna Carta were transforming political innovations that fundamentally altered the landscape on which existing and future businesses operated. A change in the federal tax law may have an incremental impact on a landscape. In the cultural arena, the Protestant Reformation and the discovery of a superior numbering system by the Hindus that became the basis for our current numbering system were transforming forces that ultimately influenced the way business would be conducted. The development of currency and letters of credit were transforming economic innovations that profoundly influenced the way businesses operated throughout the world.

In more recent times it is new technologies that have been the transforming innovations. The application of the steam engine to manufacturing made the industrial revolution possible. The development of the gasoline engine made the automobile "industry" possible and all of the complementary "industries" that it spawned. At present, it is the computer chip and the Internet that are driving many of the current competitive spaces. It is for this reason that it is especially important for the leadership of all companies to be challenging its organization to consider how technology could change its business and how it might respond to various scenarios. I do not think Hugh McColl of BankAmerica is being inappropriately concerned when he sees technology as fundamentally changing his "industry," perhaps destroying it. One possibility he envisions is that his competition in the future will not come from the banking industry but from some totally unexpected quarter.[17]

As indicated at the beginning of this chapter, turbulence can come from any one of the three areas of the landscape (Figure 5-4). However, in the short run it is most likely to come from the current and potential players. Consider the following examples:

▲ AT&T set off a brutal competition when it entered the credit card business, which continues into 2000. According to Visa USA's CEO, AT&T's aggressive marketing "changed the future landscape of the credit-card industry."[18]

▲ When Eckhard Pfeiffer became Compaq's CEO in 1991, he slashed the workforce by 12 percent and cut prices on Compaq's PCs. The result, according to *Business Week*, was that "Compaq reset the competitive landscape, forcing PC rivals to whack costs and squeeze efficiencies out of manufacturing. Those that

Figure 5-4

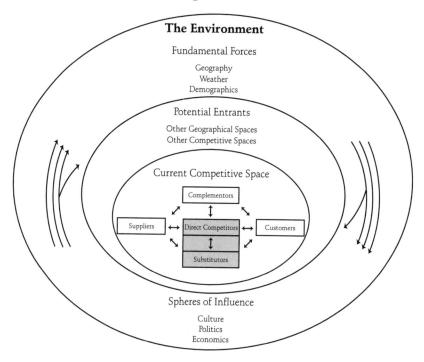

couldn't make the grade, such as AST Research Inc. and Apple Computer Inc., lost market share and were sidelined."[19]

▲ At the end of 1997, Hotmail Corp., the largest provider of free e-mail service on the Internet, agreed to be acquired by Microsoft for $385 million. According to one of the general partners at a venture capital firm that had backed Hotmail, "Once Microsoft has made its move, it becomes nearly impossible for them [other free e-mail companies] to remain independent."[20]

▲ Dell Computer has reshaped the PC industry by selling relatively low-priced, made-to-order PCs directly to customers and emphasizing rapid manufacturing and delivery. Michael Dell's company also is making the Internet an increasingly important part of any PC maker's strategy.

How Rugged Is Your Landscape?

Any organization's landscape is full of risks and rewards. Just to survive requires not only the insight (i.e., the idea of what is possible), but the capital to build an organization to exploit the idea. Then the resources are needed to convince a sufficient number of people to buy the good or service. Building the organization is a venture full of risks. The entrepreneur risks his or her reputation, time, energy, and capital. Investors risk their capital, employees risk their careers or some portion of them, and customers risk their capital to buy the new product. If the innovation is significant enough, it creates the opportunity for substantial wealth creation by those willing to take the risks.

The point of trying to analyze your landscape is not to eliminate risks but to help people within the organization better understand the risks and rewards—how rugged their landscape really is—and better cope with their landscape. In other words, people need to be realistic about the nature of their landscape and act accordingly. Some things that are appropriate for one landscape may not be appropriate for another landscape. One size does not fit all and one management fad or tool will not be appropriate for all companies. I am especially interested in the level of uncertainty or volatility of the landscape. I view the various landscapes as forming a continuum ranging from smooth to rugged.

Consider the following seven "industries," as classified by Value Line and Dow Jones: semiconductor, securities brokers, pharmaceuticals, beverages, entertainment, oil, and steel.[21] If we consider the relative degree of uncertainty facing companies in these industries, most of us would place steel toward the smooth end of the continuum, with semiconductors and financial services at the rugged end. The companies in the middle would occupy relatively fluid and changing landscapes, but they would not experience quite the sustained volatility found in technology and financial services.

Technology firms are incredibly volatile. For example, four of 1998's top ten largest technology companies in the S&P 500 were not publicly traded in 1985. IBM, even with its remarkable comeback, is about one-fifth of its 1985 index weight. The stock prices of technology firms also reflect their volatility. For example, shares of 126 technology companies that went public in 1998, by the end of September of that year were down an average of 12.8 percent, according to researchers CommScan LLC. In contrast, the Standard and Poor's 500 stock index was up 6.2 percent.[22] Even well-established technology companies such as Hewlett Packard and Apple range quite far from the S&P trend. Another indication of volatility is stock churning. A share of AT&T was held an average of 1.1 years in 1999, down from 3.1 in 1992. The average time a share of Amazon and Yahoo! were held in 1999 was seven and eight days, respectively.[23]

Internet-related companies are perhaps the most volatile. For example, Cisco stock peaked at 75³/₄ on January 21, 1997, and by April 18, 1997, had dropped 34 percent, including a 6 percent drop on April 15. Yahoo!'s stock price increased 506 percent in 1997 and, on one day in April of 1998, increased another 18 percent. Between June 10 and June 23, 1997, it had increased 29 percent.

Few companies have experienced the volatility of Netscape. When Netscape went public, its stock was priced at $14 but hit $75 before closing at $58. In 1997, Netscape got 45 percent of its revenues from browsers, but by the first quarter of 1998 it would receive none, since it was again giving it away for free to match Microsoft. On January 27, 1998, Netscape reported an $88 million fourth-quarter loss on declining sales and a loss of $115 million on sales of $534 million for 1997 as a whole. In January 1997, Netscape's stock dropped 19 percent in one day to $48. By November 1998, its market capitalization was down to $2.4 billion, from a high just three years earlier of $6 billion. According to its CEO, "When we issued Netscape stock, we gave out neck braces and seat belts."[24]

To begin to understand the level of uncertainty confronting a landscape, there are several questions that need to be answered. If the answer to any of these questions is "yes," then your organization may be farther along the landscape continuum than you thought, and you likely are operating on a fairly rugged landscape, which means more rapid and unexpected changes to confront.

1. *Is your organization facing or has it recently faced the threat of government deregulation?*

In country after country we are seeing the deregulation of such "industries" as transportation, telecommunications, electric utilities, and financial services. One impact of such political developments is to reduce a historically significant barrier to entry, thereby allowing new competitors to enter and change the landscape. For example, within a few years of U.S. deregulation of the airlines, the number of U.S. airlines almost doubled and several well-established airlines, such as Texas Air, People Express, Eastern, Piedmont, and Pan Am, were out of business. Over the next decade, we likely will see the same pattern of behavior among U.S. electric utility companies.

2. *Are the barriers to entry easy to breach in your "industry"?*

Barriers to entry are much easier to breach in most service businesses than in most manufacturing businesses. In today's world, few technology companies seem to have barriers to entry. In fact, one interesting aspect of the Internet is that it has the potential to lower barriers to entry in numerous "industries." According to Jason Olim, CEO of CDnow,

> Everyone always asks, "Where are your barriers to entry, where's your defensible position?" . . . I've always thought, 'Make socks.' Be in the least glamorous business and you'll have a defensible position.[25]

Obviously few companies, including CDnow, want to be in low-glamour, commodity businesses like socks. More and more companies are facing a landscape with few barriers. Furthermore, once the barriers have been breached, in today's world it may not cost much to increase capacity. As Olim makes clear, "To double your business, you only have to add another memory chip."[27]

3. Are significant technological developments at work on your landscape?

By definition, technology companies constantly face developments that can make their products obsolete and alter their industry. However, it is not just these companies that should be focused on such developments. According to Donald Valentine, founder of Sequoia Capital: "This dynamic—dropping prices and increasing functionality in all things digital—will crash up against more and more older industries." He adds, "The guy who runs a major airline or bank is probably clueless about what's happening around him. I don't think a lot of these CEOs enjoy facing technology. They are threatened and intimidated by it."[28] According to Hugh McColl of BankAmerica Corp., "This thing," he says, referring to technology, "is like a tidal wave. If you fail in the game, you're going to be dead."[29]

4. Is it hard to perform a meaningful, traditional industry analysis?

As discussed earlier, in more and more "industries" the boundaries are blurring. Sony is an example of a company whose most popular products have been oriented toward isolated, stand-alone, electronic entertainment so that people could enjoy it anywhere, anytime, and without having to be plugged into anything. Its future likely will be very different. According to Sony's new president:

> The digital revolution will shake our total business platform so that brand image and production power and even the best technology won't be enough. We have to recognize that in the future most of our products will become part of a larger digital network. From now on, then, Sony's work is to build bridges between computers and consumer electronics and communications and entertainment, not mere boxes.[30]

An indication that a blurring of the boundaries is happening is when analysts seem to have a difficult time accurately identifying in which "industry" you are operating and against which other companies your company should be compared.

5. *Do you find yourself increasingly worrying about companies you never before considered direct competitors?*

In working with Internet-based companies, I repeatedly heard concern expressed about the source of future competition. According to a former executive at CyberCash, "I worry about what I don't know. I worry about it every day." He adds, "Someone could change the whole landscape." Even in large, successful firms, there is similar concern. According to Hugh McColl, "I know that I've got competitors out there in the high-tech area, not the banking area, who are working this very minute to build a better mousetrap and drive me out of business."[31]

HOW FIT ARE YOU?

The third fundamental landscape question relates to relative fitness. How fit is your organization relative to the other organizations on your landscape? Within any given landscape, there are some organizations that are fitter than others. They are the organizations that so far have been able to adapt to changes and prosper. How should fitness be measured? I believe Bezos of Amazon has it right when he often emphasizes his desire "to build a valuable and lasting company."[32]

Although there are a variety of measures of fitness that an organization's leadership may choose to emphasize, I believe there are only two that are fundamental—survival and wealth creation. As the books *Built to Last* and *The Living Company* emphasize, there is much to be said for organizations that survive for long periods of time. However, there is more to fitness than survival. After all, sharks have survived much longer than human beings, but they are far from being the most interesting species on our planet.

According to Murray Gell-Mann, it is unlikely "that a truly meaningful measure of fitness can be assigned to an organism when the environment is changing, and especially when it belongs to a highly interactive ecological community of organisms adapting to one another's peculiarities."[33] Nevertheless, even he admits that a simplified discussion of fitness can be constructive and suggests that, to the extent that fitness is well-defined in biological evolution, it is connected with population size. As an aside, he suggests that wealth is a crude measure of fitness of a firm.[34]

Although companies frequently debate whether to emphasize market share or profit, the essence of Gell-Mann's argument is that adaptive companies should view growing wealth as the overriding goal. How the wealth is divided can be debated, but the real role of a business organization is to create long-term value and wealth.

In an interview I conducted in the late 1980s with Bill Marriott, CEO of Marriott Corporation, he emphasized the importance of growth. I did not get the sense that he was interested in growth just to make more money. In fact, he stressed that the real value of growth was that it gave the most capable people in the organization, the ones you wished to retain, something for which to strive. Without significant growth goals he feared that the best people would leave to find more interesting challenges somewhere else. In other words, you have to grow to survive.

The idea of growth, especially wealth creation, seems to be a powerful indication of fitness. After all, without wealth creation there is no capital to continue to invest in new opportunities, especially relatively risky opportunities. Furthermore, in a market economy, owners (especially shareholders) must be satisfied with their returns or they will shift their resources to more fit organizations or even to new competitive spaces. Again, this is not to say that other factors are unimportant. However, if I had to focus on one variable to measure fitness of an organization, it would be a measure of long-term financial success. To that end I have found a good proxy of fitness to be how the market values an organization. Such a measure not only incorporates past performance but also incorporates an estimate of future performance. Furthermore, it allows for comparisons across traditional "industry" lines.

Market value added (MVA) is the term widely used to indicate the difference between the capital investors put into a company and the money they can take out. It is the premium the market awards a company over and above the money investors have put into it. It is calculated by adding up the capital shareholders and creditors have furnished and retained earnings. This number is then subtracted from the current market value of both the company's stocks and bonds. The difference is MVA. Obviously, it fluctuates over time with the changes in the stock market. But in the long run, there is an assumption that good management will produce large, positive MVAs.[35]

Adrian J. Slywotzky, in his book, *Value Migration*, argues that company value, created by higher profits, revenues, and market share, migrates to the companies and industries with the "best business design." An example he uses is the steel industry. In 1960 eight large U.S. companies dominated the industry. Their total market value was $55 billion. By 1993 the market value was $13 billion and falling. Slywotzky believes that this value migrated to other companies and industries that had better opportunities for growth and investment return.[36]

CONCLUSION

Although historical definitions of industries may be useful for some governmental analysis, the traditional classifications are of limited value in trying to understand the future. To better understand the risks and rewards of today's world, business leaders need a useful metaphor that provides a broader picture of their world. To go back to the world of biology, the metaphor of an adaptive or fitness landscape can be very helpful.

As the landscape in which a company competes becomes increasingly volatile and complex, some species will fall off their current peaks and others will find new peaks and gradually pull the fitter agents along with them. In other words, there will continue to be great opportunities, but these will be accompanied by greater and greater risks. It is the nature of a complex world. Clearly in such a world the leadership and organizational skills required to survive—much less prosper—will need to adapt. The message is clear—managers must not get caught up in old definitions and ways of viewing their world. In turn, they must help the people in their organizations to understand the new realities.

In this chapter, I have tried to provide readers with a framework for understanding the fitness landscape on which they and their organizations operate. Specifically, I have explored three questions: What is your landscape? How rugged is it? How fit are you relative to others on the same landscape?

As discussed in Chapter Four, all companies are going to face increasingly rugged landscapes. Consequently, I have chosen to focus my research on the landscapes that are the most rugged of all—particularly the technology sector, broadly defined. I have paid particular attention to the Internet segment, which seems to be the more rugged of all as we enter the 21st century. The companies currently operating on this rugged landscape can provide some managerially useful insights to those of us whose landscapes are not yet so rugged. It is these organizational and leadership insights that are addressed in subsequent chapters.

Part III

LEARNING: ELEMENTS OF AN ADAPTIVE ORGANIZATION

Never let formal education get in the way of your learning.

—Mark Twain

Except for crisis situations, significant and large-scale organizational change toward a determined direction is extremely difficult and very rare. Even more rare seems to be the organization that is comfortable with constant change. Yet that is the essence of an adaptive organization operating on a rugged landscape. How do we begin to develop such an organization? The first step is the cultivation of a learning organization.

As Mark Twain so accurately observed, learning should be our goal, not education. This should be true for organizations as much as for individuals. Learning is at the heart of an adaptive organization. Specifically, an adaptive organization takes some common management practices and makes them aid the learning process.

Much has been written in recent years about organizational learning. For many businesspeople it has been hard to implement such a concept. I have tried to address the challenge by focusing on three common areas of management concern: strategic planning, organizational design, and organizational culture. These need to be viewed as ways to enhance organizational learning.

I wish to stress at the beginning of this section that organizational learning is not the ultimate goal. The ultimate goal is to develop an adaptive organization—one that not only survives but one that can grow, even in a constantly changing environment. We need to develop organizations that always are ready for change. The organization of the future needs to become comfortable with change—even constant change.

CHAPTER SIX

Planning to Adapt

"Strategy" probably is the most overused word in today's business vocabulary. It seems as though almost everything is "strategic." Consequently, the word has lost much of its impact. Yet the concepts associated with strategy can be especially helpful in trying to increase the chances of successful organizational adaptation. Specifically, these concepts have to enhance the learning capabilities of senior management and ultimately the entire organization.

When breakthroughs in digital technology and growing global markets can combine to change a company's landscape almost overnight, how does the leadership of a company effectively reexamine what it is doing and better position itself relative to the competition so as to more likely achieve its goals and objectives?

Consider the following Internet companies:

▲ CDnow. In August 1994, six months after Jason Olim had the idea of CDnow, he sold his first album. He recently observed "Every week is a revolution."[1]

▲ Intelligent Interaction. Yale Brown, CEO of Intelligent Interaction Corporation, reported that after a few months into his startup, he no longer thought about the future in terms of months but in terms of weeks.

▲ CyberCash. According to a vice president of CyberCash, "The Internet is growing very rapidly and companies like ours are hitched to a sky rocket; we are in for a wild ride."

▲ eBay. "In the Internet, there's a vacuum for time," says Gary Bengier, CFO of eBay. "I would say that technology companies move about ten times faster than normal companies, and Internet companies move about ten times faster than that."[2]

▲ Theglobe.com. According to CFO Frank Joyce, "We used to do five-year plans in prior companies, which were always a joke. And it's even more of a joke here."[3]

How should we think about strategy in a world where every week is a potential revolution and the future is thought of in terms of weeks?

THE EVOLVING NATURE OF STRATEGY

Today's approach to strategy is not what many business leaders learned when they were in business school or first being exposed to the practice of strategic planning. Over the past thirty-five years we have seen the emergence of at least three generations of thinking about strategy in a business context.

The first generation of thought about business strategy emerged in the 1960s and early 1970s. Its leading advocates included such organizations as General Electric, the Harvard Business School, and the Boston Consulting Group. The fundamental question posed by strategic planning at the time was: How can we position our organization to gain a sustainable competitive advantage? In many companies the approaches advocated by these pioneering organizations (experience curves, portfolio models, generic strategies, five forces, etc.) were quite helpful in improving overall organizational performance—at least for a time.

By the early 1980s many Western companies had experienced a series of environmental shocks, such as high inflation, oil embargoes, and, perhaps most significantly, growing foreign competition, especially from Japan. The traditional approaches to strategy did not seem to be working. In fact, in the early 1980s, *Fortune* estimated that less than 10 percent of companies "can fully implement" their strategies.[4]

In 1984, *Business Week* conducted a review of thirty-three strategies it had described in its pages in 1979 and 1980 and reported that "few of the supposedly brilliant strategies concocted by planners were successfully implemented."[5] They found that nineteen failed, ran into trouble, or were abandoned, while only fourteen could be deemed successful. Of the nineteen, fourteen appeared to have made the wrong assumptions about the business environment—ranging from interest rates to competitors' strategies. The article concluded that

> after more than a decade of near-dictatorial sway over the future of U.S. corporations, the reign of the strategic planner may be at an end. In a fundamental shift of power, line managers in one company after another are successfully challenging the hordes of professional planners and are forcing them from positions of influence.[6]

By the early 1980s a new approach to management had begun to emerge. Initially reflected in such books as *The Art of Japanese Management* (1981) and *In Search of Excellence* (1982), the focus seemed to shift to a more operational focus. The key question seemed to be: How do we improve our operational performance? Out of this approach came the quality movement and an emphasis on customer service, which was soon followed by an emphasis on downsizing and reengineering.

In a 1996 cover story, *Business Week* announced: "STRATEGIC PLANNING: IT'S BACK! Reengineering? Cost-cutting? Been there, done that. Now, strategy is king as Corporate America searches for real growth."[7] It reflected the fact that since the early 1990s the emphasis in a number of major businesses was beginning to shift again, with attention being focused on such concepts as core competencies and capabilities. The fundamental question was: How do we transform industries and grow our businesses? *Competing for the Future* (1994) was the best reflection of this approach.

I think this third stage now must evolve somewhat to reflect the reality of increasingly rugged landscapes. The new question, although similar to the question of growth, is: How do we grow in an increasingly uncertain world, where there are few if any sustainable competitive advantages?

What Is Strategy?

For the purposes of this book I have chosen to combine two of the early, and I think, still best, definitions of strategy into one. According to Alfred D. Chandler, formerly of the Harvard Business School, "Strategy can be defined as the determination of the basic long-term goals and objectives of an enterprise, and the adoption of courses of action and the allocation of resources necessary for carrying out these goals."[8] Henry Mintzberg of McGill University sees strategy as "a pattern in a stream of decisions. In other words, when a sequence of decisions in some area exhibits a consistency over time, a strategy will be considered to have formed."[9]

Chandler and Mintzberg are describing the same phenomenon but seeing it from a different perspective. Chandler is looking into the future—what is intended—and Mintzberg is looking backward at what actually happened. In both cases, we are interested in a *consistent pattern of decisions and actions over time that lead to the goals and objectives of the enterprise.*

In an increasingly rugged landscape the concept of strategy remains the same, but the nature of the strategic-planning process has to change. The traditional approach to strategic planning is too time-consuming and too dependent on predictions of the future. Today's business developments occur too quickly and too frequently for the traditional approach to be much help.

WHAT IS STRATEGIC PLANNING?

For me, strategic planning is the process an organization follows to try to develop a consistent pattern of decisions and actions that will increase the chances of the organization achieving its major goals.

The process of applying the various tools and techniques of strategy are most useful when they give people a better understanding of their current situation and, more important, some insights as to the questions that need to be asked to better prepare for the future. Again, the tools and techniques are especially helpful when used to facilitate adaptive behavior.

The Traditional Approach

My experience has been that strategic planning, as practiced at many organizations, is largely a useless exercise, and certainly is not a learning process. In fact it may be harmful. It may reduce the organization's ability to adapt by wasting time and increasing people's cynicism about the organization and its leadership. The result often is that people do not take the process seriously and resort to playing games; they figure out the system and try to beat it.

When I first served as a dean at a university, I had the all-too-common experience of taking seriously the annual planning process and the message from the president and provost to be innovative with our programs. The first time through the planning cycle, our team spent considerable time putting a plan together that we thought made sense for our institution. Many of our ideas, we were told, were incorporated into the university's budget request to the state legislature. Later, when we were scheduled to present our ideas to the university for internal funding of our initiatives, the president of the university did not bother to attend. Only one of his vice presidents attended our presentation, and he was planning to leave the university within a few months. Months later we learned that not only were our new initiatives not to be funded but our budget was to be cut. There was no explanation. When we appealed the decision we were again given a chance to make a presentation. Again, only one vice president attended. Within a few weeks of the last presentation, several of us had decided it was time to find more productive work or at least play other games that were more fun.

This kind of process is all too common—both in nonprofit organizations and in businesses. In the late 1980s, prior to facilitating a strategic-planning retreat for a subsidiary of a large U.S. company, I spent several days visiting with each of the executives of the firm, trying to get a sense of their view of the key issues facing the business. When I asked one of the vice presidents, "What is the company's strategy?" he responded, "It's that black book that sits on my bookshelf." The book he was referring to was a three-inch-thick notebook full of charts and tables, projecting revenues and costs into the future. When I asked him to be more specific, his response was memorable: "It's just one more event in the corporate Olympics." Strategic planning too often is a bureaucratic, mind-numbing game that is played by the same basic rules, year after year.

A Better Approach

I have been struck by the consistency of some of the comments about strategy by leaders of various Internet companies I have studied. For example, according to the CEO of one company, a strategic plan is "hardly worth writing. It changes constantly. We had one in the spring but things have changed a lot since then [three months later]." The CFO of another Internet company remarked, "I have yet to see a business plan that was implemented as written." After some refinements over the company's two-year history, he described the process at his company now as "better than the back of an envelope." Clearly the company needs a process that is helpful on a rugged landscape.

Arie de Geus, formerly of Royal Dutch/Shell, was one of the

first business writers I know to write about planning as a learning process. He also suggested that ultimately the only sustainable competitive advantage for an organization today is the ability of its managers to learn.[10] Although in today's environment we need to have everyone learning, not just managers, the process needs to begin with top management, and the best process for that, in my experience, is the strategic-planning process. In other words, strategic planning should be thought of as an organizational learning process, especially for the top management of the organization.

In *The Innovator's Dilemma*, the author talks about using "discovery-based planning" if organizations are to successfully confront "disruptive technologies." He suggests that managers should

> assume that forecasts are wrong, rather than right, and that the strategy they have chosen to pursue may likewise be wrong. Investing and managing under such assumptions drives managers to develop plans for learning what needs to be known, a much more effective way to confront disruptive technologies successfully.[11]

He also stresses that in disruptive situations, "action must be taken before careful plans are made. Because much less can be known about what markets need or how large they can become, plans must serve a very different purpose: They must be plans for learning rather than plans for implementation."[12]

As discussed in Chapter Three, agents in complex systems adapt or learn by changing their rules as experiences accumulate. To successfully learn so that they survive and prosper requires *prediction* and *feedback*. Prediction is thinking ahead; it is what helps an agent seize an opportunity or avoid getting trapped. All complex adaptive systems build models that allow them to anticipate their world, i.e., imagine consequences. That is very different from trying to predict consequences. Feedback from the environment is essential if the agent is to improve its internal models. It has to try out the models, see how well its predictions work in the real world, and—if it survives the experience—adjust the models to do better the next time. The improvement is called learning. An adaptive agent has to be able to learn quickly if it is to survive and prosper and the planning process should facilitate that learning.

KEY ELEMENTS IN A STRATEGIC
PLANNING PROCESS

As suggested earlier, it is very hard to plan in the conventional sense when operating on a very rugged landscape. By the time the staff has done a solid analysis of the "industry," or calculated an industry's experience curve, the industry has changed.

According to a survey by the Futures Group, consultants and corporate forecasters are increasingly uncomfortable looking outward, averaging a "comfort zone" of 1.7 years, down from 2 years in 1995.[13] This is especially true in technology companies. At SAS Institute, e.g., the largest privately owned software company in the United States, two years is about as far out as the company's leadership will admit to looking.[14] Even in the company that helped create the practice of strategic planning—General Electric—there is a recognition that time pressures are much greater today. According to a former GE executive, "Five years is an eternity. In fact, it's two careers in Silicon Valley!"[15]

As Netscape illustrates, in a rapidly changing environment, you can be in the Web browser business one day with no serious competitors, then within a few years, cease to be an independent organization. A traditional industry analysis in the early 1990s would not have prepared Netscape for the world of Microsoft and foreseen the great success of America Online.

If conventional planning is too time-consuming and based on too many static concepts, what are executives to do? As indicated earlier, whatever the specifics of an organization's process, it must emphasize thinking ahead and feedback. The goal is to assist managers and executives in organizations to better see both the organization and its environment—its fitness landscape. To do this well the process has to incorporate what I call active observation, "what if" questions, a clearly communicated sense of direction, and opportunism.

Active Observation

According to Holland, an "adaptive agent has to be able to take advantage of what its world is trying to tell it."[16] This means that a business organization must have good feedback from its landscape and the various agents on it. Specifically, there must be good feedback about what the other agents on the landscape are doing and about the organization's own position on the landscape. The goal is to be able to spot patterns in the overall system and thereby recognize opportunities and threats.

Peter Drucker recently observed in the *Harvard Business Review* that in human affairs, whether political, social, economic, or business, "it is pointless to try to predict the future." This is a point Drucker has been making throughout the 1990s. In an earlier *Wall Street Journal* column, he contrasted traditional strategic planning with what is needed today. Traditional planning, he argues, is based on assumptions, whether explicit or implicit, that are arrived at by asking, What is most likely to happen? He believes that when you are dealing with today's uncertainty, the right question to ask is, What has already happened that will create the future? The answer to this question defines the potential of opportunities for a given company.

To convert this potential into reality requires matching the opportunities with the company's strengths, or in today's language, "core competence." For example, by looking at demographics, Drucker believes business leaders should be asking:

What do these accomplished facts mean for our business? What opportunities do they create? What threats? What changes do they demand in the way the business is organized and run, in our goals, in our products, in our services, in our policies? And what changes do they make possible and likely to be advantageous?[17]

The next question is, What changes in industry and market structure, in basic values (i.e., the emphasis on the environment), and in science and technology have already occurred but have yet to have full impact? This should be followed by the question: What are the trends in economic and social structure? And how do they affect our business?

To answer these questions requires more than traditional market intelligence. The leadership of the organization has to understand more than the five key "industry" forces. Leaders have to understand developments in the current competitive space, and beyond it, that could change the landscape—political, social, cultural, economic, and especially technological developments.

Top management should make sure that the organization's people are constantly studying the landscape to try to spot new developments that could significantly alter it. To that end, some organizations are assigning key personnel to such a task. For example, some organizations are giving a top officer oversight of all risks, including operational and political exposure. In some cases these risk executives report to the chief executive or the board.

GE Capital incorporates risk management directly into its culture by deploying risk managers alongside business leaders at each of its twenty-seven businesses. They are responsible for checking out customers, running probabilities, and advising business leaders on every move. In each business the risk manager identifies the four or five main factors contributing to potential profitability. According to one executive, "We study the history to understand how we make money on that product." Once the profit drivers have been determined, business leaders identify alarms to alert them to any significant change. GE also uses a proprietary software tool called Globalnet to keep track of GE's exposure to every client across all lines of business.[18]

Gathering good information about developments in some competitive spaces can be very difficult. This is especially true for companies in countries without a strong commitment by the government and private organizations, such as the business press. Yet such information as exists should be aggressively sought and analyzed.

Leading technology firms seem to be especially good at gathering good information. The Futures Group, a business-intelligence consultancy, publishes an annual survey on the use of competitive intelligence in the United States. In 1997, the "savviest" player in the intelligence game was Microsoft. Of the top eight companies on the list, six were major technology companies—Microsoft, Motorola, IBM, GE, Hewlett Packard, and Intel.[19]

The leaders of these companies, which operate on one of the most rugged landscapes, have recognized that risks are everywhere: financial, technological, competitive, regulatory, legislative, political, and strategic. Within any category there are a variety of different things that could have a major impact on the company.

Understanding Competitor Behavior

Obviously competitors are an important area for observation. The new CEO of Intel, Craig Barrett, helped to advance his career as well as better position his company for the future by aggressively seeking to learn in the mid-1980s why such Japanese firms as Hitachi, NEC, and Toshiba were so much more proficient at making chips. According to *Fortune,*

> Barrett . . . took to the problem with the obsessiveness of a detective and the desperation of a graduate student. He shook down American chipmaking equipment vendors for detailed descriptions of how Japanese fabs (chip plants) used their gear. He asked big chip customers what they saw on their visits to their Japanese suppliers, toured the plants of Intel's own Japanese partners, and studied every scrap of public and academic informa-

tion about how competitors designed and managed their operations.[20]

The Internet can provide a potentially powerful avenue for intelligence gathering. Barrett's predecessor, Andy Grove, reports that he finds it helpful to scan cyberspace for indicators of trends.[21] In addition to gathering information directly from company Web sites and from news sources, some people use newsgroups to gather information about competitors and about their own company.

Competitive intelligence does not have to be a high-tech approach. For example, at GE Capital market intelligence is gathered throughout GE as part of a reciprocal arrangement with other GE businesses. Some companies find help-wanted ads to be a revealing source of information about such things as a competitor's technology and expansion plans.

I did some work a few years back with a segment of the technology sector that did not receive a lot of attention by the organizations that collect competitive data. I was impressed with this company's low-tech approach to gathering information. Someone was charged with collecting any piece of information about the various players in their "industry" that had been published in any outlet. Notebooks full of magazine and newspaper articles were developed that people regularly reviewed. Although the estimates and projections could vary quite a bit from one article to the next, the readers were trying to develop some insights about "patterns" of behavior, especially among current competitors.

It is especially important to have an understanding of various companies' histories. Again, the goal is to try to understand the patterns of behavior that characterize the way these organizations tend to operate. I often have argued that if you want to understand an organization's true strategy, look at how it has operated in the recent past, especially where it has been spending significant amounts of money and where it is hiring key people. I have found this pattern of behavior to be much more revealing about a company's likely actions in the future than reading the organization's formal strategic plan. Too often the formal plan is a public relations document, or even a political document, with little managerial significance.

Understand Key Customer Values

Active observation also requires the studying of and communication throughout the organization about the key customer values. What is it our customers really value? What are they likely to value in the near term? To answer these questions you have to be incredibly in tune with your customers. Bezos of Amazon talks about being a "customer-obsessed company":

> That's where most of our differentiation comes from. I do not believe there is another company on the Internet that thinks about, talks about, and asks about their customers as much as we do, and asks their customers as many questions as we do, and really tries just through plain old hard work to build the best possible experience for customers.[22]

I have identified three key customer values that are found on every competitive landscape and that, at a minimum, all organizations need to incorporate into their strategy—cost, quality, and convenience. I believe they are the foundation of customer satisfaction. Two more values—innovation and speed—ultimately become important to the organizations involved in a particular competitive space but may not be of immediate concern to customers.

As the reader will note in Figure 6-1, the three basic choices are depicted as an expanding triangle. This is meant to emphasize two important points. First, it is not an either-or choice. Rather, some combination of these values must characterize the product offering of the company. In other words, there are minimum levels of cost, quality, and convenience that must exist to even be in the game—sometimes referred to as "table stakes"—and those

Figure 6-1

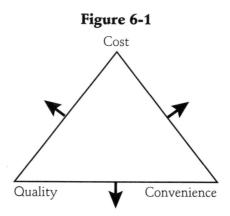

minimums are constantly increasing. In today's environment, a company cannot be the low-cost producer and completely ignore the other qualities.

There is a serious risk in concentrating on one value to the neglect of others. At Emerson Electric, Charles Knight, who once thought his company was "idea limited," now realizes his heavy emphasis on cost control in the 1980s and early 1990s was partially responsible for stifling innovation:

> It's just been amazing to be sitting in these conferences, looking at these growth programs, and thinking, "Why the hell haven't we done some of this before?" Well, we hadn't done it because we didn't have the resources to do it. And we didn't have the resources to do it because we were pounding the shit out of profit margins.[23]

The second major point I wish to emphasize with the expanding triangle is that competitors can and should continue to emphasize these three dimensions—over time. Usually through continuous improvements the frontiers of acceptable quality, cost, and convenience will expand. For example, quality likely will continue to improve over time and there will be continuous competitive pressure to lower prices, especially in a world of excess capacity. Competing companies will continually look for ways to gain an advantage, even if temporary, by emphasizing one or more of the three values.

Charles Knight offers some insight about continuous, incremental improvements. He states that leaders should

> never underestimate the cumulative impact of incremental change and the gathering forces of momentum. When you grind it out a yard at a time, you are in fact moving ahead. I can't say it will work for everybody, but at Emerson we view it as the only way to manage.[24]

This view is prevalent in a number of successful technology companies, both large and small. According to a former Microsoft employee who founded her own company, she learned from Microsoft and Bill Gates in particular the importance of "being willing to put something out there and keep building on it." She believes this approach "especially applies in small start-ups. You've got to maintain focus and keep putting one step forward—it's not a single great play or stroke of luck."[25]

HP is a good example of a technology company that has benefited from continuously improving the quality of its products. It started selling inkjet printers in 1984. At first the printers were messy and inferior, but HP kept improving them. By 1996 HP was the number one maker of inkjet printers, an almost $9 billion market, which accounted for 70 percent of all computer printers sold.

Cost

In the 21st century, no company can be viable for very long on any landscape if its products and services are not approaching the lowest cost position on the landscape. I believe that is one reason why reengineering and downsizing have been so popular in so many large companies throughout the world.

Jack Welch recognized very early in his tenure that if GE were to be competitive with strong foreign competitors, it would have to drive costs out of its businesses. In addition to being one of the first U.S. CEOs to strongly emphasize downsizing, he aggressively pushed productivity goals throughout the organization. He has stressed from the beginning of his tenure that "only the most productive companies are going to win."[26] When asked how far GE can push productivity, he responded: "After thirty years of productivity growth, nobody in Japan asks, 'Is it all over?' It's *never* over."[27]

More and more executives in the United States and Europe have recognized that if they are going to be successful, especially in global markets, they have to approach the cost structure of competitors in developing countries—even with upscale products. Nicolas Hayek, the CEO of the Swiss Corporation for Microelectronics and Watchmaking (SMH), and the driving force behind the Swatch success, believes most European and U.S. consumers may pay as much as a 10 percent premium for Swiss-made watches but no more than that.[28]

The cost emphasis is especially important among many technology companies. According to a Sony executive,

It's hard to believe how fast prices are falling. I visited a Circuit City store in Los Angeles in February and they were selling a [South Korean] full-featured VCR for $99. Ninety-nine dollars! We can't possibly make one [to sell at retail] for that, and we invented most of the technology.[29]

Leading software companies also benefit greatly from a strong cost control mindset. In 1997, Microsoft earned $.297 in profits for every dollar in sales—a margin that was not only 13 percent higher than the prior year's but almost four times the average for its industry and better than all but four Standard & Poor's top 500 companies. At the same time, the percentage of revenues going into R&D increased from 14 percent to 17 percent. According to the company's president and COO, "How do we do it? We watch costs like a hawk."[30]

Cost is more than just the direct expense of producing the good or service. It is cost throughout the organization. It is the efficient use of all resources. For example, increasing the speed of performing various administrative functions is one way to improve the overall cost structure of the organization. In 1993, Sun Microsystems took almost a month to close its books after a quarter ended. By 1996, it took only twenty-four hours to deliver preliminary figures to the CEO, giving the firm an advantage in planning for the next few quarters. Between 1989 and 1996, Sun also cut in half the time it took to receive payment after an order was issued, thereby giving top executives more available cash to invest. According to Sun's CFO, "We're spending more time managing forward instead of backward."[31]

On the Internet, cost is increasingly a key consideration. In the early days of Amazon it was not unusual for the company to offer 30 percent discounts on the prices of some books. When a serious competitor entered the market, Amazon responded by offering as much as 40 percent discounts on some books. Now it sells some books with a 50 percent discount. On an especially rugged landscape—financial services online—the CEO of Ameritrade, a cyberbroker, has joked that "by next year, we'll be paying investors to trade."[32] In fact, in 1999 E*Trade offered new customers a $75 sign-up bonus. Clearly these firms have to control costs very tightly if they are to survive.

Fortunately, the Internet also makes some significant cost savings possible. Dell Computer takes orders from end users and assembles a PC only after receiving an order. The direct contact with customers facilitates feedback that lets the company react immediately to shifting demand. According to Michael Dell of Dell Computer, "The Internet for us is like a wonderful dream come true. It's like zero-variable-cost transactions. The only thing better would be mental telepathy."[33]

Quality

In the 1980s, companies throughout the world recognized that Japanese competitors had shifted the customer value triangle more toward the quality side. (In some cases they had shifted both the cost and quality side.) For example, ten years ago I had the opportunity to become somewhat acquainted with the automobile industry in a South American country. I learned that once Japanese imports were allowed into this country, the public's perception of quality dramatically shifted from an American perspective, in which quality often meant having powerful engines, to a Japanese perspective that emphasized reliability. Once consumers had experienced reliability there was no going back. They now expected reliability. As this illustrates, there can be multiple dimensions of quality—reliability, durability, features, etc.—that competitors will emphasize. As they do so the threshold increases for all players.

From the beginning of his tenure at GE, Welch has stressed quality in addition to productivity. He believes, "If you can't sell a top-quality product at the world's lowest price, you're going to be out of the game."[34] In 1997, after many large corporations seemed to have lost interest in the quality movement, GE began a new push on quality, stressing "six sigma quality," meaning 3.4 defects per million products. According to Welch, "You have to tell your people that quality is critical to survival, you have to demand everybody gets trained, you have to cheerlead, you have to have incentive bonuses, you have to say, 'We must do this.'"[35]

In the technology sector the emphasis on quality is especially critical:

▲ Iomega Corporation, the maker of storage devices in 1997 had to recall 75,000 diskettes used with its high-capacity Jaz drive as a result of bad components. In early 1998 Iomega experienced a first-quarter loss and its CEO resigned.

▲ Motorola, although a 1988 winner of the Malcolm Baldrige Quality Award, lost some large contracts in the late 1990s because of quality problems. Motorola's cellular system would occasionally stop working, resulting in lapses that lasted between thirty minutes and two hours.[36]

▲ Hewlett Packard guarantees 99.999% reliability (five minutes of downtime a year) for certain commonly used applications. Now it is working with various partners to offer the same guarantee for systems working over the Internet.

▲ Internet companies like Amazon also recognize the importance of giving customers a quality experience. Its managers know that the Internet gives customers significant power to vent their frustrations with bad service in a way never before possible. According to Amazon's CEO, "If someone thinks they are being mistreated by us, they won't tell five people, they'll tell 5000."[37]

As with cost, quality is necessary but not sufficient to building a competitive advantage in the future. According to a former Sony executive, "The difference in quality between our products and our competitors' will be harder and harder for consumers to find."[38] Yet the push on quality has to be constant. As a senior vice president at Cisco sees it, "If we don't keep improving our technology, we'll lose our lead. Our customers won't settle for second best."[39]

Convenience

In addition to the need to emphasize the customer values of cost and quality, companies have to pay much more attention to the value of convenience. Although convenience has always been important to consumers, and some people would treat it as an element of quality, I believe that with the increasing time pressures on people and the emergence of the Internet, convenience should be viewed as a separate customer value.

The growth in two-income families as well as longer workweeks for many people have reduced leisure time from roughly twenty-six hours a week in the early 1980s to about nineteen in the late 1990s. In the same time period, consumers have reduced the time they spent on each mall visit from ninety minutes to less than an hour today. Furthermore, according to a 1997 survey by

Kurt Salmon Associates, 52 percent of consumers wanted to further reduce their shopping time.[40]

In the 1980s, Stan Davis, a futurist and former Harvard Business School professor, identified four dimensions on which companies would need to compete in the future: service (what he called "no matter"), mass customization, any place, and any time.[41] I see the last three of these as elements of convenience. Making a good or service available to customers, the way they want it, where they want it, and when they want it, is what convenience is all about.

With the growth of the Internet, it is increasingly possible for people to have more and more goods and services available in a very convenient way. For example, Amazon makes it very easy for customers to order almost any book they can think of, at any time, and have it sent anywhere. According to Jeff Bezos, "I abide by the theory that says in the late 20th century, the scarcest resource is time. If you can save people money *and* time, they'll like that."[42] He believes that if it is possible to build barriers to entry for competitors, it likely will be by offering convenience, "more selection and by making the site easier to use and more reliable."[43]

Virtual Vineyards does the same thing with wines and CDnow does it for recorded music. Both now offer a degree of customization by offering different prices and deals to its customers depending on what they've done in the past. Increasingly people are doing banking and stock trading over the Internet, right from their home or office. Customizing of information-intensive products is now possible.

It is not just individuals who value convenience but corporations as well. For example, Dell Computer is winning corporate accounts against IBM and Compaq not only because its products are priced below the competition but because it can tag and address the machines to be delivered to specific offices and load a customer's software at its factory. Later Dell launched an e-commerce Web site, Gigabuys.com, through which it will sell more than 30,000 outside products. According to one analyst,

"Through Gigabuys, Dell can build a stronger, longer-lasting relationship with customers than by simply selling them a box."[44]

Innovation

At some point on a rugged landscape, a firm will decide it can no longer grow enough by playing the cost-quality-convenience game with its existing products and will introduce a new product or service—it will innovate (Figure 6-2). Ultimately a firm reaches a point where it has pushed the boundaries of its competitive space as far as it can or wants to and decides that, if it is to continue to grow at a particular rate, it must move into a new space or perhaps create one. This usually is done by product innovation. By this I do not mean an improved version of the existing product but something new.

In many cases this will be an effort to leverage off of strength in one of the three key values. For example, in the 1960s and 1970s Hewlett Packard was very successful at producing high-quality instruments. In the 1980s, it shifted resources toward linking instruments together into systems and increasingly became a high-quality computer company. Wal-Mart's success as a low-cost retailer has been leveraged to enter the retail food business. In the Internet world, Auto-by-Tel has found that in addition to providing customers with convenient automobile shopping it can provide convenience in auto financing and insurance.

Figure 6-2

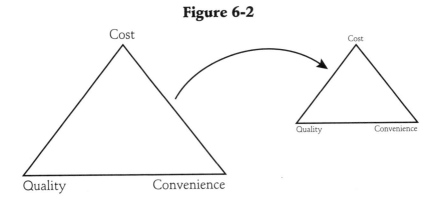

If the new product truly fills an unmet need, it finds a viable niche in an existing landscape. Ultimately, however, it may create an entirely new landscape. For example, when the first PC was introduced it may have looked like a niche in the computer landscape, but it ultimately produced an entirely new landscape. Over time, a new landscape may evolve in such a way that it combines with other landscapes, as PCs and television may be doing at the end of the 20th century.

For an organization seeking to play the innovation game, a key question has to be answered: Do we want to be the first mover? According to Daniel Hesse, President of AT&T Wireless, who introduced the Digital One Rate plan in 1998: "One thing 1998 taught us is that you can be much more successful if you dictate the terms by being first and innovating. You'll continue to see us launch new offers this year [1999] and in the future."[45]

There is no doubt that there are tremendous advantages on today's competitive landscapes for organizations that can move fast. This is especially true on very rugged landscapes, such as the Internet world. In fact, there is considerable evidence that in the world of the Internet, being first is critical. The authors of *Net Gain* believe in the importance of preemptive strategies since they see the Internet world as a world of increasing returns.[46] Economist W. Brian Arthur of the Santa Fe Institute has a similar view: "The high-technology industry is like a land race with only one prize, but that prize is a million acres."[47]

The most extreme examples of the way increasing returns work in the real world today appear in the computer software business, where establishing a big user base is the key to success. Microsoft set a standard for PC operating systems that "locked in" and consequently gave it a huge advantage in selling its spreadsheet and word-processing software.[48]

Part of the success that companies like Amazon have had is that they dared to do something the established players like Barnes & Noble and Borders seemingly were unwilling to try. Until Amazon proved that there was a large market for online book selling, the larger firms seemed to take a wait-and-see attitude. Now they too have entered the world of the Internet, but they are in a catch-up mode. It is an example of large firms ignoring a disruptive technology while a fringe company embraces it and in short order changes the competitive landscape for all.

Not surprisingly, being first is a goal for many, if not most, technology companies today. For example,

▲ Cisco's CEO—"In this industry, you have to be big and you have to be first to market with the right technology."[49]
▲ Netscape's CEO—"When you have a market changing so rapidly, you've got to be in the forefront of the change or you're going to miss it."[50]
▲ Microsoft senior executive—"The challenge is to keep pushing technology so that . . . you cause the next change."[51]

John Chambers, who had worked at IBM and Wang Laboratories before going to Cisco, places a human as well as organizational value on the importance of being first. "I learned at both companies that in high tech, if you don't stay ahead of trends, they'll destroy everything you work for and tragically disrupt the lives of your employees. I don't ever want to go through that again."[52]

Of course, there are tremendous risks to being the first mover. According to Bill Melton, cofounder of Cybercash,

> Our business is at the juncture of new technology and social change regarding how people handle money and payments. That's a very delicate position to be in. You run too slow with the technology, you don't have a defensible perimeter from your competitors. But if you run too fast, you get way ahead of the market.[53]

Not surprisingly, some established companies prefer to be a follower in the Internet world—hopefully a fast follower. They prefer to let others incur the high costs of innovation and then hope to quickly copy the work of the pioneer and improve on it, through cost, quality, or convenience. Even a follower organization, however, has to be able to move very quickly.

I am convinced that on very rugged landscapes, such as the Internet world, companies always should try to be the first mover. There are definite advantages of getting to market first. First and foremost, you likely will understand the landscape better than your competitors. According to the CEO of E*Trade Group Inc., the first brokerage service to stake a claim in online trading in 1992, by being first, "you get blood on your spear, but you know the terrain better than anybody."

Speed

Increasingly, the name of the game, whether cost, quality, convenience, or innovation, is speed—pushing faster and faster improvements. This seems especially true in introducing new products or new generations of products. Consider Sony's challenge as it moves farther into the computer business. According to one of its executives, "a television design . . . might last five or seven years. But in computers, you see [completely new hardware designs] nearly every year."[54]

In the early days of Netscape, Marc Andreessen insisted that his company release a second version of Netscape Navigator in three months and every three months thereafter. The company agreed to do it every six months. *Business Week* called the new pace "an unheard-of-pace in an industry used to two-year product cycles."[55]

Sprint used to take sixty days from the signing of a contract to completion of a networking project. Now, thanks partly to the efficiency of ordering Cisco equipment online, it takes thirty-five to forty-five days. (Sprint also has been able to cut its order-processing staff from twenty-one to six, allowing the other fifteen employees to work on installing networks, a business that doubled at Sprint in two years.)[56]

An executive with Lycos who formerly was an executive for a large automobile lubricant company, compares speed in the high-tech world to a more traditional industry: "Getting an idea to market takes seven weeks, compared to two years at a traditional corporate job."[57] Another executive who had switched from a more traditional company to a high-tech company commented, "Many classically trained consumer marketers don't cut it in high tech because of the fast pace. Because it's so quick, you don't have time to do research. You go more with intuition and instincts."[58]

At many large, traditional organizations processes are not designed for speed. For example, many strategic-planning systems require managers to make a request for resources months before they will learn whether they got the requested money or some portion of it. At companies like GE and 3M, there have been efforts to speed up the process so that people know almost immediately about the level of funding so that they can get on with it. After all, increasingly, these big companies are facing competition from small technology firms. Nevertheless, by early 1999 there was a growing sense at 3M that its processes were too slow for the increasingly rugged landscape it faced. By early 1999, not only had the company missed annual earnings projections for two years running and sales were essentially flat, but also profits declined 44.6 percent in 1998 and its stock had lost a third of its value since 1997. The results were public reports of management unrest and efforts to replace the current CEO.[59]

At some large companies there often is a desire to go slow so as to milk the profits of an older product or technology before introducing something new. This is not the case at technology leader Intel. According to Andy Grove,

> We are what we are because we push technology as fast as we can. Our whole belief is that technology is good, and more is better. How could we slow down technology? It's not good for anybody: not for the software developer, not for us, and most important, it's not good for the consumer.
>
> . . . The notion that we sit around and say: "Let's slow it down so we can charge more money . . ." I mean,

this is the room where these discussions take place, and these walls have never heard that.[60]

Some companies have a deliberate objective of making their own technologies and products obsolete. For example, Intuit commissioned a small group of engineers, dubbed the "Quicken Killers," who work apart from their colleagues, to propose alternatives to its best-selling software product—Quicken. They recognized that competitors are doing this and if competitors discover them first, Intuit will be in trouble.

Many software and Internet companies have learned to move fast by, among other things, letting internal and external customers do their market research. For example, Netscape employees used trial versions of forthcoming programs to find the bugs before customers did. In the words of one Netscape employee, "We eat our own dog food."[61] At AGCS, a telecommunications software company, before a new software product, update, or change is released to customers, it has to be installed on headquarters' equipment. Yahoo! puts new programs on its site, without research, making changes daily. Within two weeks it knows whether it has a success or a failure—and the failure gets scrapped.

These companies are constantly looking for ways to get quality products to market faster and faster. Alan F. Shugart, chairman of disk drive giant Seagate Technology Inc., may be right about how intense the race to market will become. "Sometimes I think we'll see the day when you introduce a product in the morning and announce its end of life at the end of the day."[62]

Understand Your Organization

Another element of active observation is observation of internal matters. In *On the Art of War*, perhaps the first strategy book ever written, Sun Tzu stresses the importance of not only knowing the "enemy" but knowing yourself. "Know the enemy and know yourself; in a hundred battles you will never be in peril."[63]

The founder of Amazon stresses a similar viewpoint: "You

cannot make a business case that you should be who you're not."[64] The president of a successful division of Emerson Electric makes the same point in a more positive way. He claims that he constantly "preaches" to his people the same message—"know who you are first and be it as best you can."[65]

The leaders of too many organizations fail to heed this advice. Although they may have included a "strengths and weaknesses" section in their strategic plan or have identified what they think is a "core competence" or "core skill," too often the work is superficial and more of a wish list than reality. It is absolutely essential that the leaders have a realistic view of their organization so that they can more successfully take advantage of the opportunities that the landscape may present.

Before Intuit made a fundamental shift in its strategy to take advantage of the Internet, in the words of CEO Bill Harris, "We had to think long and hard about what we did best as a company." That led Intuit to add alternatives to its traditional licensing of shrink-wrapped software—such as subscription, usage, ad, and transaction fees. By early 1999 the Quicken.com site already had signed up $60 million in ads for 1999 and 2000, and in 1998 the online mortgage center on its Web site closed $600 million in loans for partners, which included First Union Corp. and Chase Manhattan, which paid Intuit fixed fees.[66]

I have found that some organizations value having faculty at my school write case studies about them. Not only is an outsider taking an objective view of the organization and writing it up in a form that is easily shared, but he or she also sometimes benefit from listening to a class discuss the case. Whether the class consists of MBAs or executives, I have found that executives from the case company often gain insights about their company from listening to eighty to one hundred outsiders discuss their company.

In general, I have found that understanding the history of an organization can be especially useful in understanding why that organization operates the way it does today and how it might act in the future. I often have thought that the skills and insights of a historian could be especially helpful to the leaders of businesses operating on today's rugged landscapes.

What If?

After active observation, the strategic-planning process of an adaptive organization should try to answer a fundamental question: What if? There are various ways of asking that very important question. Consider the following examples:

▲ John Malone, CEO of cable giant TCI (soon to be part of AT&T), claims that the best business advice he ever got was: "Always ask the question 'If not?'"[67]

▲ Kevin Rollins, vice chairman of Dell Computer, claims his company is always "scouring for anything that could come up and bite us. In fact we ask ourselves all the time, 'What is our greatest fear?' Whenever we find something, we try to figure out how we can embrace it."[68]

▲ At GE, Jack Welch talks about how strategic planning does not focus on numbers. Rather, he and his managers get into the "dynamics of the industry." After developing a "feel for the playing field" he and his managers talk about what has happened in the past twelve months and what is likely to happen over the next three years. Equally important, they explore what "we want to do to change the game" and what competitors could do.[69]

However the question is worded, we are trying to get at what we will do if in spite of our active observation, we might have missed something. Few people have good plans for when their assumptions are wrong and unexpected developments occur.

In a 1997 *Forbes* article, the author contrasted the planning approach for Boston-based firms to those in Silicon Valley. He described the Boston firms as more likely to depend on traditional approaches to planning that assume one can predict with some regularity the occurrence of certain events. By contrast, Silicon Valley firms were more likely to put little stock in predicting but emphasize the importance of quick responses to rapid change.[70] In other words, they are more adaptive.

Andy Grove certainly reflects the Silicon Valley approach. He points out that no amount of formal planning can anticipate the major changes that affect businesses, what he calls "strategic inflection points." Yet he does not advocate doing away with planning. Rather he stresses the need to plan the way a fire department plans. "It cannot anticipate where the next fire will be, so it has to shape an energetic and efficient team that is capable of responding to the unanticipated as well as to any ordinary event."[71]

Scenario planning is one way to help ask the "what if?" question. According to Arie de Geus, formerly with Royal Dutch/Shell, scenarios "provide tools through which the nonfashionable and weak signals may be picked up and considered without overwhelming the managers who use them." He adds, "In the process, the managers develop a language in which they can later communicate among themselves about the subject, to arrive quickly at decisions."[72] He also believes that we

> will not perceive a signal from the outside world unless it is relevant to an option for the future that we have already worked out in our imaginations. The more 'memories of the future' we develop, the more open and receptive we will be to signals from the outside world.[73]

It is important to keep in mind that scenario planning is not about predicting the future. Rather it is about thinking of "what ifs?" If it helps managers reduce the ambiguities and uncertainties by even 10 percent, that can be very important to an organization. According to Paul Saffo of Menlo Park, California's, Institute for the Future, "We don't live in a deterministic world; the best any of us can do is postulate reasonable alternatives and warn our clients what they should keep their eyes on."[74]

ARTICULATE A CLEAR DIRECTION

The objective of active observation, both internal and external, and asking "What if?" is to be able to articulate clearly a successful direction for the organization—establishing, among other things, the goals of the organization.

Before the term "strategy" was widely used in business, organizational leaders and scholars clearly thought about what we now call strategy and wrote about it. Consider three of the classics in management literature—Peter Drucker's *Practice of Management*, Chester Barnard's *Functions of an Executive*, and Henry Fayol's *General and Industrial Management*. If you compare Drucker's activities of a manager to Barnard's functions of an executive and Fayol's managing director (as seen in Exhibit 6-1), one common activity stands out—setting direction and objectives. This is the heart of strategy in any organization and on any landscape. It is about determining, communicating, and supporting a clear and consistent direction for the organization.

Practitioners and writers use lots of words to describe various elements of strategy—strategic intent, mission, vision, goals, objectives—and those words can have very specific meanings in some organizations. For example, in some organizations, "goals" are more long-term targets than "objectives." In other organizations, they seem to be used interchangeably. Yet regardless of the terms and the process used, at the core we are talking about providing a clear sense of direction for the organization—a sense of what is to be important to the people in the organization and, at least indirectly, what is not important.

Microsoft's new vision ("vision version 2"), articulated publicly in early 1999, is to become more customer focused and less product focused. According to Microsoft's president, Steven Ballmer, it was "needed to give people a beacon that they could follow when they were having a tough time with prioritization, leadership, where to go, what hills to take."[75]

Jack Welch has done this better than any CEO of a major

Exhibit 6-1

Tasks of a General Manager—Peter Drucker (1909–)

Set Objectives
Organizes
Motivates and Communicates
Establishes Yardsticks
Develops People

Functions of an Executive—Chester Barnard (1886–1961)

Maintenance of Organizational Communication
Secure Essential Services from Individuals
Formulates and Defines Purposes and Objectives

General Principles of Management—Henri Fayol (1841–1925)

Division of Work
Authority and Responsibility
Discipline
Unity of Command
Unity of Direction
Subordination of Individual Interest to General Interest
Remuneration of Personnel
Centralization
Scalar Chain
Order
Equity
Stability of Tenure of Personnel
Initiative
Esprit de Corps

Sources: Peter F. Drucker, *The Practice of Management,* New York: Harper & Row Publishers, 1954; Chester I. Barnard, *The Functions of the Executive,* Cambridge, MA: Harvard University Press, 1968; and Henri Fayol, *General and Industrial Management,* London: Sir Isaac Pitman & Sons Ltd., 1949.

company that I know. When he first became CEO of GE, he articulated a goal of becoming "the most competitive business enterprise in the world."[76] He stressed,

> A decade from now I would like General Electric to be perceived as a unique, high spirited, entrepreneurial enterprise . . . a company known around the world for its unmatched level of excellence. I want General Electric to be the most profitable, highly diversified company on earth, with world-quality leadership in every one of its product lines.[77]

He also divided all GE businesses into three circles—(1) core, (2) high technology, and (3) service. Only the businesses that dominated their markets were put in the circles. He made it clear to people throughout GE that, under his leadership, being number one or number two in market share was the overriding goal. Those businesses that were not number one or two in market share had to be "fixed, closed or sold."

Make Your Goal(s) Simple

It may sound simple, but the articulation of a mission or overriding goal(s) can be especially challenging in an organization struggling on a rugged landscape. Andy Grove stresses that to make it through a "hostile landscape" successfully,

> your first task is to form a mental image of what the company should look like when you get to the other side. This image not only needs to be clear enough for you to visualize, but it also has to be crisp enough so you can communicate it to your tired, demoralized and confused staff.[78]

Grove believes it is important to be able to "answer in a single phrase that everyone can remember and over time, can understand to mean exactly what you intended."[79] But he acknowledges that it is not enough to articulate what will be. He adds,

> What you're trying to do is capture the essence of the company and the focus of its business. You are trying to define what the company will be, yet that can only be done if you also undertake to define what the company will *not* be.[80]

According to CEO of Daimler-Chrysler, Jurgen E. Schrempp, a key to running a "global, multicultural business" is to "see your goal clearly. But you've got to deliver it just as clearly to clients, employees, shareholders, politicians, labor unions, analysts, the media."[81]

The CEO of SatCon Technology, a maker of electromechanical products for markets ranging from aerospace to autos, stresses what he calls "the elevator story":

> You have to be able to describe to the person standing next to you what your company does before he gets off at the next floor. It's got to be simple. If it's too complex, then something's wrong.[82]

The leaders at several large organizations I have examined have been especially successful at articulating a clear direction for their employees. For example, for more than a decade Emerson Electric has been very successful in driving throughout its scattered workforce the mission of being the "best cost" producer. British Airway's goal has been to become "The World's Favourite Airline." Canon's goal was to "Beat Xerox." Dell Computer also keeps its message clear and simple: "We sell custom-made computers directly to our customers."[83] For Intel, as it evolved from a semiconductor memory company to a microprocessor company, the mental image Grove stressed was "Intel, the microcomputer company." Bezos of Amazon talks of his company as "not a book company" but a "customer company." He adds, "Our vision is that we want to be the world's most customer-centric company. . . . [W]e focus incessantly on trying to get the customer experience right."[84] Gary Hamel and C. K. Prahalad call these statements "strategic intent . . . an animating dream."[85]

It is not just leaders of large organizations that need to have a clearly articulated direction. Every entrepreneur also should be able to state his or her direction clearly, in just a few sentences. According to Roger Ailes, who created what is today known as CNBC, "You have to be able to crystallize your idea in a memo, spelling out your vision in a dramatic way."[87]

Make Your Goals Understood by All

At the corporate level, especially in organizations with relatively diverse product lines, there seems to be real value in a clear goal that everyone can understand. As described earlier, few large and diversified organizations have done as well in recent years as GE. Nevertheless, 3M and Daimler Benz are led by CEOs who have understood the power of a clear goal.

▲ At 3M, there long has been a clear goal to have a certain percentage of revenue coming from products that did not exist a few years ago. For many years, the goal was 25 percent of revenues from products that did not exist five years ago. Under its current CEO, Desi DeSimone, the goal is 30 percent and four years. He also has stressed, "We're going to do two principal things: be very innovative, and satisfy our customers in all aspects."[86]

▲ When Jurgen Schrempp became chairman and began rebuilding Daimler-Benz in the mid-1990s, he decreed that each of Daimler's twenty-three business units had to earn at least 12 percent on its capital employed.

Whether or not we like the GE, 3M, or Daimler-Benz goals or mission, or think they are the right ones, it is hard to say we do not understand them.

The crystallizing of an idea for outsiders is a particular challenge for the leadership of many Internet companies. Although they usually do not have a problem with employees understanding the mission (the employees themselves are often technically oriented people with whom the employers work closely), they often have problems with such outsiders as venture capitalists. Because many of them are dealing with products that are hard for nontechnical people to grasp, it frequently is hard for them to raise the kind of venture capital that they think should be possible.

It is not surprising that Amazon and Yahoo! were much more successful than many in raising early venture capital and selling stock. They could describe their mission and products in terms that most people could understand (book retailer and index, respectively). Companies that sell some new form of entertainment or that sell some way of measuring the number of hits on a Web site and turning that into useful marketing data seem to have had more difficulty clearly communicating their direction to outsiders.

Incorporate Values

Ideally, the planning process results not only in goals but also in a statement of values. Are there some fundamental values in which we believe? The message needs to be simple so that it can be easily articulated and understood; it must be stated in broad and clear terms. To illustrate, consider the U.S. Declaration of Independence. It is a great strategy statement. It not only sets a clear goal—independence—but it identifies the values the new venture embraces—life, liberty, and the pursuit of happiness.

Unfortunately, as important as a clear sense of direction is, if you asked employees of most organizations what is the overriding mission or goal of their company, you will not find a consistent message. In a survey of U.S. businesses conducted in 1996 by *CFO* magazine, 79 percent of respondents thought having a clear vision statement played a "significant" role in their company's effectiveness and 91 percent thought their company had a "clearly articulated statement of its mission." Yet when asked, "What percentage of people within your organization clearly understand the vision?" 71 percent of senior management, 40 percent of primary operating managers, and, most telling, only 3 percent of the general employee base were thought to understand the mission.[88]

This is one reason it can be especially helpful to involve a mix of people in the strategy development process. Although the direction can be dictated by the CEO, developed by a small team of executives, or recommended by consultants, it has been my experience that only when you develop the direction with large and diverse groups are you likely to test your assumptions and identify areas where there may be real differences of opinion or perceptions about key issues facing the organization. At Intuit, e.g., the CEO involved seventy staffers, or 10 percent of headquarters staff, in designing the new Web-based strategy. After six months they agreed on one and then helped to sell it to their coworkers.[89]

BE OPPORTUNISTIC

Consider the following technology companies and their recent history:

▲ *Hewlett Packard.* In the 1970s Hewlett Packard was in the business of making scientific instruments. By the 1990s it was considered by many to be more of a computer company. With its recent emphasis on printers, it could wind up a photography or consumer electronics company.

▲ *Compaq.* In the 1980s, this company was transformed from being primarily a maker of portable PCs to a maker of a full range of PCs. By the late 1990s, it was earning significant revenues selling servers and, in 1998, acquired DEC to have a stronger presence in the corporate market.

▲ *Microsoft.* Within a matter of months, Microsoft went from having little focus on the Internet to having every product plan and marketing strategy include an Internet component.

▲ *Yahoo!* Started as a Web navigation guide, the company began
adding electronic mail, chat, and other communications functions through its Web site. In early 1998, Yahoo! Inc. and MCI
Communications Corporation announced plans to collaborate
in launching a new online service.

Technology companies, especially Internet-based companies,
have to be prepared to change directions quickly. Their world can
change almost overnight. According to Dan Heath, president of
the Internet Society, "If you're unwilling or unable to constantly
change, beware, because you can't dominate."[90] Rob Thatcher,
vice president of Fusebox, a company that initially focused on
CD-ROM and multimedia ideas before turning to the World Wide
Web and then virtual-reality programs, puts it more sharply: "It is
not just that you cannot dominate. You cannot survive."[91]

Increasingly companies will have to be opportunistic in their
approach to strategy. As the landscape changes, the winners will
be those who can improvise rapidly to turn the change into an
opportunity rather than allow it to threaten the organization.
More important will be the ability to cause the major changes on
the landscapes. Are there elements of the landscape that can be
exploited to create new opportunities, even if they only give temporary advantages?

I like Microsoft's approach to planning. According to a former
Microsoft executive and current CEO of an Internet company,
"Steve's [Ballmer, Microsoft's president] invention is: Don't have
an elegant plan. Do the smart, obvious thing. Then fix it as you
go."[92] It is a perspective reinforced by Microsoft's head of human
resources: "We have directions we're going in, but beyond that,
things are constantly changing, you're always making course corrections."[93]

A key change at GE under Jack Welch is that the strategic-
planning process now allows for midcourse corrections based on
new developments and new information. Executives are no longer
as locked into their numbers as they once were. They can be more
opportunistic.

The U.S. Marines may have the right perspective. According to their manual: "We have already concluded that war is inherently disorderly, and we cannot expect to shape its terms with any sort of precision. We must not become slaves to a plan. Rather, we attempt to shape the general condition of war; we try to achieve a certain measure of ordered disorder."[94]

William Brian Arthur, Stanford University economist and active member of the Santa Fe Institute, has captured this point very well. It is a message every business executive should consider.

> If you think that you're a steamboat and can go up the river, you're kidding yourself. Actually, you're just the captain of a paper boat drifting down the river. If you try to resist, you're not going to get anywhere. On the other hand, if you quietly observe the flow, realizing that you're part of it, realizing that the flow is ever-changing and always leading to new complexities, then every so often you can stick an oar into the river and punt yourself from one eddy to another.
>
> So what's the connection with economic and political policy? Well, in a policy context, it means that you observe, and observe, and observe, and occasionally stick your oar in and improve something for the better. It means that you try to see reality for what it is, and realize that the game you are in keeps changing, so that it's up to you to figure out the current rules of the game as it's being played. It means that you observe the Japanese like hawks, you stop being naïve, you stop appealing for them to play fair, you stop adhering to standard theories that are built on outmoded assumptions about the rules of play, you stop saying, "Well, if only we could reach this equilibrium we'd be in fat city." You just observe. And where you can make an effective move, you make a move.

THE NEED FOR AN EVOLVING
STRATEGIC-PLANNING PROCESS

Not only must the strategy adapt, but the very process by which strategies are developed must change regularly. This is especially true for large organizations.

Companies that are successful on a rugged landscape not only try to simplify the process and adapt it to fit the landscape but are constantly evolving the system. After all, smart people in any organization will find ways to "game the system." After people have participated in an organization's planning process once or twice, they begin to see how the process really works and often resort to playing the game. For example, if everyone gets 50 percent of what they asked for last year, they will ask for twice as much this year. If people are rewarded for meeting their goals, they will set goals they are assured of meeting, rather than setting "stretch" goals. These are rational responses to a static system.

General Electric, perhaps the corporate father of U.S. strategy practices, seems always to be changing its strategic-planning process and its emphasis. Soon after Jack Welch became CEO, he stopped monthly financial reports and simplified the planning process by reducing the traditional, multivolume planning documents to small "playbooks" that summarized key strategic issues and actions. He also dropped the requirement that every business have a strategy review each year. It now depended on how rugged or smooth the landscape was. A smooth one might be reviewed every two or three years, whereas a rugged one would be under continuous review. In recent years it has moved away from a numbers exercise to emphasize the "dynamics of the industry."

From the late 1970s to the present, GE's strategic-planning system has gone through numerous changes. It is as though every time people get used to the system, some aspect of it changes. The system used by Reginald Jones in the late 1970s was different from what he inherited in the early 1970s. The system that Jack Welch uses now is different from what he used in the early 1980s.

One thing, however, seems constant at GE during the past quarter of a century—an emphasis on trying to understand what is happening externally and internally, giving people a clear message about what the company is trying to achieve and letting people know how resources will be allocated. Those seem to me to be the hallmarks of a good strategic-planning process.

CONCLUSION

George Bernard Shaw may have been right: "A good battle cry is half the battle." On rugged landscapes strategy cannot be a long-term, detailed plan. More and more it is a good battle cry—a short statement of direction that guides and inspires a series of short-term decisions and actions as people try to adapt to unexpected developments.

I do not mean to suggest that all of the traditional strategy tools and frameworks are useless. In fact, I believe quite the contrary. They can help leaders and their employees better understand their landscapes. I like the description of strategic planning offered by the CEO of British Petroleum: "We see strategy as applying a series of frameworks that help us constantly reexamine what we are doing relative to what the world can offer and what our competitors are doing."[95] In essence, he views the strategic-planning process as a learning process. This approach seems particularly appropriate in a rapidly changing world.

Whatever tools and techniques are used, the goal of the strategic-planning process should be to stimulate thinking and learning about the business—what we and our competitors likely *will* be doing as well as what we *are* doing. More and more, strategy will mean using whatever tools and frameworks we can get our hands on that will help us consider the future of our organization in light of an increasingly rugged landscape—then taking action.

The CEO of a successful insurance company in the United Kingdom, owned by GE Capital, talked to me a few years ago about how his approach to strategy had changed in recent years. It was no longer the traditional approach to developing a detailed plan, such as he followed when he first became head of the firm. After great upheaval in his landscape, brought on by a recession and new government regulations, he no longer sees value in a detailed strategic plan. Now, he has "the plan" put on one page and widely distributed and, in his words, "We get on with it." I think he is right. The key increasingly is to get on with it—take action when you can and correct things when necessary.

In many ways, strategy on today's increasingly rugged landscapes should be viewed more like guerrilla warfare than conventional warfare. As a first step, the forces need to understand the landscape, the ultimate mission, the values being fought for, and then be trained to improvise—to adapt. Now we can turn our attention to the forces required to operate effectively on a rugged landscape.

CHAPTER SEVEN

Creating an Adaptive Culture

O rganizations, like organisms, have to keep evolving if they are to survive. Each change on the landscape, whether caused by our own actions or the actions of others, carries with it the potential for significantly altering the lives of all agents. Only those agents that can adapt to the new reality will survive and prosper.

What is needed in this kind of environment is an organization staffed by people who can respond to the uncertainty in a positive way rather than being frightened by what may lie ahead. V. Gordon Clemons, the CEO of CorVel, recognized by *Forbes* as one of the 200 best small companies in America in 1997, has the right perspective. He claims,

> I have a healthy tolerance for the volatility that's created with growth. I accept the "mess of success." I'd rather have that than the smoother environment that tends to come from less growth.[1]

I have found what seems to me to be a fairly large proportion of such people in technology companies, especially Internet com-

panies. The most successful of such people have what one Internet executive described as a "strong stomach for chaos." The
hallmark of an adaptive culture is one where people are comfortable and can succeed in the middle of uncertainty, ambiguity, and
change. How do we build such a culture?

STAGES OF AN ADAPTIVE CULTURE

Becoming comfortable in an adaptive culture is not easy, especially for those individuals who have spent much of their career in
large organizations. Tim Brady, Yahoo!'s vice president of production who had earlier worked at Motorola, found "getting used to
that constant pace of change, accepting it, and not getting uncomfortable was a big challenge. It was personally hard to get used to
the speed, accepting it with grace and trying to use it to your
advantage."[2] What more and more companies will need in the
21st century are organizations full of people who can make the
adjustment.

I want to stress at the beginning that it will be neither quick
nor easy. It is a major cultural change for most organizations. For
many people in the organization, it will be a major achievement
if they reach an intermediary stage that my colleague Dianne
Houghton calls "resiliency." Here, people may not embrace and
welcome constant change, but they can deal with it without
being constantly worn down by it. Ultimately, however, the organization has to be made up primarily of people who are very comfortable with constant change. These are the people who can help
the organization to adapt, not just adjust to a one-time change.
Reaching this stage may take large traditional organizations years,
even with superior leadership.

Whereas Arie de Geuss wrote of learning managers as a competitive advantage, Jack Welch believes that an "organization's
ability to learn, and translate that learning into action rapidly, is
the ultimate, competitive advantage."[4] The point is that from the

newest hire to the CEO, each person in the organization needs to see learning as a key part of his or her job.

The CEO of British Petroleum believes that "learning is at the heart of a company's ability to adapt to a rapidly changing environment." He adds, this means "in order to generate extraordinary value for shareholders, a company has to learn better than its competitors and apply that knowledge throughout its businesses faster and more widely than they do."[3]

The challenge for organizational leaders is to help create a learning culture. In Chapter Six, I discussed how the strategic-planning process needed to be a learning system if top management is to have a reasonable chance of succeeding on a rugged landscape. In this chapter, the focus is on creating an organization full of people who can succeed on such a landscape. Before leaders can begin to shape such an organization, they must understand what it looks like. In general, it is an environment that not only encourages individual learning but also encourages individuals to share their learning with other employees. I believe there are three distinct stages that organizations will need to go through to become a learning organization.

Stage 1: Encourage Individual Learning

Every organization has a culture. In the book *Corporate Cultures*, values are described as the "bedrock" of any corporate culture. They provide a "sense of common direction for all employees and guidelines for their day-to-day behavior."[5] The power seems to lie in helping to make the organization's direction clear for employees in their day-to-day work.

Traditionally, many of us have believed that strong cultures were better than weak cultures. That is only part of the story since strong cultures can offer serious resistance to change. What is needed are cultures where people accept change as inevitable and hopefully even enjoy some aspects of change. These are cultures where people like to learn new things.

Clearly an important first step in creating a learning culture is to *hire smart people*. According to the head of Microsoft's human resources department, "It all starts with a great hire" and a great hire tends to be a "super-smart" person who can adapt to the near monthly-revolutions in technology and in the business.[6] At Enews, the CEO says he looked for "good, smart people who are willing to work." A CEO of another Internet company says he looks for "good, smart people who can move from job to job." The cofounder of Broadcom stresses his company's commitment to recruiting "the best talent on the planet, period." He also points out that "it's not enough to offer very smart people lots of money. They want to work in an exciting environment with other smart people."[7] In many of these companies, the hiring process seems to place much more emphasis on how prospective employees think and attack problems than the specifics of what they know at the present time.

Merely hiring smart people is not enough. They have to be *encouraged to keep learning*. This is particularly important in technology companies. Bill Gates has stressed that

> in a technology business everybody has to acquire knowledge at a prodigious rate. At Microsoft we read, ask questions, explore, go to lectures, compare our notes and findings with each other, consult experts, daydream, brainstorm, formulate and test hypotheses, build models and simulations, communicate what we're learning, and practice new skills.[8]

To keep learning requires that those smart people be given the freedom and are encouraged to *experiment*—not just when things are not going well but all along. According to Andy Grove of Intel,

> Ideally you should have experimented with new products, technologies, channels, promotions and new customers all along. Then when you sense that something has changed, you will have a number of experiments

that can be relied on to expand your bag of tricks and your organization will be in a much better position to expand the scope of experimentation and to tolerate the increased level of chaos that is the precursor for repositioning the company in a new business direction.[9]

Experimentation will result in failures. The key is for people to *learn from their failures*. Bill Gates has the right idea. When he was informed by a product manager in 1989 that there was a major bug in a product and it would have to be recalled, Gates reportedly told him, "Well, today you lost $250,000. Tomorrow you'll hope to do better." According to Gates, "It's important to acknowledge mistakes and to make sure you draw the right lessons from them."[10] A vice president at Microsoft makes the case very clearly: "If you fire the person who failed, you're throwing away the value and learning of the experience."[11]

Stage 2: Share Individual Learning

Too many organizations never reach the later stages of encouraging individual learning—experimentation and learning from failures. Yet learning organizations go farther. They find ways to share the individual learning that has occurred. Learning by individuals is important but if that learning is not shared with others in the organization, the return on the investment is much less.

A key to creating such an organizational learning environment seems to be the practice of "flocking." In Arie de Geus's most recent book, *The Living Company*, he cites the work of Allan Wilson, a zoologist/biochemist based at the University of California at Berkeley, for insights about how learning can occur for the organization, not just the individual. He reports that "birds that flock . . . seem to learn faster. They increase their chances to survive and evolve more quickly." By flocking he means bringing people together so that learning can be disseminated among them. "Flocking depends on two of Allan Wilson's key criteria for learning: *mobility* of people and some effective mechanism of *social transmission.*"[12]

3M provides a powerful example of a large organization that facilitates mobility and social transmission. It not only maintains a database of research at 3M, but conducts the equivalent of trade shows and academic conferences for 3M people to talk and hear about the work that is going on by others throughout the company.

GE also utilizes a number of ways to encourage mobility and social transmission. Well-thought-out transfers of key managers, the now-famous "workout" sessions and, perhaps most important, the use of its executive education center seem to be keys to GE's recent success. According to Jack Welch: "The enormous advantage we have today is that we can run GE as a laboratory for ideas. We've found mechanisms to share best practices in a way that's more trusting and open."[13]

Stage 3: Leveraging the Learning

Institutional learning seems to require flocking. For this to succeed on an organizational level, we have to create ways for people to easily share with others in the organization what they have learned—both the successes and failures.

Again, 3M provides a useful example. If a 3M research project fails all of its tests, the work is not necessarily discarded. Others may have ideas about how the work could be used. For example, the phenomenal success of Post-it® Notes was partially the result of an adhesive that did not stick very well. Because it was so different from most 3M adhesives, the scientist involved continued to examine its properties and tell others about it. Eventually someone else had an idea of using the poor adhesive to make temporary bookmarks, which then evolved into a product for notes, which then evolved into one of the most successful products in 3M's history.

3M's work with microreplication (the covering of surfaces with millions of precisely made minuscule structures) is another example of shared learning about a technology that was not viewed as a great success in its early stages of development. Work on the technology started in the early 1960s, but for almost twenty years it was used for little more than lighting systems. By the mid-1990s it was being used in numerous products, allowing 3M to sell close to a billion dollars worth of microreplication products and with the possibility of selling $10 billion worth by the turn of the century. According to the head of the lab responsible for the technology and who invented the first product using microreplication, "We didn't sit down and say, 'Microreplication is the next thing to do.' It doesn't work this way. It evolved. It reached a critical mass. And it suddenly proliferated."[14] It clearly would not have proliferated if ways had not been found to share what was learned over two decades.

The CEO of Buckman Laboratories, a specialty chemicals company, states the challenge of shared learning very simply: "If you can't maximize the power of the individual, you haven't done anything."[15] It is through large scale shared learning that the power of the individual is maximized. In encouraging such a learning environment, leaders can help to minimize the probability of future failures and, more important, increase the chances that new ideas will be commercially successful.

Yet few companies make much of an effort to encourage this and even fewer do it well. Part of the challenge is the organizational tension between short-term financial considerations and long-term investments. It requires a willingness to make investments up front in people. This usually pulls them away from "productive work" or "billable hours" for some period of time. Bob Buckman of Buckman Laboratories, who has built one of the most frequently benchmarked knowledge sharing systems in the world, sees the challenge as adopting a new mindset:

> When we invest in smokestacks, we depreciate that investment over time, while investments in people development are traditionally considered expenses. You need to shift from an expense philosophy to an investment

philosophy. In this era of cutting expenses, that's difficult but if we're not prepared to shift priorities, then we'll never make it a major component of what we deliver in the way of value-added to the customer.

Furthermore, developing a sharing culture takes time. There will be no shortcuts. Like any major cultural change it is easily a three-to-five-year process. Many executives and managers are just not willing to spend that amount of time on matters that do not have an immediate measurable impact on the bottom line. Consequently, they will never develop an adaptive organization.

KEY VALUES OF A LEARNING ORGANIZATION

Jack Welch has observed that "every organization needs values, but a lean organization needs them even more." He adds, "Values are what enable people to guide themselves through . . . change."[16] To make large scale shared learning a reality, organizations must encourage and reward at least four core values: external focus, diversity, responsible risk taking, and openness.

External Focus

As has been emphasized earlier in this book, when discussing strategy, people throughout the organization must have an eye primarily focused on the outside landscape, not the internal politics of the organization. In too many organizations the focus is just the opposite—internal considerations. A friend of mine who formerly ran a consulting firm that did a considerable amount of strategic planning facilitation remarked recently to me that she found much of the discussion in these sessions tended to focus on "us, us, us."

For GE's Welch, the ability to make significant change, what he calls "fundamental change," requires an external focus:

Most bureaucracies—and ours is no exception—unfortunately still think in incremental terms rather than in terms of fundamental change. They think incrementally primarily because they think internally. Changing the culture—open it up to the quantum change—means constantly asking not how fast am I going, how well am I doing versus how well I did a year or two before, but rather, how fast and how well am I doing versus the world outside.[17]

An external focus is critical for small firms on rugged landscapes. According to an executive at CyberCash, it is especially important for team leaders to be market sensitive: "You need very sophisticated team leaders. They need to be sensitive to the marketplace and always thinking ahead."

This perspective requires first and foremost a *customer orientation*. Intuit illustrates a simple approach to achieving this perspective. According to Scott Cook,

We think it is important for those who touch the product—the product engineers and the marketing people—to do the research. We want them to make the phone calls, sit with the customers in usability training and handle calls. If you really want to create change, you must produce a feeling in the employees' guts as to how our customers really feel about the product.[18]

An external perspective also requires a keen *awareness of competitors*. Emerson Electric offers a good example of how this can be done for people on the factory floor. The company's relentless emphasis on cost is brought down to the level of the individual employee by showing employees how each of Emerson's products compare to competitors' products, component by component. One of the things this changes is the perspective of employees. Rather than seeing the cost push as just a management driven effort to increase profits, they can see it as landscape or competitor driven. If they are going to be viable on their landscape, and certainly if they are to be among the fittest, they have to at least equal and hopefully beat what their competitors are doing.

As discussed in Chapter Six, the use of scenarios can be an effective way to engage a significant number of people in the organization in thinking about external forces that can shape their future. Peter Schwartz, formerly with Royal Dutch/Shell, believes "scenario thinking" can "help you watch for things out of the corner of your eye." He believes it is important to "keep your eyes open so you can act in a timely manner and change strategy if it turns out you're wrong."[19] Scenario planning is not just for the senior leadership of an organization. Leaders need to find ways to involve most of the people in the organization in such an exercise.

Diversity

As discussed in Chapter Three, evolution by mutation and selection alone is limited to searching locally in the space of possibilities, guided only by the local terrain. The adapting population could benefit from what Kauffman calls "a God's-eye view" where it can "behold the large-scale landscape features—see where to evolve rather than just climbing blindly uphill from its current positions, only to become trapped on poor local peaks."[20] He believes that in biology, if an adapting population is to "see beyond its nose," mating probably is the answer, i.e., recombination between organisms at different locations on the landscape. Only then can its gene pool be enriched.

In the mid-1990s, Intel reportedly experienced a few problems in exploiting the impact of the Internet. Andy Grove saw that the best course of action was recombination with new organisms. He believed that the appropriate action to deal with the new challenge was "to update our own genetic makeup, to be more in tune with the new environment."[21] Whatever form corporate mating takes, the goal is to enrich the corporate gene pool. It is absolutely essential in today's business environment.

A diverse workforce, including different races, sex, age, skills, experiences, geographical backgrounds, may be politically correct at the end of the 20th century, but I believe it is essential to competing in an uncertain environment. The objective is not just to have diversity of personal characteristics but to have a diversity of ideas, skills, and experiences that can add economic value to the organization. Because of the different life experiences and different perspectives that can be brought to bear on a problem or challenge facing the organization, diverse people with very different perspectives may identify new and previously unconsidered options.

At Microsoft, e.g., Bill Gates has even gone so far as to hire a few managers with experience in failing companies because he wants to have people around who understand how such companies often are able to be creative in such a difficult situation, if they are to survive.

As will be discussed in Chapter Eight, there also are advantages to linking up with other organizations, especially if they have a good gene pool. In some cases this will involve forming alliances with organizations that can help us learn new things. For example, in the 1970s many successful Japanese companies were willing to form alliances with U.S. and European firms as a way of learning how to operate in new markets.

Responsible Risk Taking

It is critical that organizations on rugged landscapes create a climate that encourages risk taking. I do not mean a culture that encourages high-stakes gambling all the time—betting the company on every roll of the dice. Rather, it means creating a climate that allows people throughout the organization to take risks appropriate for their role.

According to James Clark, cofounder and chairman of Netscape, the Internet's first brand name,

> It took a lot of courage to initially give away our Web browser and to let people download it for free. Most

business people would have resisted, wondering how that could ever be profitable. But you've got to recognize the Internet for what it is—a massive distribution channel. So we threw a lot of seeds into the electronic wind, and they took root in organizations all over the world. That established Netscape as an instant brand name—perhaps faster than any other in history.[22]

At Clark's level he could afford to bet the company. At lower levels we want people to be able to try new things too but on a smaller scale. For example, the Post-it success started when a 3M employee "bootlegged" the project by working on it without official support.

Post-it was not an isolated 3M case. In the early days of the company, a laboratory technician began working on a solution to the problem automobile manufacturers and repair shops were having as they tried to keep colors of two-tone cars from running together. Although the technician was ordered by an executive to stop and devote full concentration to 3M's core business at the time—abrasives—the technician continued to work on his idea in his spare time. He ultimately came up with 3M Scotch masking tape and later Scotch cellophane tape. These products were 3M's first nonabrasive products.[23]

Clearly there is a need for guidelines—an articulation of what are appropriate risks for various levels in the organization. Furthermore, if regular reviews are built into the system, people can be both encouraged to pursue promising options and discouraged from pursuing less promising ones before investing too many resources.

Although it is desirable to eliminate much of the employment risk faced by employees who try new things, especially when they think the new things may be in the organization's best interest, we need to recognize that their actions are never without some risk. They certainly risk their time and reputation when pursuing a new product or new technology.

Accepting Failures

A key element of an adaptive organization is an acceptance of the fact that there will be failures. Adaptation occurs as a result of learning—and learning rarely occurs unless mistakes are made. In the words of Jean-Louis Gasse'e, former president of Apple's product division and founder of Be Inc., the computer startup: "It's hard to learn when you succeed."[24] I think it is one reason successful companies often miss the next innovation. They often stop learning.

Even executives as successful as Bill Gates and Michael Dell have experienced several failures. For example, Microsoft Network, the company's Internet service, has struggled to compete against America Online. Also, Corbis, Gates' solely owned company that has been buying or making licensing deals for digital rights to a range of image sources, is not yet financially successful. Sidewalk, Microsoft's chain of local arts and entertainment sites, has lost millions of dollars. At Dell there was an unsuccessful effort to enter retailing, and it did poorly with a line of notebook computers.

3M has been the best large company that I know of at encouraging systematic risk taking and accepting the reality that there will be failures. Here innovation is viewed as a numbers game—the more tries the more successes. In the words of a common saying at 3M: "You have to kiss a lot of frogs to find a prince." Implicit in this viewpoint is the acceptance of failures. In fact, the acceptance of failure is almost as old as 3M itself. The company started with a mistake. Founded to mine corundum, the ore was soon discovered to be low grade. To survive, the company found ways to use the ore in sandpaper. According to Lewis Lehr, 3M's CEO in the 1980s, "If one doesn't make at least some mistakes, there is no progress."[25]

Support for Risk Taking

To create a risk-taking environment means finding ways to actively and visibly encourage and support people who want to try new things and reassuring them that they will not be punished for good-faith efforts that fail. After all, big breakthroughs often seem to evolve from a trial-and-error process, and luck and accidents often are factors.

Microsoft stresses the importance of reassurance. According to Gates, "It's . . . important to make sure that nobody avoids trying something new because he thinks he'll be penalized for what happens if it doesn't work out." He adds, "Almost no single mistake is fatal."[26] The failure to take risks, however, can be fatal to an organization on a rugged landscape.

Again, 3M provides some useful insights into mechanisms for supporting individuals willing to take risks. If employees at 3M have an idea for a product or technology, there are multiple avenues for funding—formal support from management, Genesis grants awarded by a panel of scientists, bootlegging, etc. If a new business venture fails, people are assured of receiving the equivalent of their old jobs back.

Support for risk taking is reflected in the attitude expressed by 3M's current CEO—L. D. DeSimone. He stresses how important it is to "appreciate the curiosity of your people."[27] The way to truly appreciate the curiosity of your people is to encourage it and to positively respond to it.

I believe that a key element in supporting risk taking is holding people responsible for their failures. If people take risks and through incompetence or unethical actions the venture fails, they must be held responsible. To do otherwise undercuts the very culture you are trying to create.

Openness and Trust

The three values just discussed—external focus, diversity, and responsible risk taking—are not very useful unless there is an open climate that encourages debate and discussion about critical issues. At the foundation of every long-term successful company, after all else is stripped away, there has to be mutual respect and trust between management, employees, and customers.

The leadership of the organization sets the tone for openness. At Intel, Andy Grove certainly set such a tone. According to a former Intel employee, Grove "constantly challenges you: 'What's your problem? What's your plan? What are you going to do about it?' He's always looking for the problems. Pretty soon he uncovers one you haven't found." He added, "Like Andy, I don't let them [people] off the hook. I've got to make it wrong not to talk about problems."[28]

At GE, Jack Welch has worked hard to push the Work-Out program as a way of opening up debate and discussion needed to get good ideas on the table. These never ending series of town meetings, in which employees propose changes in work processes and bosses are required to approve or reject them on the spot, are one of GE's ways of getting at the ideas of more people. According to Welch,

> Work-Out will expose the leaders to the vibrations of their business—opinions, feelings, emotions, resentments, not abstract theories of organization and management. Ultimately, we're talking about redefining the relationship between boss and subordinate.[29]

He also sees it as a way of getting "rid of thousands of bad habits accumulated since the creation of General Electric."

Like GE, Emerson Electric has discovered that a basic but powerful way of building trust is to regularly ask employees for their input and then respond to their concerns. Every two years, each of Emerson's more than 70,000 salaried and hourly employees are asked to fill out lengthy opinion surveys. They are asked such questions as: "Is the plant manager competent and doing a good job?" and "If you were starting over, would you go to work for this plant again?" The surveys are more than an employee relations ploy. If more than a third of the responses to the above questions are negative, the division manager must come up with a proposal for correcting the defects.[30]

Building trust with employees of new acquisitions can be a

real challenge. At Cisco, before any employee in a newly acquired company can be terminated, both CEO Chambers and the former CEO of the newly acquired company must give their consent. "It tells new employees that Cisco wants them, that Cisco cares about them, and that we're not just another big company," says Daniel Scheinman, vice president for legal and government affairs. "It buys the trust of the people . . . and their passion is worth a lot more than any of the downside legal protection."[31]

Mutual respect and trust are not easy to achieve and even harder to maintain in the modern organizations in which most of us work. Saying you trust is easy but acting on that trust can be very difficult. Alan Weber, the former editorial director of *Harvard Business Review*, explains why:

> Trust is tough because it is always linked to vulnerability, conflict, and ambiguity. Vulnerability is a pre-condition of trust. Before any two people can form a personal bond, they must first open themselves up, let each other know "where they stand." But that creates the possibility of disagreement and conflict. Indeed, healthy conflict is a sign of the existence of trust. It shows that two people care enough to disagree. Finally, trust acknowledges the inevitability of ambiguity. No two people will see the same event in the same way or have the same feelings about it. Trust admits to that ambiguity and strives to negotiate it.[32]

I believe that the key elements of trust within an organization are *fairness* and a sense of *partnership*. Without these, communications efforts and new initiatives likely will be seen as cynical, manipulative, and self-serving.

According to Jack Welch, "trust is enormously powerful in a corporation." However, he believes that "people won't do their best unless they believe they'll be treated fairly." By that he means that there is no cronyism and everybody has a real shot. The only way I know to create that kind of trust is by laying out your values and then walking the talk. You've got to do what you say you'll do, consistently, over time.[33]

The authors of *The 100 Best Companies to Work for in America* report on several ways that successful companies foster a culture where people feel a sense of partnership—a feeling that "we are all in this together."

In the best workplaces, employees trust their managers, and the managers trust their employees. The trust is reflected in numerous ways: no time clocks, meetings where employees have a chance to register their concerns, job posting (so that employees have first crack at openings), constant training (so that employees can learn new skills), and employee committees empowered to make changes in policies, recommend new pay rates, or allocate the corporate charity dollars. Trust, in the work place, simply means that employees are trusted as partners and recognized as having something to contribute beyond brawn or manual dexterity or strong legs and arms.[34]

In today's environment, especially in technology- and information-intensive businesses, organizations need to find ways to encourage key employees to stay. After all, talented employees are the key to their success. Consequently, in spite of a growing sense in the modern business world that organizational loyalty is no longer important, I believe it is essential to a learning culture. Developing a sense of partnership seems to be key.

Building a partnership with employees requires finding ways to help employees closely identity with the organization. Good wage and benefit packages are necessary but not sufficient. To hire and retain the people they will need for the 21st century, companies must find ways to deal with two fundamental characteristics of today's skilled knowledge workers: They have other attractive career options and time is their scarcest resource.

Treat Employees as Owners

One way leading technology companies try to provide an incentive for people to identify with the company, and hopefully resist the opportunities that other companies may offer them, is through profit sharing and especially stock options. It is estimated by some that the average technology company distributes about 3.3 percent of its stock in the form of employee options each year. Employee ownership is a profound example of how the Information Age has changed the nature of the modern corporation.

Microsoft has always been pay-as-you-go since the company was founded, with no long-term debt. So why did the company go public in 1986? The major reason was, according to CFO Michael Brown, to create a vehicle to share ownership with employees. He observed:

> For pure Information Age companies, the principal barrier to entry is the ability to concentrate intellectual property. When these companies go public they don't do it to raise proceeds to build plants. They do it to monetize the value of their employee ownership programs. Microsoft was incorporated to create a vehicle to share ownership, not to ramp up production. And the principal reason we went public was to monetize the value.[35]

In 1997, ownership of Microsoft was split roughly fifty-fifty between people who invested financial capital in the company—outside shareholders—and people who invested human capital—employees and founders. Since 1990 the company has issued 807 million stock options to employees—worth $80 billion if they were exercised in late 1998. By the late 1990s it was estimated that Microsoft had created 5,000 millionaires and 3 billionaires.

At Cisco, more than 40 percent of the forty million stock options granted in 1997 were to employees below the managerial level. By some estimates, the first 1,500 employees of the company were millionaires in early 1998 based only on their Cisco stock. Similarly, Intel reportedly has produced thousands of millionaires, and in early 1997 Intel announced that it would grant potentially lucrative stock options to virtually all of its 50,000 employees. When UUNET went public in 1995, its CEO insisted that employees receive the block of stock normally reserved for special friends of the company.

Stock options are now reaching far beyond Silicon Valley. GE now gives options to more than 20,000 employees, versus just 200 in the 1980s. IBM announced in early 1998 that it was breaking with tradition and opening its stock-option programs to nonexecutives. The number of employees who get stock options will triple—that is on top of a 100 percent increase in 1997. IBM planned to set aside 2.5 percent of its outstanding shares for employees, up from 1.8 percent in 1997. It also was increasing its merit-pay pool by $2 billion and its performance-related bonuses by 30 percent to $1.3 billion.

Under Jurgen Schrempp, Daimler-Benz became the first German company to offer stock options to management. He was able to push the plan through against the opposition of union leadership and a significant number of the company's board members. He also was able to push through an incentive pay plan that rewards employees based on their contribution to overall profits. In 1998, 150,000 employees qualified for a bonus, based on 1997 results.

In some of the smallest Internet companies I have visited, even in some that had not yet gone public, there was a desire to treat employees as owners. Brian Hecht, the CEO of Enews, talked about wanting to give stock options since he was "demanding stock option behavior." His reasoning was based on a desire for a sense of ownership. "It's seven o'clock at night. Do you stay and finish the project, or do you go home, rent a movie, and sit on the couch for the rest of the night?" He remembered when he was in that position at a prior company and the movie often won.

Microsoft's CFO has recognized an important characteristic of many of today's successful technology companies: "Fifteen or twenty years ago a person was either an employee or he was unemployed. Now look around: People are owners, managers, and employees—sometimes all three in the same hour."[36] A sense of partnership requires recognizing and rewarding the overlapping roles of owners, managers, and employees.

Treat Employees as Time Constrained

According to Marc Andreessen, cofounder of Netscape, technology startups "demand virtually a Herculean effort from all their employees."[37] I think this is true of all successful startups. Although the pay may be good, the workdays can be incredibly long, especially during the time the organization is most vulnerable—at its beginning and when a new product is being developed and introduced and when it is under attack.

In today's world of two working spouses and more-demanding jobs, time has become a particularly scarce commodity. Many leading technology companies are trying to ease the time constraints on their employees with a variety of benefits. For example, at Netscape a Winnebago stocked with dentists showed up twice a week for workers who could not find time for checkups. At 3Com Corporation, employees can get film developed at the company store and their car washed in the parking lot. Engineers at PointCast have access to washers and dryers during the workday.

Few companies go as far as SAS Institute. It owns thousands of developable acres and sells employees plots at steep discounts to encourage them to put down roots close to the office. Two doctors and ten nurses staff a 7,500-square-foot medical center. There is a state-of-the-art nursery school and day-care center with one staff member for every three children. Parents are encouraged to visit their children during the day and they often take them to lunch at SAS's giant cafeteria. A private junior and senior high school is being built on the edge of the SAS campus. SAS owns a country club where employees can join at a discount from the initiation fees that non-SASers pay.

Similarly, WorldCom recently announced that it planned to build a high-technology campus for as many as 30,000 employees in Northern Virginia that would include restaurants, stores, and health clubs that would cater to young, well-educated, high-tech employees. According to the company's request for zoning approval, "Many of these employees are younger, single and more technologically oriented and more highly educated than the average employee in a manufacturing environment." Furthermore, these employees are "relatively highly paid, work long, irregular hours, and participate in a broad range of challenging educational, recreational and diversionary activities."[38] They are just the kind of employees more and more companies will need to hire in the 21st century.

CONCLUSION

In GE's 1998 annual report, in the letter to the shareholders, Welch observes that

> early in the next century, Japan will rebound. Oil prices are bound to rise again. Inflation is probably not dead. But spending a lot of time putting too fine a point on the "how" and "when" any of these might happen is less important than growing a culture that is both challenged by the unexpected and confident in, as well as capable of, dealing with whatever comes along.[39]

In a world of constant change, many aspects of an organization have to change. It requires an organization made up of people who are willing and able to change. That is a fundamental characteristic of an adaptive organization.

A few things will need to remain fairly constant. In fact, it is these relative constants that help the people of the organization deal effectively with the changes they confront. I believe the core values we have explored in this chapter will need to be constant in any organization that succeeds long term in the 21st century. The ways in which these values are implemented and perhaps interpreted may change as the landscape changes, but they remain the core of the organization. In Holland's words, they are what allow the organization to retain a "coherence despite continual disruptions," i.e., a "pattern in time."

Now we turn to an exploration of some of the organizational characteristics that can facilitate the development of an adaptive culture.

CHAPTER EIGHT

Structured for Adaptation

One of the inherent weaknesses of many large organizations that try to compete on rugged landscapes is that they cannot adapt fast enough. Even very well-run companies can have difficulty. As Jack Welch has pointed out, General Electric is a "magnificent high tech company as long as it takes a long time and a lot of money."[1]

Increasingly, companies on rugged landscapes must operate in a fast-forward mode. Regis McKenna, a Silicon Valley veteran, argues that companies need to be organized to conduct business in real time because "the competitive environment will no longer tolerate slow response or delayed decision making."[2] His and Jack Welch's observations raise the question: How do you organize for speed and uncertainty? Stated differently: How should a business operating on a rugged landscape be organized?

There clearly is no right answer to this question about organizational structure, although a lot of organizations seem to be searching for the right structure. I do believe, however, that whatever the structure, it must make possible quick and effective responses to new developments. In other words, businesses on a rugged landscape need to be organizationally flexible enough to meet massive and rapid change.

In this chapter we explore some organizational concepts and practices that can help to more rapidly leverage the learning that is going on, both by leaders and employees, in the adaptive organization.

THE GOAL: OPERATE AT THE EDGE

As discussed in Chapter Three, complex adaptive systems, such as business organizations, function best at the edge of chaos. The results of Kauffman's and Holland's work suggest that the very highest fitness occurs precisely between ordered and chaotic behavior—at the intermediate transition called "the edge."

Kauffman reports that "networks in the regime near the edge of chaos—this compromise between order and surprise—appear best able to coordinate complex activities and best able to evolve as well." It is as though a position in the ordered regime near the transition to chaos affords the best mixture of stability and flexibility.[3] Thus, the transition between order and chaos appears to be the regime that optimizes average fitness for the whole system. He notes that as each population within a system is evolving, if each population happens to climb to a fitness peak that is also consistent with the peaks located by all its coevolving partners, then all the populations will stop coevolving. "Each species at its own peak is better off not changing as long as the other species occupy their own peaks."[4] In this situation the population is in an ordered regime. An organization in such a situation is "too rigid, too frozen in place, to coevolve away from poor local peaks."

Unfortunately, too many organizations try to adapt when they are in an "ordered" regime. To put this into organizational terms, as an organization evolves, if the people within the organization reach a state where most if not all are satisfied with their current performance, they are in a state of complacency. They are in an ordered state. We have all seen organizations that reached such a state. For whatever reason, most employees are pretty content with things the way they are. Their attitude seems to be: Why change?

Other organizations create so many rules and regulations that the organization cannot adapt even if many of its people would like to. Some observers believe AT&T has had this problem. According to Tom Evslin, who founded and ran WorldNet, AT&T's 1-million-subscriber Internet access division and who left to found ITXC Corp., a seller of Internet telephone calls to telecommunications companies at wholesale, "I left because you needed 17 approvals for a decision."[5] In Kauffman's words, such an organization is too far into a "frozen ordered regime." It is too rigid to coordinate the complex sequences of activities necessary for development.

Unless there is constant vigilance, complacency seems to be an inevitable result of organizational evolution. Jack Welch offers a good explanation for this fact of organizational life:

> As institutions prosper and get more comfortable, the priority begins to shift gradually from speed to control; from leading to managing; from winning to conserving what has been won; from serving the customer to serving the bureaucracy. We begin to erect layers of management to smooth decision-making and control all that growth, and all it does is slow us down.[6]

In contrast to the ordered regime, there is a chaotic regime. If most or all of the species never settle down but keep chasing receding peaks, according to Kauffman, they are forever doomed by their own best efforts to deform the landscapes of their neighbors, and thus by indirect feedback loops, their own landscapes. "All keep struggling uphill, Sisyphus-like, forever." The various agents "climb and plunge on heaving fitness landscapes and therefore have low overall fitness." On such a landscape, a small change can cause major turmoil within the system.

To put this into organization terms, if most people in an organization are constantly introducing changes that also change the landscape, the organization will not be very fit. Many of us have observed this phenomenon in relatively young, high-growth organizations. It also can be found in organizations where there is very weak leadership and everyone is "doing his or her thing." Here the challenge is to rein in some of the chaos without stifling the people involved.

Between these two states lies the edge of chaos, where our adaptive organizations have to be. It is here that we find enough order for stability but also find flexibility and surprise.

THE NEW ORGANIZING PRINCIPLE: STRUCTURE FOLLOWS LANDSCAPE

When I was earning my MBA in the 1960s, the traditional view of organizational structure was that structure should follow strategy. The assumption was that once an organization had formulated its future long-term game plan, the organizational structure should be designed to support the implementation of that plan. Such an approach sounds very reasonable. However, it has at least two fundamental weaknesses. First, it assumes that there is a right structure for the implementation of a particular strategy. There is little evidence to support this. Second, even if there is a right structure, the time required to reorganize the company, especially a large organization, can run into years. Not only can the original plans be out of date by the time the reorganization is complete but the cost involved in a massive reorganization, both financial and personal, can be prohibitive.

By the time I received my Ph.D. in the 1970s, it was common to hear a different view of the strategy-structure argument: Strategy follows structure. The argument was that the structure of an organization could greatly influence the strategy that a company is likely to develop. For example, a company that is organized around traditional functions, such as marketing and manufacturing, may develop a somewhat different strategy than one organized around customers or regions. Although there is some truth to such an argument, it offers little concrete help to corporate leaders who are looking to improve the performance of their organization.

I believe it is more accurate to say that structure influences strategy and strategy influences structure but *both* should be influenced by the landscape. In other words, as can be seen in Figure 8-1, both structure and strategy should adapt to the landscape.

I believe this point is at the heart of an argument Clayton Christensen makes about managing disruptive technological change. He believes commercializing disruptive technologies "requires implanting the projects that are to develop such technologies in commercial organizations that match in size the market they are to address."[7]

There seems to be a growing recognition that, for large organizations, the more traditional structures, such as a functional organization, may be unable to respond fast enough to unexpected developments. Likewise, a strong regional focus in an increasingly global marketplace, may lead to very slow responses. This was clearly demonstrated by the problems that Philips, the electronics giant headquartered in the Netherlands, had in coordinating multiple country operations to compete with a global player like Sony in the 1960s and 1970s.

In many large companies, the traditional functional structure seems to be losing out to a more process-oriented organization.

Figure 8-1

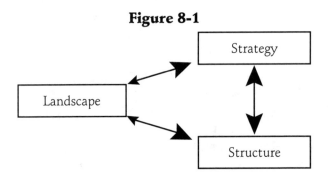

The attention in recent years on core competencies, core skills, core capabilities, etc., is a response to the organizational challenge of dealing with a rapidly changing landscape. The idea seems to be that although products, customers, and markets may change, certain core elements are less likely to change in the short run. Unfortunately, a lot of companies have struggled to "operationalize" these new concepts. They are intellectually appealing but extremely difficult to implement in a managerially meaningful way.

ORGANIZATIONAL GUIDELINES

So what can the leadership of an organization operating on a rugged landscape do about its structure? I think there are at least five general characteristics of an adaptive organization's structure: It tends to be relatively decentralized, have high spans of control, make extensive use of temporary structures, have a powerful information system, and constantly evolves the structure.

Decentralize

A general rule of organization should be that the more rugged the landscape, the more decentralized the organizational structure. According to Reinhard Mohn, chairman of Bertelsmann Foundation, which controls more than two-thirds of the stock of the German media giant Bertelsmann, "Centralist leadership structures are no longer capable of meeting the requirements in today's competitive environment. We must have the courage to decentralize responsibility. Creative people need freedom!"[8]

I think Mohn would approve of Intuit CEO Scott Cook's description of his company: a "collection of entrepreneurs."[9]

Another company Mohn would likely approve of is St. Louis–based Edward Jones. Operating on the rugged landscape of financial services, it had a pretax return on equity of 39 percent in 1996 and has not been below 29 percent in recent years. The company's goal is to have 10,000 brokers by 2004. Not only does the company have a clear focus (conservative long-term investments for rural and suburban customers), but it has an organizational structure that has been called "a confederation of highly autonomous entrepreneurial units bound together by a highly centralized core of values and services."[10] It is a network of thousands of brokers, each of whom has his or her own wired office.

Some of Kauffman's work reinforces a widespread perception that a decentralized structure is the way to go, especially on rugged landscapes. He has studied models with nonoverlapping "patches," or smaller units, such as profit centers. He finds that breaking an organization into patches, where each patch "attempts to optimize for its own selfish benefit, can lead, as if by an invisible hand, to the welfare of the whole organization."[11] When the system is broken into well-chosen, nonoverlapping domains or patches, each adapts for its own selfish benefit, yet the joint effect is to achieve very good results for the whole collection of patches.

This raises a fundamental question: What is the right number and size of patches? According to Kauffman, the answer depends on how rugged the landscape is. His studies suggest that if the landscape is highly correlated and quite smooth, the best results are found in a more centralized system. But as the landscape becomes more rugged, reflecting the fact that the underlying number of conflicting constraints is becoming more severe, it appears best to break the total system into a number of patches such that the system is near the phase transition between order and chaos. For example, one might expect more centralization in an aerospace business like Boeing than in an electronics instruments company like Hewlett Packard. As the conflicting constraints become worse, patches seem to become "ever more helpful," leading Kauffman to conclude, "Patches, in short, may be a fundamental process we have evolved in our social systems, and perhaps elsewhere, to solve very hard problems."

In a real-world example of this, Lt. Col. Douglas Macgregor, author of *Breaking the Phalanx,* has found success in the U.S. military with smaller combat units. He believes that the key to his success is linked to the size of his organization. He finds that combat units in today's environment must react much faster to keep pace with the flood of data that new information technology is making available. Therefore, divisions of 18,000 soldiers are too cumbersome and have too many layers of command for modern warfare. He recommends that divisions should be broken down into agile "combat groups" a third the size. These smaller units also would be harder to find and less susceptible to chemical and biological attacks.[12]

Smaller patching systems that are poised on the edge of chaos may be extremely useful for two related reasons. First, such systems rapidly attain good compromise solutions. Second, and even more fundamental, such poised systems should track the moving peaks on a changing landscape very well.

Make Good Decisions

I use the word "good" in describing decisions rather than the word "best." Although it probably always has been true in business it is especially true on rugged landscapes that management can never know, even with hindsight, what would have been the best decision. Could the company have done better? Who knows? The key is to strive for good decisions—the best you can make with the information you have at hand.

As is increasingly obvious from studying successful high-tech companies, it is essential to be close to the action. In an organizational sense, this means that on rugged landscapes it is critical to have people on the ground who can make decisions. In the overused term of the 1990s, people need to be "empowered." The people who are closest to customers and other players on the landscape should have a better feel for what are the needs and wants of the various players and thereby have a better chance of making sound decisions.

Part of the success of GE's move to Strategic Business Units (SBUs) in the 1970s was no doubt attributable to the fact that general managers, who were closer to their customers than corporate management, now had more control over their own resources. They also could be more responsive to those customers than had been true under the departmental structure that preceded SBUs.

The CEO of Cybercash, who operates on a very rugged landscape, has made it clear to his people that centralization is to be avoided at all cost. According to one of his executives, his view is: "over my cold, dead body." Within a few years of its founding, the company had already experienced a major reorganization that shifted power away from the top to strong general managers, each responsible for a specific product.

Track the Landscape

Closely related to finding a sounder solution is the ability to track the moving peaks of the landscape. If the landscape changes because of external forces or even actions by one of the current players on the landscape, the detailed location of local peaks will shift. According to Kauffman, a "rigid system deep in the ordered regime will tend to cling stubbornly to its peaks." What you want, he would argue, are "poised, edge of chaos systems" that "track shifting peaks more fluidly."[13]

In general, the more decentralized an organization, the more likely that someone in the organization will pick up on a shift in the landscape. An organization with dozens of relatively small business units, as opposed to one or two large units, likely will cover a larger portion of the relevant landscape and perhaps pick up small shifts before they become landslides. The former head of GE Capital, Gary Wendt, told people running its many businesses, "It's their responsibility to be looking for the next opportunity. Where is their customer moving? What are their needs?" While his role was to provide the broad direction, he wanted his general managers to be tracking the landscape.[14] The 1999 reorganization at Microsoft has a similar objective. In Bill Gates' words, it emphasizes that the customer is "at the center of everything we do."[15] If so, you need to have authority assigned to people closer to the customer.

We have all seen large companies whose executives, far removed from the day-to-day world of the customer, decided what the customer wanted, when people much closer to the customer had a very different and more accurate view.

A decentralized organization also is likely to be able to make a modest local adjustment to accommodate a shift in the landscape, rather than waiting for a much larger organization to decide centrally to respond. Should there be a major change in the overall landscape, a decentralized organization may already have some experience in dealing with the change as a result of an early adjustment. In fact, the likely reaction of a large organization is to ignore a small shift. Later, the larger structure may have to undergo a significant organizational change in a relatively short time, if it is to adapt successfully.

I believe part of Sony's phenomenal success with PlayStation was the result of PlayStation's parent company being a separate subsidiary with considerable autonomy. Likewise, part of the early success that IBM had in the PC business was attributable, in part, to setting up an almost independent operation in Florida, far removed from corporate management, to develop and make their PCs. The company became less successful in the PC business as it drew the new organization more into the corporate fold.

In early 1999, Microsoft announced plans to reorganize from three divisions based on technology to four groups based on customer service. At about the same time, Hewlett Packard announced that it was splitting into two companies—one focused on computers and related products and the other on medical products and test and measurement devices. Both companies' actions reflect a realization that the landscapes are different for each unit. For example, the changes at Microsoft seem to suggest that landscape-altering developments in the near future are more likely to come from the markets and customers than from new technologies.

To go back to an earlier military analogy, decentralization is like having a band of guerrilla fighters on the ground. The odds are good that they will know better how to proceed in the immediate conflict than will leaders who are far removed from the likely battlefield. As discussed in earlier chapters, for this to work, those on the ground have to understand the ultimate mission and have been properly prepared for the task at hand.

Increase the Span of Control

According to Arno Penzias, Bell Lab's chief scientist, "The problem with hierarchies is that people at every level have the power to say no. You have to get to the person who can say yes."[16] This seems to get at the heart of organizing for a rugged landscape. In an adaptive organization, a primary concern has to be: How can we facilitate faster, yet effective, decision making? A conscious effort to increase spans of control can help.

In the 1990s we saw numerous companies go through what became known as downsizing or delayering. In most cases the objective was to reduce costs. Frequently this also resulted in increasing spans of control which, if management was willing to delegate, allowed people closer to the landscape to make decisions and thereby increase the speed of decision making. Since there were fewer levels of managers to sign off on decisions, the speed of response could be faster.

In addition to speeding up decision making, there are longer-term organizational advantages to increasing the span of control. One such advantage is identifying and developing good executives. According to Jack Welch,

> When you take out layers, you change the exposure of the managers who remain. They sit right in the sun. Some of them blotch immediately—they can't stand the exposure of leadership. I firmly believe that an overburdened, overstretched executive is the best executive, because he or she doesn't have time to meddle, to deal in trivia, or to bother people. Remember the theory that

a manager should have no more than six or seven direct reports? I say the right number is closer to 10 to 15. This way you have no choice but to let people flex their muscles, to let them grow and mature.[17]

According to the CEO of AlliedSignal, one of the keys to his success in turning around his troubled company was more delegation. As he tried to "fashion . . . a responsive organization, one that can not only respond to customers, but can anticipate what customers are going to want," he found that a lot of the things that "had to do with too much supervision" were "slowing us down." Consequently, he too widened the span of control so that "instead of a person having three people reporting to them, more typically now it's ten."[18]

This emphasis on few levels is particularly striking in large, successful technology companies. For example, Bill Gates has long had a goal for Microsoft "to have no more than six levels of management between me and anyone in the company."[19] One of Nabuyuki Idei's first actions after becoming president of Sony in 1995 was to remove a layer of management that had existed between Tokyo and its top U.S. chiefs. At Wang Laboratories, its current CEO, Joseph Tucci, started the company's turnaround in part by reducing the levels of management between himself and the lowest-level employee from seven to three.

Most of the Internet companies I have studied also seem to stretch their few managers. For example, at Amazon, it was not until after the company had been in existence almost two years that a significant number of new executives were hired.

Delayering by itself will not solve the problems of centralization that face many large companies. It fact, it may be especially detrimental to an organization operating on a rugged landscape unless two important considerations are kept in mind. First, if senior management still insists on making most decisions, the speed at which decisions get made will still be slow. Second, if all redundancy is lost, an organization may not be able to respond fast enough to new developments. For example, when an unexpected development arises, if there are no resources that can be freed up immediately to respond, the organization can fall behind those that can move quickly.

Use Temporary Structures as Much as Possible

When unexpected developments arise, how fast can your organization respond? Again, Internet companies may be a good sign of what is to come. According to the vice president of a New York–based company that does programming for the World Wide Web, "It is definitely a changing environment every day, and you have to be willing to change, or else you'll go under. . . ." He adds, "It's the type of thing where one of the things I think of tonight on the ride home we could sell tomorrow."[20]

Clearly, large organizations cannot respond that quickly, but it is important to find ways to increase the flexibility of the organization. Adaptive organizations must be flexible. I believe a concerted effort to use a variety of temporary structures can help the leaders of large organizations increase speed and organizational flexibility.

Use Teams and Project Management

In recent years there has been a great deal of attention focused on the use of teams and project management. Intel uses "task-based management"—temporary teams drawn from a range of disciplines to form around specific business issues. In Andy Grove's words, these teams attack issues much like "a person's body mobilizes its antibodies" to attack a biological invader.[21]

I was especially impressed with the approach taken by Oticon Holding A/S, a Danish maker of hearing aids. Although relatively small in size, with sales of about $200 million, it has introduced several major product innovations, including the first digital hearing aid. In 1990 the CEO, Lars Kolind, set about to reinvent the company, which was in trouble at the time. He not only abolished the formal organization but also declared that projects would be the defining unit of work and that project teams would form, disband, and form again as required. The project leaders had to compete to attract the resources, including people, to deliver results. Project owners (members of top management) were there to provide advice and support but make few decisions. With a hundred or so projects at any one time, and most people working on several projects at once, it has been described as "a free market in work."[22]

Oticon also makes heavy use of mobile phones within the building, and the company's physical space encourages freedom in that it uses uniform mobile desks and state-of-the-art, networked computers. People can move their "office" where they need to be for the duration of the project. According to the company's R&D leader, "When people move around and sit next to different people, they learn something about what others are doing. They also learn to respect what those people do."[23]

The U.S. Marines have an organizational structure that typically has six layers of management between a private and the colonel commanding his or her regiment. Furthermore, it is broken down for administrative purposes into divisions and battalions. Such traditional structures, however, do not seem to reflect the way the marines function in action. They seem to think in terms of more fluid, customizable groupings. Furthermore, when the action begins, the layers reportedly collapse on an as-needed basis. Marines at all levels start making decisions in response to a rapidly changing situation without consulting the chain of command. According to a major general, "If your decision-making loop is more streamlined than your enemy's, then you set the pace and course of the battle."[24]

Frank Walker, president of GTW Corp., a seller of project-management consulting services and software, has identified four basic levels (and types of careers) that are common in a project-oriented world: (1) The top level of CEOs, presidents, and executive vice presidents who set strategy; (2) resource providers such as CFOs, CIOs, human resource executives, and vice presidents of expert staffs, such as marketing and engineering, who develop and supply talent and money; (3) project managers who buy or lease money and people from the resource providers and put them to work; and (4) the talent who may report to a functional boss but spend much of their time on project teams.[25] If he is right, we are not only looking at much leaner organizations in the future but also a different way of thinking about peoples' careers.

We also will be looking at an increasingly important role in the organization of the future—the project leader. In working with teams, the team leader will become less of a traditional manager and become more of a troubleshooter and facilitator, what some have called an "enabler." A software development team leader at Ericsson Radio Systems sees his role correctly.

> They (team members) know what they need to do. They have the skills and training to go do it. I'm just here to make sure that if they hit a snag, I can help them over it. And I have to make the major decisions on whether we do a go or no-go. I've been on both sides of the fence. The worst thing in the world when I was a developer was to have someone looking over my shoulder.[26]

As will be discussed in Chapters Nine and Ten, this change will have significant implications for the role of leaders.

Outsource

We are seeing more organizations move toward outsourcing noncore elements of the business. Even in relatively stable landscapes, such as that occupied by automobile manufacturers, you can see the advantages of such an approach. The old GM model of a high degree of vertical integration, which worked so well in the relatively stable world of Alfred Sloan, will have trouble competing in the 21st century. Competitors such as Toyota and Ford are much more willing to subcontract out noncore work to others but tightly manage their network of suppliers. For example, in the late 1990s, Toyota produced about 30 percent of the parts that went into its cars, compared with about 65 percent for GM.

This move toward outsourcing can have significant cost advantages. For example, in 1997, Ford, with much more subcontracting than GM, had a pretax profit for every vehicle that was $978 higher than GM's—up from $613 in 1993.

There are similar examples in the high-tech world. For example, by outsourcing production of 70 percent of its products, technology leader Cisco has quadrupled output without building new plants and has cut the time it takes to get a new product to market by two-thirds, to just six months.

A practice that has been embraced by a significant number of high-tech companies, including Microsoft, AT&T, Hewlett Packard, Intel, and Boeing, is the use of long-term temporary employees. Microsoft may be the leading practitioner of temps among high-tech companies, employing about 5,000 temps alongside its 17,000 domestic employees. This includes 1,500 temps who have worked for at least one year. (In May 1999, a three-judge panel of the U.S. Court of Appeals for the Ninth Circuit ruled that workers who are on the payroll for more than a few months, even if independent contractors, are entitled to the same benefits as permanent employees.)

Organizations likely will continue to look for ways to outsource work that is noncore. At a minimum, the leadership of any company in the 21st century would be wise to evaluate the benefits of having certain administrative support activities handled by subcontractors as opposed to in-house staff.

It is important to recognize that outsourcing does not mean abdicating responsibility. Even if a function is considered noncore, if it is done poorly, the customer will see it as a failure of the primary company. Furthermore, creating a harmonious environment in which employees from various organizations have to work together can be a challenge.

Form Alliances

Sometimes the relationships with other agents on the land-scape take on a formal role, ranging from contractual but nonex-clusive arrangements to formal partnerships. In the world of technology, these alliances are becoming a way of life. In fact, I suspect alliances are likely to be much more common on rugged landscapes than large-scale mergers and acquisitions. For example, Sony has formed alliances with Intel, Microsoft's WebTV, Qual-comm Inc., News Corp., and Fuji Television Network—just to name a few. Between 1996 and 1999, Intel invested $2.5 billion into 200 small companies. Microsoft invested in or acquired ninety-two small companies in a recent five-year period.

Alliances are a way of *spreading risks*. This seems particularly common among businesses that are trying to stake out a niche on the information/communications landscape. Their leaders know there are lots of potential ways the landscape could evolve, so they form alliances with various agents that have different skills: If the market moves in any particular direction, at least their companies will have a presence there. They will not be isolated on a small hill, far from the highest peak on the landscape.

In the Internet world these alliances can be especially critical. Over and over again we see small companies trying to form alli-ances with larger players as a way of *gaining additional resources* and *gaining legitimacy*. An example of the latter was Enews part-nering with both Amazon and HotBot—both better-known com-panies at the time. In 1997 it teamed with American Family Publishers, a discount subscription distributor. CyberCash formed early alliances with VeriFone, Cisco, RSA, and Intel to raise capi-tal. In addition to capital, some organizations form alliances to have access to another company's skills and technologies.

It is critical that, before rushing into alliances, the various parties have realistic expectations about the relationship and be able to use it to learn. The experience of Auto-By-Tel, one of the leading auto-sales services on the Internet, is all too common. Ac-cording to its president, Peter Ellis, Microsoft was "picking our brains" during the year and a half that the two companies collaborated. They split after a disagreement over strategy. He adds, "When they call you up, you think it's great, but in reality, the dance will soon turn into a nightmare."[27] Obviously Microsoft got more out of the relationship than did Auto-By-Tel.

According to John Chambers, CEO of Cisco, a firm that as of 1997 was number 1 or number 2 in all but one of the seven major equipment markets in which it competed, "Partnering is our heritage. Very few people in this industry partner well, so it's a huge competitive advantage."[28] He adds that IT industries have been transformed by the Internet into a "diverse ecosystem" in which the important thing is not so much the "technologies you own as how well you can work with the other players."[29] According to his chief technology officer, "At a lot of technology companies, it's a sign of weakness to have to look outside for technological help. John has instilled a culture in which it's not a sign of weakness but a sign of strength to say, 'I can't do everything myself. I will find a partner and trust myself to be able to manage the process.'"[30]

Chambers believes there are four key elements to making a strategic partnership work:

> First, you and your partner have to have the same overall vision of where things are going. Our key partners agree on the potential for network commerce and high-quality multimedia over the Internet. Second, both sides have to see a short-term benefit come from the relationship, and by that I mean real sales. Third, you both also have to see long-term wins. And fourth, your organizations have to have chemistry—they have to share similar values. All our key partners are a lot like us: aggressive, technologically strong, and very focused on the customer.[31]

According to the founder of a Cisco-acquired company, "Cisco makes every acquisition feel they're part of the company. It represents the best of Silicon Valley culture."[32]

Microsoft has not always had the best relationships with its partners. But in the mid-1990s, one senior executive reportedly began pushing Microsoft people to think about those relationships—if for no other reason than Microsoft's own long-term benefit: "I made [Microsoft executives] list the three good things for the other side" before approving a deal, he said. "I was trying to make [Microsoft] aware that if the other guy didn't profit, it wouldn't be a good, long-term partnership."[33]

It is not just technology companies and small companies that are recognizing the value of alliances. In recent years, GE has been particularly successful in Asia, after a tough start, by avoiding investing in one central factory that would serve the entire continent. Instead, it has proceeded country by country and region by region and formed joint ventures with local companies that have a grip on national and regional markets. In Europe, GE Capital, which contributes approximately 40 percent of the profits of GE, has made more than 100 acquisitions over a recent three-year period, both full takeovers and equity stakes.

It is essential to recognize that, whether we like it or not, the connections between the players in the global marketplace are increasing. Consequently, they must be actively managed. In general, corporate leaders should be asking explicitly two questions: What kind of relationship do we want with the other players on our landscape? How can we best achieve a relationship that is satisfactory to us?

Develop Powerful Information Systems

A common definition of information is that it is the reduction of uncertainty. In many ways, the organization of the 21st century, facing great uncertainty, will be defined more by its information systems than by its organization charts.

Both Kauffman and Holland have done work suggesting the importance of an exchange of information between adapting agents in a system. It seems particularly important to have all the agents in a system who are trying to coordinate behavior, let other agents know what is happening to them. The receivers of this information can then use it to decide what they are going to do. This is especially powerful when the receivers base their decisions on some overall specification of a "team" goal.[34]

The U.S. Air Force has adopted this procedure to allow pilots to coordinate mutual behavior largely in the absence of ground control. The pilots talk to one another and respond preferentially to those nearest them, and achieve collective coordination in a way loosely analogous to flocking behavior in birds.[35]

We see evidence of the corporate success of such a practice at 3M. Not only is there a clear team goal—30 percent of revenue has to come from products that did not exist four years prior—but there are numerous opportunities for the exchange of information about what each is doing. As mentioned in Chapter Seven, there are technology councils, technical forums, in-house trade shows, a corporate technical directory, video conferencing, etc., to further the exchange of information—especially about technologies.

Similarly, at General Electric, the goal is clear: Be number 1 or number 2 in market share. There is also a concerted effort to widely exchange information—both internal and external—through the use of its world-class executive training center and such initiatives as workout.

At Microsoft, Bill Gates stresses the importance of information technology and systems to facilitate learning. Although he acknowledges that many of the techniques employed by Microsoft to facilitate individual learning go on in the best classrooms, he believes there is "a critical difference."

> At Microsoft these learning activities get a boost from the latest computing and telecommunications technologies. Microsoft succeeds because its employees learn efficiently, in part by using information tools.[36]

Few companies have taken the idea of using technology to facilitate information exchange as far as Buckman Laboratories International of Memphis, Tennessee. Its success in the specialty chemicals business has been attributed in large part to a knowledge network, called "K'Netix." According to its CEO, Bob Buckman, the knowledge network that his company developed is a pillar of the corporate culture and in many ways is the organization. His basic philosophy is, "How do we take this individual and make him bigger, give him more power? How? Connect him to the world." He says, "I realized that if I can give everyone complete access to information about the company, then I don't have to tell them what to do all the time. The organization starts moving forward on its own initiative."[37] The objective behind the knowledge network at Buckman is clear: "Effectively engage on the front line" in serving the customer.

There have been a number of companies that tried to develop such knowledge-sharing systems but have failed because they did not recognize the cultural issues associated with implementation. As Buckman has observed, "What's happened here is a 90 percent culture change. You need to change the way you relate to one another. If you can't do that, you won't succeed."

The advent of groupware software, such as Lotus Notes, can be a powerful tool for facilitating this exchange of information. Other software products seek to provide organizations with the ability to do even more than share databases and send messages. They basically are redefining the workplace. Such products have the potential to fundamentally change the workplace by destroying the traditional command and control structure so common in large organizations. Unless these products are combined with clear team goals, however, they can be detrimental to the organization.

An Evolving Organizational Structure

Just as with the strategy of the company and the strategy formulation process, I believe organizational structures must keep changing. The right organizational perspective is to see the organization as an evolving organism whose structure must constantly adapt to facilitate growth.

At many Internet organizations, a changing structure is relatively easy to accommodate but still a challenge. The former CFO of CyberCash described the first few years of his company's life as "absolute chaos." He pointed out that "the people who have trouble here are those that think you can organize this." He added, "However, you have to keep trying."

It is the larger organizations where there is a real organizational challenge. Yet some of the best have found ways to do it. For example, at 3M when a product reaches a certain level of sales it becomes a department. At another milestone a new division is formed, then groups. According to a former CEO of 3M, "Over the years we've discovered that when a division reaches a certain size, it has a tendency to spend too much of its time on established products and markets and a lesser amount on new products and businesses."[38] When the new businesses are broken out and new managers assigned, he reports that "we find, almost without exception, that the new division begins growing at a faster rate. We also stimulate the established division to find other new products and markets which will help it meet our growth objectives."[39]

Few companies go as far as Oticon Holding, but maybe more should. In the mid-1990s, CEO Las Kolind feared his company's project teams were hardening into something close to departments. In response he "exploded the organization" by relocating people based on the time horizons of their projects. Within three hours, more than a hundred people had moved. Kolind describes it as "total chaos" but stresses that "to keep a company alive, one of the jobs of top management is to keep it disorganized."[40]

On a smaller scale, Nokia announced in 1998 that all of the top managers of the company's main division were to switch jobs. According to CEO Jorma Ollila, he was "removing people from their comfort areas."[41]

A word of caution is in order. It is not enough just to change the structures—people need to understand what is going on. When Andy Grove talked about the possible need to rethink Intel's entire corporate organizational structure and modify it, he observed, "Thousands of our employees would need to understand why we would tinker with what has worked well for us in the past."[42]

In general, I believe constantly evolving organizational structures are the future, especially in organizations that are information or knowledge based. More and more corporate executives will need to be able to describe their organization the way Microsoft's COO, Bob Herbold does: "Microsoft is very good at reorganizing. This is the kind of thing we do all the time, to group people to do the best job possible to get good products to market."[43]

However, like the employees at Intel, people need to be told why the changes are necessary. In other words, they need to understand what is happening to the landscape on which they operate, before they can help the business adapt.

CONCLUSION

At 3M, the story is told of a reporter who repeatedly asks 3M's president for an organizational chart of the company. He finally asks if the company really has an organizational chart. Supposedly the president replies, "Oh, we have one all right, but we don't like to wave it around. There are some great people who might get upset if they found out who their bosses are."[44]

As 3M leadership has long recognized, the key concerns about organizational structure are more than the focus of the various boxes, their size, and to whom each reports. The key is to do as 3M tries to do—whatever will enhance speed and flexibility so that the organization can respond to its changing environment faster than its competitors—enhance adaptation.

Arie de Geus, in his recent book, *The Living Company*, uses the word "tolerance" to describe one of the key factors that long-term surviving corporations have in common. He stresses that tolerance was "the core quality that made it possible to diversify and decentralize, yet still manage the entity as a whole." He found such companies to be "particularly tolerant of activities in the margin: small, seemingly strange businesses that might have been pruned off the corporate rosebush elsewhere."[45] Tolerance, he believes, can only exist in an organization "where people recognize the value of creating space for innovation."[46] The organizational guidelines discussed in this chapter are ways of encouraging such organizational tolerance.

As we move away from a world made of fairly smooth landscapes where people have jobs they do every day, new organizational structures and practices will be required. The efforts will have to be supported by the leadership of the firm. After all, it is the leaders who will be the major influence in creating and communicating the strategy, helping to shape the culture and changing organizational characteristics.

Leadership in an adaptive organization requires a set of skills and aptitudes that are different from that of traditional organizations. After all, they are trying to operate at the edge of chaos. It is the role of the leader in an adaptive organization that I turn to now.

Part IV

LEADERSHIP: PERSONALLY SHAPING THE ADAPTIVE ORGANIZATION

Courage is resistance to fear, mastery of fear—not absence of fear.

—Mark Twain

It is not enough just to create organizational structures, processes, and cultures that are *able* to respond to change. Adaptive organizations must be *willing* to change constantly, even be desirous of change. This willingness to change must be constantly reinforced by the leadership of the organization. It is a never-ending struggle. It requires courageous leaders. After all, in complex adaptive organizations, leaders never know exactly what will happen as a result of their actions. Successful leaders, whether of new ventures or well-established companies, find ways to cope with their fears of the unknown.

This section recognizes that the leadership challenges of change are quite different depending on whether we are considering a small, startup venture or a well-established organization. Clearly, many of the challenges of leading Amazon.com are quite different than those of leading Intel or General Electric.

CHAPTER NINE

Leadership in the Beginning

I f you spend much time with small Internet firms you cannot help but be impressed with the anxiety that some of their founders feel about their companies' future. They know that without the ability to rapidly adapt to the unexpected, their business could easily go under in a very short time frame. Even the leaders of successful companies like Yahoo! worry. According to cofounder Jerry Yang, he still worries "if we'll be around in three to four years."[1]

Netscape is a classic example of what Jerry Yang was talking about. As noted earlier in this book, Netscape experienced extreme volatility in its short history. Not long before its acquisition by America Online in late 1998, Marc Andreessen observed,

> This is going to sound weird, but the gut-wrenching tension has decreased over time because survival has become less of an issue. Before you ship a product, you're operating on borrowed time and borrowed money. You don't have a business. All you've done may go up in smoke. You may not be there in three months. That's

gut-wrenching. There's a good amount of pressure now, but it's not the same. If you put $200 million in the bank and do a $400 million-a-year run rate, you're not going to disappear overnight. You may be gone in twelve months, but not overnight.[2]

This chapter is devoted to exploring the leadership challenge at the beginning of a venture—that time that Andreessen calls the most "gut-wrenching" for business leaders. One Internet CEO graphically expressed the challenge of his company's early days, using a football analogy: "Because it was all self-funded, it was fourth and ten with no time-outs."[3] What are the key tasks for a leader of a new venture who has no "time-outs"?

Although this chapter is especially appropriate for those individuals who are involved in a startup venture, whether as an entrepreneur or product champion within an established company, it also can be useful for the leaders of established organizations. It is important for them to think about how their organizations got to where they are today and how new ventures should be nurtured.

FUNDAMENTAL TASKS FOR THE LEADER OF A NEW VENTURE ON A RUGGED LANDSCAPE

I see three fundamental tasks associated with ensuring that the new organization adapts and survives its early days: identifying a viable niche, securing the key resources, and building relationships with other players on the competitive landscape. These three challenges will continue to be important throughout the life of the organization but are particularly critical in the early stages of a new venture—when it is least fit.

Identify a Niche

Each new venture, whether a new company or a new product, has to find a niche to fill. As discussed in Chapter Three, the competitive landscape, like Darwin's biological landscape, finds each new business or venture trying to "wedge itself into the filled nooks and crannies of the tangled bank of life, struggling against all others to jam itself onto the wedge-filled surface of possibilities."[4]

Successful entrepreneurs must first spot an opportunity on their landscape that they believe they can successfully exploit. These spots almost always are perceived as small niches in a larger landscape and usually are niches that larger organizations do not see, underestimate the potential importance of, or cannot successfully exploit. In fact, with disruptive technologies, the most powerful protection that small entrant companies enjoy as they build the emerging markets for disruptive technologies is that "they are doing something that it simply does not make sense for the established leaders to do."[5]

To illustrate, consider the experience of William Melton, cofounder of CyberCash. He watched the growth of the Internet in the early 1990s and recognized a niche that was not being served:

> Most of the banking world at that time was not paying attention to this new phenomenon, and most of the people in the Internet were not paying attention to payments. And so there seemed to be a gap that needed to be filled.[6]

Over time, what started as a niche may come to dominate the landscape and even change it, as personal computers have done for the computer landscape.

Even Microsoft started as a niche player. As teenagers, Paul Allen and Bill Gates saw a 1972 article in *Electronics* magazine announcing that Intel had released the 8008 microprocessor chip. Then, in 1974, the same publication announced Intel's new 8080 chip, which was ten times more powerful. According to Gates, most people in the computer industry, including Intel, saw it as only "an improvement in chip technology." He added,

> But Paul and I looked past the limits of that new chip and saw a different kind of computer that would be

> perfect for us, and for everyone—personal, affordable, and adaptable. It was absolutely clear to us that because the new chips were so cheap they would soon be everywhere.[7]

Gates and Allen believed they could come up with new and innovative software for machines based on the new microprocessors Intel was developing. According to Gates, "And why not? The microprocessor would challenge the structure of the industry. Maybe there was a place in the new scheme of things for the two of us." When IBM failed to emphasize software and DEC failed to embrace the personal computer, according to Gates, "they made room for the likes of Microsoft."[8] Armed with that insight, the next year they started the company that would become Microsoft. They were able to "jam" themselves "onto the wedge-filled surface of possibilities" ignored by much larger "species" on the landscape.

The technology sector is full of nooks and crannies into which entrepreneurs have been able to wedge themselves. They have recognized the power of a focus strategy. Michael Dell, founder of Dell Computer, is another good example. His company's success resulted from the fact that his people "believe in focus." He also stressed that the companies that have won in PCs and networking "were not the broad, diversified General Motors of computing. They were the fast, flexible, focused companies— Cisco, Compaq, Dell."[9]

Even large organizations have recognized the power of focus. At GE, Jack Welch has identified focus as his company's key to winning in "mature" industries. He believes GE has been successful by taking

> industries that may not be perceived as growth industries and pick the growth elements of those industries and get on them. For example, plastics. We are on every PC that's being sold today, with a high margin product.[10]

The same can be true for growth businesses. GE Capital Services, the $33 billion division of General Electric, is run as a collection of niche businesses. According to an executive at GE Capital, "Customers say our niche approach is what helps us win market share."[11]

Andy Grove has argued that Intel's focus on microprocessors "has been the single factor most responsible for Intel's success" since the mid-1980s.[12] He also makes the case very well for why focus is so important. He has observed that "hedging is expensive and dilutes commitment. Without exquisite focus, the resources and energy of the organization will be spread a mile wide—and they will be an inch deep."[13] Contrast this view of the world with that expressed by Compaq's recently dismissed CEO. At the time of Compaq's acquisition of Digital Equipment in 1998, Eckhard Pfeiffer claimed, "We want to do it all, and we want to do it now."[14] Especially in the early days of an organization, the exquisite focus is critical.

I see at least three keys to a successful niche strategy. First, a successful niche has to *serve the unmet needs*. It helps if, in the words of Douglas Leone, a partner with a Silicon Valley venture capital firm, the "customers are experiencing pain."

> We look for markets where the customer has a problem he understands. You don't want to go selling to a customer and saying, by the way, do you know you have a problem with your FTP software? You want immediate pain and . . . a wealthy set of customers.

He adds, "Most pain can be anticipated over a period of twelve, twenty-four, and thirty-six months. It doesn't have to be understood by all. It has to be well understood by a group of people that can launch a company."[15]

The Internet has given a wide range of startup companies the opportunity to reduce customer pain. For example, the founders of Enews recognized that small-circulation publications had difficulty in obtaining shelf space on traditional newsstands. From that base it has expanded to carry all kinds of publications. Auto-by-Tel recognized that there were a significant number of cust-omers who disliked the traditional haggling process of buying a new car.

The second key to a successful niche strategy is to *build on innovation*. It usually is an innovation that creates niches; a differ-ent way of doing something. It may be the result of a new tech-nology or a new distribution channel or simply a process that enables an organization to do something more efficiently or effec-tively than its competitors. It is rare to find a successful venture that merely copies what another firm is doing.

The third key to successfully exploiting a niche is for the lead-ership of the organization to *make hard choices*. Which niches will the organization attempt to serve? Of necessity, this means being pretty clear about which niches one will *not* attempt to serve.

Organizations generally have a far better chance of success if they focus their energies around a subset of the potential market, especially in the early days and then grow from there. A 1996 article in *INC* magazine ("Just Say NO") focused on "why not all business is good business" and reported on seven CEOs and the sales they "refused to make."[16] More companies need to say no and have the discipline to stick to it.

To illustrate, consider Open Market, an Internet startup formed in April 1994. According to its founder and Chairman Shikhar Ghosh, when Gary Eichhorn became chief executive in December 1995, he said, "We were doing way too much." Eich-horn focused the Open Market on developing ready-to-use soft-ware that allowed companies to easily sell products to consumers who visit their Web site. Perhaps more important, he stopped ef-forts in all other areas, which meant walking away from its service-oriented business, or 80 percent of Open Market's reve-nues. According to Ghosh, "The companies that survived focused on one area and then put a lot of resources behind it."[17]

Similarly, in the early 1980s, Emerson Electric's executives, who were responsible for developing and implementing a new strategy for its recently acquired Skil power tool division, chose not to serve some segments of the power tool business but to focus on the rapidly growing hardware stores and home centers. When several of the mass merchandisers sought out Skil to buy their products, they were turned down—as much as $100 million in additional revenue or a third of company revenues at the time. Skil management believed that if it was to increase Skil's fitness, it had to focus its resources where it could receive the greatest help from others on its landscape—particularly the emerging distribution channel of hardware/home center stores.

Understandably, many businesspeople have trouble turning away business. Too often they try to be all things to all people—to serve all customers. They want to hedge their bets. We have all seen new startups that tried to chase every opportunity that came along and in the end failed because they did not have the resources to do so.

Kauffman's research on complex systems demonstrates that there are benefits to ignoring a subset of customers. In dealing with complex problems he argues that "the best solutions may be found if . . . different subsets of constraints are ignored at different moments."[18] In other words, you should not try to please all of the people all of the time.

Securing Key Resources

Although all successful organizations get their start by finding niches, those that are to adapt and hopefully become the fittest have to be effective at exploiting the resources of their existing landscape. Before an entrepreneur can turn an idea into a business, he or she has to create an organization according to Gerhard Schulmeyer, CEO of Siemens Nixdorf, the giant European computer maker. "The corporation exists insofar as it provides a place where the individual can do what he is good at, at a lower cost than he could do it alone."[15]

Organizations, like species, must attract the key resources needed to sustain life and allow the organization to grow. They have to secure the necessary resources to build a growing business and use them wisely.

Many good ideas never get funded and many of those that are funded fail. One venture capital firm estimates that it reviews 3,000 business plans each year and ends up funding just twenty. Another culls through 1,600 to come up with ten worth reading.[19] If a venture capital firm is successful 15 percent of the time, it has a pretty good record. Thus, lots of people with ideas never secure the resources needed to develop a viable organization, and many of those that do secure resources do not necessarily succeed.

The Small Business Administration has estimated that less than 1 percent of new businesses ever break even and less than 1 in 1,000 goes public.[20] Even those startups that reach the stage of going public have a high failure rate. If you look at the history of technology IPOs from 1980, there has been approximately a 40 percent failure rate. It appears to be even higher for Internet IPOs—approximately 60 percent.

I find that the successful leadership of a viable startup has two key priorities: *employees* and *cash flow*. These are the two strategic or core resources that should occupy a significant amount of any leader's time, but especially the leader of a startup.

Even in large and diversified organizations like GE, leadership places great emphasis on allocating these two resources. According to CEO Jack Welch, "People say, Jack, how can you be at NBC, you don't know anything about dramas or comedies . . . Well, I can't build a jet engine, either. I can't build a turbine. Our job at GE is to deal with resources. . . ."[21]

The allocation of these two critical resources—employees and cash—are at the heart of what leaders do. In rugged landscapes especially, the risks and rewards for proper stewardship of these resources can be tremendous.

Drawing on our biology analogy, it can be helpful to think about these resources as sources or forms of energy. Energy is defined as the capacity to do work or stored work. In any organization there have to be at least two forms of energy: people and cash. People are like kinetic energy or the energy of motion; cash is like potential or stored energy, which can be used at a later time.

People

Hiring good people is the key to any organization's survival, especially in its early days. After all, they largely will determine the "genetic makeup" of the organization. Employees who do not get along with the founder will not survive and those that do are likely to advance faster and be given the opportunity to hire others. The people who stay and advance will influence more and more people, thereby shaping the organization.

It is not surprising that a key admonition that Bill Gates gave to a key executive in the early days of Microsoft was to "keep hiring smart people as fast as you can."[22] According to Steve Jobs, cofounder of Apple, "Silicon Valley is a meritocracy. It doesn't matter what you wear. It doesn't matter how old you are. What matters is how smart you are."[23]

I found the same attitude in many of the Internet companies I studied. For example, CyberCash executives talk about "hiring up"—hiring people below a manager who are smarter and more capable in a certain area than the manager. Amazon has a similar approach. According to an early Amazon employee, "One of his [Bezos] mottoes was that every time we hired someone, he or she should raise the bar for the next hire, so that the overall talent pool was always improving."[24] The CEO of Enews, says "it's all talent in this business." He stresses the importance of "liking the people you work with. Is this someone who I want to burn the midnight oil with?"

You see evidence of a similar attitude at some of the best-managed large companies. They are able to pick from the best job applicants. In a poll of Japanese college students, Sony has ranked number 1 in the world for preferred employment. In some years, 3M receives more than 100 applications for every one technical opening, and its turnover rate among professionals, including managers, often is less than 4 percent. There is virtually no turn-over among senior management.

Securing good employees is only part of the battle. Retaining them, especially those with special skills and abilities, is critical. As discussed in Chapter Seven, many of the leading technology companies emphasize some degree of shared ownership. According to Bill Gates, shared ownership "has contributed more to our success than anyone would have predicted."[25] It is a powerful way of increasing the chances that key employees will have a direct stake in the company fitness. If the company succeeds, they succeed.

In the most rugged landscapes, you cannot attract the capital without the people. Thus, I have come to believe that people are *the* strategic resource. I have found over and over in the world of the Internet that investors invest their capital largely on their assessment of the people behind the new venture and not the technology or product. Even in a large but entrepreneurial organization like 3M, the corporate resource allocation process often seems to be a bet on the person behind an idea—the product champion—rather than the technology. In the language of the racetrack, they bet on the jockey rather than the horse.

Cash

Good people cannot be retained if they do not have the resources to do what needs to be done. On a rugged landscape the successful organizations must be able to survive the rough times, which are inevitable. This requires access to cash. Yale Brown, co-founder and CEO of Intelligent Interactions, put the case for cash very clearly: "Cash is key, without it, you'll die; it is the life blood of a small business."

One of Bill Gates's early policies for Microsoft was to "always have enough *cash* [Gates's emphasis] on hand to be able to run the company for at least a year even if no one pays us."[26] Microsoft continues to emphasize free cash. As of mid-1996, Microsoft had

$6.9 billion in cash on its balance sheet, approximately $14 billion in late 1998, and $22 billion in mid-1999.

It is not just Microsoft that has this philosophy regarding cash. It seems to be common at many successful high-tech companies. For example, in early 1998 Compaq had $6 billion in the bank and almost no debt. SAS Institute, Inc., with 1996 sales of at least $600 million in revenues, has never borrowed money or had to acquire equity capital at high prices, except for a mortgage on its first office building that was long ago repaid. In early 1998, Amazon had approximately ten times the cash that Barnes & Noble and Borders had. In early 1998 America Online had $750 million on hand. In early 1999 Intel had nearly $11 billion in cash.

Dell Computer has been effective not only at raising external capital, but at squeezing cash out of existing operations. It has a cash-conversion cycle (the difference between the time it pays its competitors and the time it takes to get paid) of negative-eight days. In addition, management hopes to squeeze even more cash out of the business, as it plans to measure parts inventory in hours instead of days. According to its CEO, Michael Dell,

> Seven days doesn't sound like much inventory but 168 hours does. In a business where inventory depreciates 1 percent per week, inventory is risk. A few years ago, no one in this business realized what an incredible opportunity managing inventory was.[27]

This is on top of an already impressive record. In 1993 Dell had $2.6 billion in sales and $342 million in inventory. At the end of 1997 it had $12.3 billion in sales and $233 million in inventory. By contrast, Gateway 2000, which also sells direct to customers, had $6.3 billion in sales and $249 million in inventory. Another way to compare Dell's performance in the area is inventory turns. In early 1999, Dell's rate was approximately sixty per year compared to Compaq's fourteen.

I was recently struck by an observation made by the author of *The Innovator's Dilemma*:

The dominant difference between successful ventures and failed ones, generally, is not the astuteness of their original strategy. Guessing the right strategy at the outset isn't nearly as important to success as conserving enough resources (or having the relationships with trusting backers or investors) so that new business initiatives get a second or third stab at getting it right. Those that run out of resources or credibility before they can iterate toward a viable strategy are the ones that fail.[28]

It was interesting to find that in a number of cases, too much cash could be a problem for a new venture. A high-level executive at one Internet company observed that, because his company had been so successful in raising funds, he feared people did not have the sense of urgency that he thought would be necessary for long-term success. Similarly, Douglas Leone, a Sequoia partner, believes most venture-backed startups are overcapitalized. "I tell them [startups] to spend money very carefully. Spend the money in a narrow focus, one product, one application, one target set of customers."[29]

The same problem can be created at large organizations. At 3M, the product champion behind the phenomenal success of Post-it® Notes observed that the beauty of bootleg projects is that they "allow you to keep a low profile during the time when the early, tough problems arise that require creative solutions." He added, "Throwing a lot of money or people at the task doesn't speed it up, but it does cut down on management's ability to afford to be patient."[30]

▲ ▲ ▲ ▲ ▲

Good relationships with such internal agents as employees and stockholders or investors are especially important for a successful beginning (and long-term survival) for the organization. If the organization is to survive and grow, it must be able to quickly adapt to the changing landscape around it. Unless the people in the organization are able to adapt to new developments, the organization cannot adapt. Even if the people are willing to adapt, if the organization does not have the cash to manage during the time of adaptation, it will not survive. Thus, building good relationships with the key resource providers—employees and providers of capital, especially stockholders—is critical. However, it is not enough.

Building and Managing a Web of External Relationships

Even with a viable niche, good people and adequate cash, it is impossible for organizations on the most rugged landscapes to survive and prosper unless they establish reciprocal relationships with other members of the landscape. The external relationships with other members of the landscape are especially critical in the early life of the business—relationships with customers, suppliers, and even competitors and complementors. It is impossible for an organism to "go it alone" on a volatile landscape. It needs a web of external relationships.

As discussed in Chapter Five, organizational leaders have to think about not only with whom they need to establish relationships but what type of relationships they want and the risks associated with various relationships. After all, any of these agents can potentially change the landscape.

Customers Are the Key External Relationship

In recent years, we have seen much attention focused on building strong customer relationships. Such an emphasis is absolutely necessary on a rugged landscape. If I had to prioritize the external relationships in terms of importance, customers would rank number 1.

There is a fundamental force at work today—customers have more power than ever before. The worlds of Compaq and Intel in the 1990s were a fight for control of a landscape that they once dominated. Yet, at least in the case of Intel, the immediate challenge was not a direct attack by a competitor but a change in the power position of a customer that competitors could try to exploit for their own advantage.

This power shift has been brought on by at least two major developments. First, most competitors now offer fairly similar products. In other words, there is relatively little differentiation in the customers' minds between many competing products. Second, and most important, we are living in a much more interconnected world of information and communication, unlike anything we have seen before. Customers can more easily compare existing products.

At Intel, in spite of its heavy promotion of the Intel brand, most individual customers still bought an IBM computer or a Compaq computer—not an Intel chip. Furthermore, the PC industry was increasingly becoming a commodity business, which gave the individual customer lots of choices. Although the individual consumer might pay a little more for an IBM with an Intel chip, he or she would not pay a lot more. If there were questions about the quality of the premium-priced Intel chip, customers would easily switch brands.

It is not just technology companies that have had to deal with a shift in power to customers. Consider the case of American Express. In spite of American Express's success with its Travel and Entertainment cards, by the end of the 1980s, the bankcards Visa and MasterCard controlled almost two-thirds of the market. In addition, several large players had entered the credit card business—Sears, Prudential, J. C. Penney's, Spiegel, General Motors, and most significantly, AT&T. The latter offered a card "free for life" for those who signed up the first year and used it at least once a year. They also offered a 10 percent discount on AT&T's long distance calls, plus many of the services that American Express had been offering. By 1990, it was estimated that there were 400 million retail cards, 245 million bankcards, 120 million oil cards and 30 million travel and entertainment cards in circulation in the United States alone. The average consumer was estimated to have eight cards, including 2.5 bankcards. Individual customers now had multiple choices and merchants had choices too. If customers, including high-income customers, did not carry an American Express card, they carried either Visa or MasterCard. Many carried all three. Individual customers and merchants could choose to use whichever one gave them the best deal. The annual fee charged to card holders and the higher fees charged to merchants by American Express made their card less attractive to many customers.

One of the challenges faced by technology companies is that their leaders often become enamored with their technology. Leaders of technology firms often have to learn, as did Sony's founders and Motorola's current leadership, that technology is not particularly important unless the customer wants it.

▲ Akio Morita, cofounder of Sony, realized in the early days of his company that "having unique technology and being able to make unique products are not enough to keep a business going. You have to sell the products, and to do that you have to show the potential buyer the real value of what you are selling."[31]

▲ Motorola failed to give some of its biggest corporate customers what they wanted in the mid-1990s—digital cellular phones. Although it had approximately 60 percent of the U.S. analog market at the time, by failing to listen to its customers, it seems to have been in a catch-up mode ever since and is no longer delivering the financial results investors came to expect of Motorola.[32]

This seems especially true with many Internet companies. Intelligent Interactions is a good example. According to Matt Walker, cofounder of the company, "The real trick is not the technology, but knowing what the [customer] requirements are." According to his cofounder, Yale Brown, some of their early struggles resulted from being more focused on the technology than the customer. "We thought we had a beautiful baby, but quickly found out not everyone thought our baby was beautiful."

There is an important balancing act that technology companies have to master. If they blindly follow the direct feedback they receive from their existing customers, they may miss the next big breakthrough. They need to be thinking and listening to the needs and interests of potential customers as well. As Christensen points out in *The Innovator's Dilemma*, by continuing to support the needs of current customers, a company often continues to improve an existing technology but ignores a new technology that may completely disrupt the landscape.

Good technology companies in general and Internet companies in particular have a lot to teach companies in less-rugged landscapes about building customer relationships. Not only do their customers have lots of options, but one of the challenges of the Internet world is that many of the companies have to try to balance a wide variety of customers. For example, VirtualRadio has to manage artists and individual fans. Amazon management not only has to worry about the individuals who buy books, but the company also has to satisfy associates who refer individual buyers to Amazon. In addition, it is heavily dependent on wholesalers and publishers for its success. Cybercash has to sell its products to banks, merchants, and individuals. In other words, increasingly companies have to manage a network of customers.

Another common characteristic of startup Internet companies, as they relate to customers, is the focus on market share. In the short run, the fittest Internet startups seem to emphasize market share over profits. Amazon's leadership frequently speaks of the need to sacrifice profits to grow volume, as does the leadership of CDnow. Netscape was willing to give away its browsers to customers to create a significant lead over its competitors.

As discussed in an earlier chapter, fitness means growth. If a company is to be fit, it has to grow, and that means increasing its market value. In the early stages of a company's development, that generally requires building market share.

To build this share quickly, successful Internet companies in particular seem to emphasize five key customer initiatives that I believe all companies should consider: providing good content, building customer confidence, involving the customer, studying the customer, and quickly responding to customer problems.

A Positive First Experience

Good content on the Internet is critical to laying the foundation for market share growth. Raul Fernandex of Proxicom, the first Internet firm to win a Clio award for Internet advertising, believes that "what you want to do first is get people there. Compelling content gets people to your site."[33]

CDnow has worked to provide compelling content by having a content editor with a group of stringers who will tell the customer which album is, according to its CEO, "best for you." According to one of its founders, "I'd rather take advice from a guy who writes for *Rolling Stone* than some kid in a mall making minimum wage."[34]

Amazon has been a leader at providing compelling content. It strives for lots of information in a simple format that is not cluttered with elaborate graphics. According to its CEO, "The No. 1 thing we work on is making the store a fun place to be."[35] He also stresses, "If your site is confusing or otherwise hard to use, you won't get a second chance with most people."[36]

He also believes in the importance of allocating resources to support the customers' experience. He claims that in the offline world, 30 percent of a company's resources are spent providing a good customer experience and 70 percent goes to marketing. But online, he says, 70 percent should be devoted to creating a great customer experience and 30 percent should be spent "shouting" about it.[37]

IBM struggled with its Web site in 1998. That year its most popular feature was the search function, and its second most popular was the "help" button. According to IBM's vice president for Internet operations, "Most people couldn't figure out how to navigate the site." After a complete redesign that cost millions and involved more than 100 employees for ten weeks, help-button usage decreased 84 percent and sales increased 400 percent.[38]

Even in non-Internet companies the message is the same—make the customers' initial experiences especially interesting and simple to access. Then keep emphasizing the experience.

Building Customer Confidence

Hand in hand with market share is giving the customer confidence to deal with you. Building a brand name is one especially important way to build customer confidence. Leading Internet companies such as Netscape, Yahoo!, and Amazon have built global brand names in a relatively short time frame. For example, soon after going public in 1996, Yahoo! spent $5 million to promote its name on television. E*Trade has tried to build brand awareness by offering a mock trading game that by the fall of 1997 had attracted 35,000 players. It also allowed investors who were hesitant to leave their brokers to open shadow portfolios to see what hands-on trading would be like.

Jeff Bezos of Amazon believed that print ads in publications like *The Wall Street Journal* and the *New York Times Book Review* were most likely to instill confidence for his early customers:

> If you see the ad in print several times and then see the banner on a Website, you might decide to buy something. But when the advertising's just Web-based, it's not crystal clear to the viewer that this is a real business. There are no products in the window, no other customers, no proof you are giving your credit card number to a real company.[39]

Involving the Customer

As the customer gains confidence, the next step is to actively engage him or her. Some of the best Internet companies look for ways to involve the customer in more than just a transaction. In the words of one Internet CEO, "Once they come, you have to provide the tools for people to interact with the company, the products and, especially, each other."[40] Often the goal is to create a community—what Bezos of Amazon refers to as a "virtual community."[41]

Few if any Internet companies involve customers more effectively than Amazon. It tried to create a sense of fun for customers by such activities as compiling a list of the twenty most obscure titles that were sought, giving prizes for best reviews, having a book-writing contest, and holding random drawings for free books.

Amazon not only encourages customers to write book reviews but has found a way to turn customers into salespeople through its Associates Program—third-party Web sites that can earn money by linking and sending book-buying customers to Amazon's site. According to Amazon's CEO, "We pay the fee because our Associates provide a service. They place the books in an editorial context that enables the customer to make a purchasing decision, and they bring the customer to the table."[42] He adds, "We may not know what the best book on model rocketry or Labrador Retrievers is. But there's already a Web site out there run by a passionate person who does."[43]

Amazon also knows that building confidence means not taking advantage of customers and giving them some control in the relationship. Although Amazon makes good use of e-mail, according to its founder, "The key to success is keeping the e-mail process firmly in the hands of the customer. They have to actively sign up for it."[44]

Studying the Customer

Part of building the relationships with customers is to actively study them. It is perhaps the best way to learn a great deal about the future of your business. At Intuit Corporation, the software maker best known for Quicken and now an emerging Internet-based company, its founder, Scott Cook, stresses the importance of listening to customers. "There are plenty of advisors out there, but I believe that all the real learning comes from consumers."[45] His company conducts both customer interviews and surveys.

Amazon uses an automated service that informs customers of newly published books and provides them with reviews and recommendations based on their past purchases. Bezos also finds that e-mail offers "a tremendous amount of feedback from your customers." The "semi-anonymity" of e-mail, he believes, "allows people to say what they really think."[46] It is a view shared by Yahoo! According to Tim Brady, Yahoo's third employee and vice president of production, "We get hundreds of thousands of e-mails each month, and we make use of the information that says 'I want this' and 'I want that.' Users are great. The time they spend to tell us what they want is unbelievable."[47]

Jim Goodnight, cofounder of SAS, has mandated that every suggestion a user makes be written down. Once a year these suggestions are sorted, ranked, and then placed on a ballot that is sent out to every SAS customer. The survey results are then analyzed. The top ten suggestions are almost always implemented. Goodnight puts all of this effort into the proper context: "It's an amazingly effective business practice, listening to your customers." The results prove him right. In 1996 SAS reportedly had a 95 percent lease renewal rate.[48]

John Chambers, CEO of Cisco, has the right idea about why such studying of customers is so important: "There is nothing more arrogant than telling a customer: 'Here is what you need to know.' Most of the time you are not going to be right."[49]

Taking Care of Customer Problems

Part of the challenge of building strong customer relationships is to make sure customers are not mistreated. The first challenge is to try to prevent problems. Unfortunately, technology businesses always have customers with problems. Consequently, the second challenge is to try to quickly resolve any problem.

The best technology companies not only look for ways to resolve the problem but turn those problems into future opportunities. Scott Cook of Intuit offers a good example of how a customer problem can be turned into an opportunity:

> At Intuit, there was one newspaper story talking about a bug in one of our tax products. I saw the article at eight in the morning on the day the article came out. By 3:30 that day, Intuit sent out a press release announcing the bug and four others that we found out about over the course of the investigation. We announced a complete program of 800 numbers where customers could get replacement products without being grilled about what their software was doing. We also re-announced the fact that we have always guaranteed our tax software; if a user ever pays interest or a penalty because of an error in our software, we pay it for him. And we did all this even though the bugs only affected less than one percent of our total users. In the tax season, our market share went from 60 to 80 percent.[50]

It is a classic case of making a silk purse out of a sow's ear.

Companies need to find ways to make sure customer satisfaction is high on employees' radar screens. Leading technology companies have done so.

▲ At Cisco, every manager's compensation is directly tied to customer satisfaction. The company surveys clients each year, polling them on approximately sixty performance criteria. According to the CEO, "If a manager improves his scores, he can get a fair amount. But if the scores go down, we'll take money out of the manager's pocket."[51]

▲ Sun polls its workers as often as monthly via an e-mail questionnaire about "performance inhibitors" that have gotten in their way in the past month. The result, which Sun calls an "employee quality index," is part of a broader quality initiative that also gauges customer loyalty.[52]

▲ Dell tied bonuses and profit sharing to service improvements of
  at least 15 percent in 1998. Success was measured by shipping
  deadlines, fixing machines on the first try, and getting repair
  people to customers within twenty-four hours.

  I like the philosophy expressed by Buckman Laboratories'
CEO, Bob Buckman. He believes that the "number of people in
the organization working on the relationship with the customer,
relative to the total organization, will determine the momentum
of the organization." He also stresses, "If an employee is not effectively engaged with the customer, why are they employed?"[53]

Other External Relationships

  Although many of the quality programs adopted by companies in the 1980s emphasized the importance of managing both
customer and supplier relationships, too many companies still neglect to actively manage the supplier relationship.
  Companies such as Toyota have a lot to teach other companies about supplier relationships. To illustrate, the CEO of a Toyota supplier has contrasted the common approach: "How can I
club you into submission?" to Toyota's approach: "How can I
help you be better." To prepare his company to be a supplier, he
had two Toyota engineers spend seven months in one of his
plants, improving processes, materials management, and quality
in preparation for a Toyota contract—even though the plant was
then making parts for a competitor.
  In addition to customers and suppliers, organizations on rugged landscapes need to actively manage relationships with competitors and complementors. Unfortunately, relationships with
these two landscape participants often are largely ignored.
  With both competitors (including substitutors) and complementors, it is especially important to think of how we might be
able to work together. Consider the 1980s fight in the consumer
electronics business over the video tape recorder. Although Sony
thought its Beta format was superior, it failed to convince enough

other industry players, and ultimately customers, to back its technology. Sony lost to a better-organized effort that supported VHS. We have seen a similar situation in the DVD introduction. There was Sony and Philips arrayed against Toshiba and a much larger and more diverse group of players that included competitors and customers. The Toshiba technology seemed to be prevail.

At a minimum, companies will want to think through how other competitors are likely to interpret their actions and how they might respond. Are there aggressive moves that they can make that may not provoke a severe retaliatory response from all or even one of their direct competitors?[54] After all, one day they may be willing to work together in a more collaborative relationship. The nature of relationships can change rapidly. For example, when Netscape was seen as a threat to Microsoft, it was not unusual for companies like Sun, IBM, and Hewlett Packard to support them. But as Netscape began to move into corporate markets, the support was less enthusiastic.

As for complementors, at a minimum, it seems that organizations should want to build cooperative relationships so that if new developments are under way, they will at least know about them in time to make the necessary adjustments. Ideally, they might even be consulted and work together with these organizations to improve the competitive landscape for both. From my observations, this advanced insight is one of the reasons so many small Internet companies want to establish a relationship with Microsoft and Intel. For example, Rob Glaser, formerly of Microsoft and later the founder of RealNetworks, a firm that develops software for receiving multimedia over the Internet, describes a key element of his strategy as "coopetition" with other players. Specifically, when it comes to Microsoft, he observes, "They are neither friend nor foe, but Microsoft is most certainly the environment we live in." He adds, "It's how we work within that environment that will make all the difference."[55]

Andrew Grove has the right idea about understanding and managing the network of relationships on a rugged landscape. In contemplating the future, especially the impact of the Internet on his company, Grove observed,

> We have a whole slew of new fellow travelers that we need to get to know, to cultivate and learn to work with. The list includes software companies that we never had anything to do with in the past. It includes telecommunications providers that are in the process of upgrading their networks. It extends further afield to advertising and media companies that want to learn about our technology, and advertisers who have paid no attention to the computing world until now but suddenly realize that they had better start.[56]

A clear understanding of just what kind of relationship we want with each of the other firms on our landscape is needed. Microsoft seems to have a pretty clear picture of other leading technology firms and the kind of relationship it wants. At a recent investment banking conference in San Francisco, Microsoft Chairman Bill Gates showed a slide listing more than a dozen of high tech's most important companies. "These are all partners," he said, "except for IBM, which is both a competitor and a partner." He paused. "And Sun. They're just a competitor."[57]

Clearly, the power and visibility of large firms make external personal relationship building much easier for the CEO of a Fortune 500 company than for a small startup company. Yet this network is especially critical for small companies. For example, in the high-tech community of Northern Virginia, an organization known as The Potomac KnowledgeWay was formed specifically to help such leaders form better contacts with others who might be able to help their companies achieve their goals. Whether such organizations exist in your area, a key task for the CEOs of small companies is to find ways to build external networks. These relationships are key to adapting.

Luck

I think it is important to acknowledge another important factor in the successful beginning of any new organization—luck. We all know it is a factor in any organization's success, but few leaders of businesses or writers about business seem to want to talk about it. Yet to be intellectually honest about the world around us requires us to acknowledge the role of luck.

Paul Newman, the actor and businessman, caught my attention with a quote about luck:

> Few successful people like to mention it, but let's be honest. Luck plays a big part in everything. Right place, right time, left turn rather than right turn, avoidance of illness, the right genes, all luck. We ought to think about it before we pound our chests.[58]

One of the most obvious areas of luck is in the genes inherited. We have no control over the genes we inherit. Clearly some are better for given environments than others. If the genes are not good, an organism will have difficulty surviving, even in the short run. The same is true of new organizations. If the founder and his or her first hires are not up to the task, i.e., they cannot adapt to their landscape, the organization will not survive.

There also is luck in timing. In more common language, it helps to be at the right place at the right time. In the biological world, Kauffman talks about "community assembly": How do stable communities of species come together? Although the answers are not known, he illustrates the phenomenon by describing a patch of prairie that is surrounded by a fence so that certain types of small animals can no longer enter the plot. Over time the kinds of plants in the plot will change. After some time, if the fence is removed, allowing the same set of small animals back onto the plot, many people would expect the plot to go back to the original community of plants. Yet, according to Kauffman,

It appears that this intuition is wrong. Typically, one gets a *different* stable community! It seems that given a "reservoir" of species that can migrate into a plot or patch, the community that forms is deeply dependent on the sequence in which species are introduced.[59]

In other words, you cannot always put an ecosystem back together with only the final species in the community. He refers to this as the "Humpty Dumpty effect."

This helps me to understand why merely hiring away some good people from a strong firm may not allow one to reproduce their success. Timing may not be everything but it is very important and often timing is a matter of luck—right place, right time.

CONCLUSION

Comedian Sid Caesar once commented: "The guy who invented the first wheel was an idiot. The guy who invented the other three—he was a genius." Henry Ford did not invent the automobile. He mass-produced it and sold it to millions of consumers. Bill Gates did not develop the first computer operating system. He made his system widely available.

To have a successful new venture requires more than just a breakthrough idea or technology. The real rewards go to the person or persons who understand how it can be used. Even more rewards go to those who can build the organization that can successfully oversee its large-scale introduction onto the landscape. After all, the company that invented portable computers— Osborne Computer—survived less than three years. In the semiconductor businesses, firms such as Unisem, Advanced Memory Systems, and Mostek are no longer around. Intel and Microsoft, however, have survived and prospered. They adapted.

New ventures, whether new companies or new products,

benefit greatly from a successful start—but survival and growth require much more. The things leaders should focus on in those early years have been the emphasis of this chapter. In the next chapter, the attention shifts to the things a leader in an established organization should emphasize.

CHAPTER TEN

Leadership in a Complex Environment

A s the various populations on a fitness landscape adapt and are able to climb to higher and higher peaks on their landscape, climbing to new heights becomes harder—but not impossible. This is especially true in the world of business. For companies like Microsoft and General Electric to continue to experience double-digit growth is much harder today than when they were much smaller companies. Clearly, this makes the task of leadership in a large corporation every bit as challenging as that of starting a new venture. The nature of those challenges are, however, quite different.

The challenge of leading large corporations on increasingly rugged landscapes is similar to that of other competitive environments where the records get harder and harder to set. In the world of sports, for example, it seems that records advance in very small increments. Occasionally, however, there is a breakthrough effort that "rewrites the record books," such as Mark McGwire's 1998 home run record of 70. In many cases the performance cannot be repeated for some time to come. It is as if a variety of circumstances came together at the right time and right place. However, it is not just luck. The athletes were ready for that magical moment.

I think the same is true for business organizations. The moment when the business breakthrough will be achieved cannot be predicted, but the organization can be ready to take advantage of the opportunity when it arises. Whether in sports, biology, or business, the truly successful players are part of what I call an "environment of success."

LEADING IS ABOUT CREATING AN ENVIRONMENT OF SUCCESS

Executives at 3M often describe their role in leading their company as providing an environment or a climate—what one former executive called a "climate for achievements" that "stimulates ordinary people to produce extraordinary performance."[1] The following are some selected quotes from various 3M executives that suggest to me a different way of thinking of leadership:

> Head of R&D: "We're managing in chaos, and that's the right way to do it."
> Head of organizational learning: "[A]n environment to free up your imagination—that's the whole idea."
> Head of international operations: "We go in helping to shape but not shaping."
> Vice chairman: "[I]t's almost alive, always ebbing and flowing."
> CEO: Innovation "tells us where to go; we don't tell innovation where to go."[2]

Leadership on a rugged landscape seems to require constantly working to shape an environment where change always is possible and usually is occurring. But it is an environment that also is finely balanced between surprise and order. When 3M's CEO talks about the foundation of 3M being "innovations and stability," he is describing, in organizational terms, the edge of chaos—a mixture of stability and flexibility; a compromise between order and surprise.

Using different language but describing a similar balancing act, Andy Grove talks about the importance of an organization being able to deal with debate and disagreements over an uncertain future, but also being able to rein in chaos and pursue a "determined march." The determined march and the environment of chaos are the equally important sides of the leadership coin. In an interesting choice of words, Grove describes an organization that can balance such qualities as "a powerful adaptive organization."[3]

I am convinced that the role of a business leader in the 21st century will be to create and nurture an environment that allows the organization to operate at the edge of chaos; a place where fitness can be at its highest. To successfully lead in this type of environment requires a nontraditional view of leadership. Rather than the "hero" as a lone figure trying to control the organization or drive the record-breaking car, the leader will be a catalyst and facilitator.

In this chapter I identify ten activities that leaders of large organizations can emphasize to help shape a coherent environment that can handle constant and significant change and thereby achieve breakthroughs. Many are applicable to small organizations but are especially applicable to larger, more complex organizations.

Build and Manage a Network of Personal Relationships

Just as business organizations need to have a network of relationships with other key agents on their landscape, so business leaders of established organizations need a network of relationships if their tenure at the top is to be successful. According to a classic *Harvard Business Review* article by John Kotter on the role of general managers,

> Effective GMs allocate significant time and effort when they first take their jobs to developing a network of co-operative relationships among those people they feel are needed to satisfy their emerging agendas. . . . . After that, their attention shifts toward using the networks to both implement and help in updating the agendas.[4]

Similarly, Andy Grove describes managers in Silicon Valley as "a node in a not-so-crisply defined network."[5] Jurgen Schrempp of Daimler-Chrysler talks about spending 40 percent to 50 percent of his time "networking."[6]

Building and maintaining this network of relationships involves more than just establishing relationships with direct reports. It includes establishing relationships with people throughout the organization as well as carefully chosen outsiders who can help people in leadership positions achieve their organization's goals. It may involve building relationships with people already in the organization, but it also may require replacing people who may not be as helpful in the future as they will need to be. People more in tune with the challenges of the future may have to be added to the network.

Kotter found that the best managers "ask, encourage, cajole, praise, reward, demand, manipulate, and generally motivate others with great skill in face-to-face situations." He also found that they rely more heavily on "indirect influences" than less capable managers who are more likely to rely on a "more narrow range of influence techniques and apply them with less finesse."[7] In other words, effective leadership is a very subtle process of building and utilizing a network of agents throughout the organization.

Study the Landscape

Although the future cannot be predicted at the edge of chaos, one thing is clear from the work that has been done on complex systems—there are patterns of behavior. That does not mean that they are easily seen at any point in time. It does, however, mean that many companies need to devote more resources and more CEOs need to devote their time to trying to understand the landscape on which their organizations operate. A key role of leadership in an adaptive organization is to be a student of the landscape.

Such leaders have to be intellectually honest about what they see around them. What are the developments, patterns, and trends among our competitors, both current and potential? What about our customers? Or our suppliers? What might they mean for us and our current strategy? How can we use these insights not only to respond to changes but to shape the future in our favor? As mentioned in an earlier chapter, leaders need to frequently ask themselves, and others, "What if?"

Unfortunately, too few corporate leaders seem to find the time today to study their landscape as carefully as is needed. According to Peter Drucker,

> I find more and more executives less and less well informed [about the outside world], if only because they believe that the data on the computer printouts are ipso facto information.
>
> I tell all my clients that it is absolutely imperative that they need a few weeks each year outside their own business and actively working in the marketplace, or in a university lab, in the case of technical people. The best way is for the chief executive officer to take the place of a salesman twice a year for two weeks.[8]

In Silicon Valley it is not uncommon for leaders to take short sabbaticals so that they can gain new perspectives. Bill Gates takes biannual "think weeks." Andy Grove talks about supplementing "management by walking around," which was an early Silicon Valley practice, with "management by reading around." He believes that surfing through a high volume of electronic communications leads to the occasional "random insight" that may help him gradually reposition Intel's strategy.[9]

Jack Welch talks about using travel to "regenerate." He says he keeps asking himself,

> 'Are you regenerating? Are you dealing with new things? When you find yourself in a new environment, do you come up with a fundamentally different approach?' That's the test. When you flunk, you leave. Three or four times a year, I hop on a plane and visit something like seven countries in fifteen days. People say to me, 'Are you nutty?' No, I'm not nutty. I'm trying to regenerate.[10]

One large professional service firm I know has developed what some partners refer to as a one-week "partner re-tread" program. It also developed a series of short, focused executive education courses after surveying clients about what skills and insights they would value from partners.

How can leaders help people understand what their landscape is like if the leaders cannot see what is happening—internally and externally—to the organization? Leaders need to be constantly exposed to insiders and outsiders who can help them better understand their landscape.

Set High Expectations

John Kotter also writes about the role of managers in "setting agendas" that are made up of "loosely connected goals and plans that address their long-, medium-, and short-term responsibilities."[11] For senior business leaders, increasingly detailed agendas are being replaced with much shorter agendas. Often they take the form of broad goals or targets and these goals frequently are "stretch goals."

GE was one of the first organizations to institutionalize the idea of stretch goals. According to Jack Welch, stretch means "moving beyond being as good as you have to be—'making a budget'—to being as good as you possibly can be: setting 'impossible' goals and going after them."[12] He says it "means that we try for huge gains while having no idea how to get there—but our people figure out ways to get there."[13] He adds, "If you do know how to get there, it's not a stretch target."[14]

Welch likes to illustrate stretch with an insight gained from a trip to Japan where he saw a new VCR by Toshiba. "They had a stretch goal: Produce it with half the parts, in half the time, at half the cost. They sent a team away to design the new model and ended up reducing the number of parts by 60 percent and producing it in one year instead of the usual two."[15]

More and more corporate leaders seem to be adopting stretch goals. In 1991, 3M's CEO raised its corporate goal of generating 25 percent of its sales from products introduced in the last five years to 30 percent in four years. In 1992, Boeing's CEO set a stretch goal of reducing the cost of manufacturing a plane by 25 percent by 1998 and reducing the time needed to build a plane from 18 months in 1992 to 8 in 1996. In 1993, Hewlett Packard vowed to go from a marginal PC maker to a top five player by 1997. By 1997, it was the world's number 3 supplier of PCs and in September of that same year announced its goal of being number 1 in four more years. Michael Dell wants his company to grow at twice the PC market growth rate.

According to *Fortune*, the reason for the growth in the use of stretch goals is that "executives are recognizing that incremental goals, however worthy, invite managers and workers to perform the same comfortable processes a little better every year. The all-too-frequent result: mediocrity."[16]

Stretch targets, like Craig Breedlove's 1963 rule-breaking run or Richard Noble's breaking of the sound barrier, require a major shift in the thinking of top management. It calls for revolutionary thinking.[17] According to Jack Welch,

> Incremental change doesn't work very well in the type of transformation GE has gone through. If your change isn't big enough, revolutionary enough, the bureaucracy can beat you. When you get leaders who confuse popu-

larity with leadership, who just nibble away at things, nothing changes. I think that's true in countries and in companies.[18]

For stretch goals to work it is essential that the leader believes the goals are attainable. According to Marc Seriff, America Online's first head of technology, "In a little company everybody's got to believe. But there needs to be somebody who believes no matter what. That was Steve [Case]. Steve believed from the first day that this was going to be a big deal."[19]

Get Out of the Way

Perhaps the hardest suggestion I will make in this chapter to many business leaders is to let go. In the words of an executive at 3M, "Managers must set goals, then get out of the way."[20] On a rugged landscape leaders have to trust that the people in the system will do good things more often than not.

On a rugged landscape I believe a top-down, command and control system generally will do more harm than allowing people at lower levels to make some mistakes—especially in an organization with capable people. It is a viewpoint that has long characterized 3M. According to William L. McKnight, an early CEO of 3M,

> Mistakes will be made. But if the person is essentially right himself, I think the mistakes he makes are not so serious in the long-run as the mistakes management makes if it is dictatorial and undertakes to tell people under its authority, to whom responsibility is delegated, exactly how to do their jobs.[21]

Getting out of the way can be a very scary thing to do at first. Many traditional executives see it as giving up power and control. I believe that it actually increases the power inherent in the system and that the leaders never had the real control that many thought they had.

Again GE and 3M leaders provide some useful insights:

▲ According to Jack Welch, the "whole management philosophy" of GE is "getting great talent, giving them all the support in the world, and letting them run. . . ."[22] He believes that "strategy follows people; the right person leads to the right strategy."[23]
▲ When a reporter asked the vice chairman of 3M "What is a 3M business?" the executive replied, "None of us is foresightful enough to decide . . . because our people might find some way to make whatever they're doing work."[24]

Even in some of the small, startup Internet companies I have studied, there is a recognition that the CEO will not have all of the good ideas. According to one such CEO, he tells his team, "any idea is a good idea now. There are no unreasonable ideas." According to another CEO, "No one could master all the skills going on around here. It makes me excited that other employees know things I'll never know."[25]

Intuit's founder, Scott Cook, describes a way of visualizing an organization where top management gets out of the way:

> I think of an organization not as a hierarchical triangle but as a circle with the leaders in the middle and the customers scattered around the perimeter. As the circle gets bigger, the leaders become subtly insulated from the customers. So I think the role of the leaders in a growing organization is to push the decision-making and control out to the edges as much as possible.[26]

This is similar to Sam Walton's philosophy that helped lead Wal-Mart to fundamentally change the retailing landscape. When Walton was building Wal-Mart into the leading retailer in the United States, he often talked of "servant leadership." He saw the role of the leader as one of providing workers with whatever they needed to serve the customer in the stores—merchandise, capital, information, inspiration—and then get out of the way.

Be Available

Getting out of the way does not mean abdicating responsibility. The leader of a firm on a rugged landscape has to be available to help others, especially customers and employees. Implicit in Cook's circle and Walton's servant leadership is a leader who is actively engaged.

The technology community is filled with executives who reflect this. Eric Schmidt, the CEO of software maker Novell Inc., reportedly met with more than 25,000 customers and flew more than 200,000 miles during a recent twelve-month period.[27] John Chambers of Cisco spends as much as 55 percent of his time with customers and receives every night, 365 nights a year, voice mail updates on many of his fifteen key clients.[28] He also claims to have visited the heads of ninety of the world's biggest phone companies in a recent one-year period.[29] Jack Welch reportedly spends 20 percent of his time visiting with customers.

Sometimes being available is as simple as asking questions or sharing information. According to Hewlett Packard Chairman Lewis E. Platt, "I don't create business strategies. My role is to encourage discussion of the white spaces, the overlap and gaps among business strategies, the important areas that are not addressed by the strategies of individual HP businesses."[30] At GE, the CFO talks about the importance of corporate management helping to "spread best practices across our businesses."[31]

Other times it is as simple as listening to people and letting them know how to reach you when they need help. UUNET's CEO rejected the idea of a security door to the executive suites because he wanted employees to be able to visit him anytime. Jerry Kalov, CEO of Cobra Electronics Corp, has a phone extension that is not screened by anyone, and it is given only to employees.

An executive of a small company that I interviewed a few years ago has his home phone number printed on his business cards so that customers and employees can reach him at any time.

He also occasionally calls his own office telephone number and asks, in a disguised voice, to speak to himself just to make sure that his staff is not protecting him too much from calls.

Choose the Measures on Which to Focus

What does your organization measure most carefully? Many companies spend an inordinate amount of time developing and studying traditional financial measures. Yet, according to the Conference Board's research director for corporate governance and strategy,

> Traditional measures . . . do not capture key business changes until it is too late. They reflect divisional, not cross-functional, processes within a company; and often they fail to cope with hard-to-quantify assets such as intellectual capital.[32]

According to GE's CFO, the "market is moving so fast" that a "cost accounting system or some other system that you designed five years ago may not be even remotely close to being accurate or meaningful in today's environment, because the world has changed."[33]

In rapidly changing landscapes, those traditional measures can be especially misleading. Consider the difference between Microsoft and IBM. In 1998, Microsoft's asset base was approximately 20 percent of IBM's but its market value was more than 200 percent higher. Investors clearly were valuing something that conventional accounting techniques did not capture.

Too often leaders forget that financial numbers are an abstraction, they are not reality. Furthermore, they often give an illusion of precision. They also are historical and can blind leaders to future changes. When American Express was experiencing a competitive crisis in the early 1990s, one of its executives commented, "Our return on equity had been in excess of 20 percent a year for decades. The attitude was, 'Who can argue with those numbers?' "[34]

I find that a rapidly changing landscape requires organizations to have simple measures. Leaders at companies such as Microsoft and GE certainly support this view. According to Microsoft's CFO,

> [A]s the rate of change in the information age accelerates, we have to keep our internal financial statements simple and meaningful, and our external reporting documents as basic as generally accepted accounting principles permit. By doing this, we provide our managers and investors with the figures they need to make informed decisions on how best to allocate scarce resources.[35]

GE's CFO suggests looking at such measures as time and customer satisfaction:

> We as finance people have to recognize that there are more measurements than machine output per labor hour, or contribution margin on widget A. There's a whole range of things that are becoming more and more important to managing the business. The focus on time, for example. . . . . Similarly, are we as good understanding how we measure customer satisfaction as we are measuring returns in customer concessions?[36]

I like Jack Welch's emphasis on three key measures: cash flow, customer satisfaction, and employee satisfaction. According to Welch,

> Too often we measure everything and understand nothing. The three most important things you need to measure in a business are customer satisfaction, employee satisfaction, and cash flow. If you're growing customer satisfaction, your global market share is sure to grow

too. Employee satisfaction gets you productivity, quality, pride, and creativity. And cash flow is the pulse—
the key vital sign of a company.[37]

I do not mean to suggest that traditional financial measures
are unimportant. They may not be particularly helpful in leading
the organization but they are very important to outsiders. For
example, under 3M's current CEO, the financial goals are tough
and traditional: 10 percent growth in earnings per share; return
on equity between 20 percent and 25 percent; return on capital
employed 27 percent or more; and sales per employee to rise by 8
percent a year. According to CEO DeSimone: "3M needs its financial characteristics to be exceptionally good because the company is hard to understand."[38]

Communicate a Direction

As discussed in Chapter Six, an organization needs to have a clear
direction. A key role for any leader, but especially the CEO of a
large, established organization, is to be able to articulate the *business direction and goals* clearly to interested parties, both internal
and external to the organization.

Too often, leaders think they have a clear direction for the
company but in reality have trouble communicating it to others.
Leaders may forget that others have not thought nearly as much
about the challenges and opportunities facing the organization as
they have.

I have been particularly impressed with some large organizations whose leaders can briefly and clearly describe their strategic
direction. As was discussed earlier, most people at GE and 3M
have little doubt about the ultimate goals of their respective companies.

What is especially impressive is when people throughout the
organization can clearly articulate the direction. When Reg Jones
implemented GE's strategic-planning process in the early 1970s,
he insisted that each of GE's general managers be able to describe

their business strategy to others without resorting to overheads or other aids. When Emerson Electric purchased the Skil Corporation in the 1970s, the management team that developed the new Skil strategy eventually put the strategy on two flip-chart pages and trained the sales force to go out to customers and explain it.

This ability to communicate a clear direction is essential at all levels of leadership, even at the level of project leader. According to Pamela Lopker, the president of QAD Inc., a developer and supplier of integrated business software and services, "I've never had a project completed successfully where someone couldn't articulate what they were doing." She adds, "If someone can't explain to me what they are doing very simply, and show me milestones between now and when they finish it, I just don't believe them."[39]

In technology companies, communicating a clear direction often requires an ability to articulate the *technology vision* of the company. According to Netscape's CEO, Jim Barksdale, Marc Andreessen's role was to be Netscape's "principal technology visionary." He "articulates in practical, pragmatic terms how his vision can become a real product. He's also a spokesman and an evangelist, and he does lots of sales calls and public presentations."[40]

At Sony in the late 1980s, Akio Morita, chairman and cofounder of Sony, saw one of his roles as being the "company philosopher." He believed that particularly in a "highly technical enterprise," philosophy was "needed to place technical developments within the entire texture of modern social existence. The philosopher must see technology in its human context so as to guide the aims of engineering."[41]

The senior leadership of most Internet companies I studied was shared between a chief executive officer who handled business matters and a chief technology officer. The former could explain the intended business direction of the company and the latter could explain the technology vision.

Ideally, leaders should go beyond just helping people understand the direction, whether it is the overall business direction or the technology direction. They should help others in the organization understand what is happening around them, i.e., understand their *landscape*. For example, when Welch took over GE, he began to talk about a "much smaller world, where winners and losers would be more clearly defined, with no place for also-rans."[42] Grove believes that "sharing a common picture of the map of the industry and its dynamics is a key tool in making your organization an adaptive one."[43]

Hamel and Prahalad in *Competing for the Future* suggest that a senior management team should be willing to spend about 20 percent to 50 percent of their time, over a period of several months, to build a corporate perspective on the future. They report, however, that on average less than 3 percent of senior management's time and in some cases less than 1 percent is spent on building such a perspective.[44]

Good leaders do not have to be great speakers or even have outgoing personalities. They do, however, have to find a medium whereby they can effectively communicate the message that they think is at the heart of the organization's direction, whether business direction, technology vision, or the landscape. They need to actively look for a variety of ways that are effective for them to communicate, both by words and deed, what the important dimensions of the business are. For example,

▲ At Hewlett Packard, every department holds "coffee talks" on a regular basis, where top management discusses with employees not only what is happening in their departments but what is happening in the company as a whole.

▲ At GE, there are unexpected visits every week by the CEO to plants and offices, luncheons with several layers of the organization, and countless handwritten notes to GE people.

▲ An Internet company in Washington, DC, holds weekly meetings with all employees to discuss the status of various projects and what is happening to their business.

▲ An Arizona-based software company holds regular "ask Jack" (the CEO) meetings with employees at all levels and the head of R&D holds "Bud Time" meetings (Bud is his name) with all departmental employees.

The more forums management can hold, the better. According to an employee I interviewed at a telecommunications company, "If you just had one mechanism, somebody would miss that meeting or they would miss that channel of communications, so I think redundancy is important." Because his organization utilized numerous forums, he could say, "I don't hear a lot of complaints from people about how, 'Hey, I didn't hear about that.'"

The message not only has to be communicated often but it has to be consistent and simple. According to Welch of GE,

> You've got to be out in front of crowds, repeating yourself over and over again, never changing your message no matter how much it bores you. You need an overarching message, something big but simple and understandable. Whatever it is, every idea you present must be something you could get across easily at a cocktail party with strangers. If only aficionados of your industry can understand what you're saying, you've blown it.[45]

As a child it was common to hear the following homily: "Actions speak louder than words." Leaders need to constantly remind themselves of the basic truth in this saying. Regardless of how many memos are written or speeches are given, insiders and outsiders will pay much more attention to what the leader does or does not do, than to what he or she says. The energy and the time spent on those actions signal to the organization what the truly important things are in the company.

Employees come and go, people forget, and circumstances change. If the direction is not communicated clearly and often, people in the organization will get lost in fairly short order.

Be Decisive

In Chapter Seven, the importance of developing a culture that fosters such qualities as open debates, experimentation, and learning was stressed. Such a culture is necessary but not sufficient. Otherwise universities would be the fittest organizations in the world.

One of my frustrations with the academic world is the slowness with which decisions are made, even on relatively minor administrative issues. Too many presidents, deans, and department heads want to form task forces to study (and study again) an issue; they seem to want to avoid making a hard decision. Shortly after I was named interim dean of a business school, I was confronted with a serious disciplinary problem. One faculty member had charged another faculty member with threatening him. When I asked other deans at the university, "How do you recommend I handle such a situation?" everyone's advice was "keep it off your desk." Their other recommendation was to appoint a faculty committee to study the situation.

Debate and study have to lead to action. I was impressed with advice given to Fred Smith, the CEO of Federal Express, when he was serving in Vietnam. A sergeant reportedly told him, "Lieutenant, there's only three things you gotta remember: shoot, move, and communicate."[46] For me, one interesting aspect of this advice is that survival begins with action. Decisions have to be made before things start to happen.

In the 1980s, the Walt Disney Company fought off two hostile takeover attempts and received new management—Michael Eisner and Frank Wells. The two produced a dramatic turnaround in a very short time. *60 Minutes* then did a feature on Eisner. In the course of the program, a very successful movie director, who was being courted by several studios, was interviewed. He reported that when he had pitched his latest idea to Eisner, it was rejected. Yet, the director was looking to continue to work with Disney, because, he observed, Eisner "wasn't afraid to be decisive and go on."[47]

Many business writers and leaders have explored the importance of values in a modern organization. A clearly understood set of values is vital to an organization on a rugged landscape. When surrounded by great uncertainty, people find it very helpful to know what the organization "believes in," even if they do not always know what the next actions will be.

Articulated values are meaningless, however, unless they are consistently reflected in hard decisions. Again Jack Welch has an interesting take on this issue:

> You've got to be hard to be soft. You have to demonstrate the ability to make the hard, tough decision—closing plants, divesting, delayering—if you want to have any credibility when you try to promote soft values. We reduced employment and cut the bureaucracy and picked up some unpleasant nicknames, but when we spoke of soft values—things like candor, fairness, facing reality—people listened.[48]

In most organizations the key leadership decisions involve resource allocation. As discussed earlier in the book, leaders have to regularly make decisions about where capital and people are to be assigned. In other words, which products, businesses, departments, and people are to be given access to scarce resources, and which are not.

The poor performance of many companies often can be attributed to the failure to secure the needed resources or make the hard decisions about which activities to support and, more important, which ones not to support. I have heard of organizations where every department received 50 percent of the capital that was requested because the company's leaders could only raise half of what was asked for and they thought everyone receiving the same percentage was fair. Clearly that is a prescription for disaster—especially on a rugged landscape.

On rugged landscapes leaders have to be decisive. More and more, difficult decisions will have to be made faster and with less information than most leaders would like. Over the years I have had the experience of using case studies with various groups of MBAs and executives. In virtually every group there are people who say, "I can't make a decision about this case because I don't have enough information." Business leaders on rugged landscapes never have all the information they would like to have. Yet for their companies to be successful they have to make big decisions and increasingly do it quickly.

I was impressed to learn that some U.S. Marine officers have been trained in mock trading sessions at the New York Mercantile Exchange. According to a Brig. General involved in the program, "If we could see how the traders process information and do trading in chaotic situations, we could probably learn from them and translate some of those things into the combat operations center." Another officer observed,

> We're trying to learn from them . . . how to make better decisions. That's what this game is all about. They absorb a certain amount of information, they figure out what should be the right decision and they make it. Our problem is we don't have enough practice making decisions normally to get that kind of confidence.[49]

Marines speak of the 70 percent solution, by which they mean an imperfect decision but one that can be made immediately. According to another marine officer, "Everyone is always looking for the perfect truth, but you never have it. Even if you did have it, the other guy is up to something, so by the time you execute it, your truth isn't perfect anymore."[50] Marines also limit the amount of time to be spent in developing a plan. In describing a planning session with a group of marines, the author of a recent article reported that "whatever mission the marines put together . . . they have three hours to decide on and plan it and three hours to prepare it." If the group determines that certain aspects of the mission require clarification from headquarters, they do not wait long for the answers. "If and when the answers eventually come in, the marines will adjust their mission on the fly."[51]

A similar approach seems to be found at many technology companies. For example:

▲ When CyberCash leaders decided they wanted to buy IC Verify Inc., a maker of software payment systems, they completed the $50 million deal over a weekend. According to James Condon, president and chief operating officer, "We met for the first time on Friday evening, negotiated all day Saturday, and closed the deal on Sunday." He added, in a regular company "if you take four days to make a decision, you're doing pretty well. If you take four days to make a decision at an Internet company, you're a dead company."[52]

▲ At Netscape there were impromptu meetings aimed at getting quick decisions. They called it "surround-sound" management. When an issue came up, such as what to charge for a new program, somebody called a meeting of key people. According to *Business Week*, "They swarm on the problem for 20 minutes, come to a conclusion, and separate."[53]

There are some significant advantages to rapid decision making. For one, you are more likely to stay ahead of the competition. Intel's new CEO, Craig Barrett, while acknowledging the risks associated with spending billions of dollars on new chip plants stresses, "If we didn't we couldn't possibly reap the benefits. . . . [T]he worst thing we can do is stop too soon and let someone else pass us."[54]

Marc Andreessen, formerly of Netscape, sees another advantage. "One of the advantages of moving quickly is if you do something wrong you can change it. What technologies tend to do is they tend to make a lot of mistakes . . . but then we go back and aggressively attack those mistakes—and fix them. And you usually recover pretty quickly."[55]

This willingness to make quick decisions and then improve on them needs to be found not only at the top of the organization but throughout. Several years ago, I had the opportunity to spend some time with managers and executives of a successful supplier to the automobile industry that had implemented a quality program that had dramatically improved the company's performance on many dimensions, including financial. When a plant manager was asked about his role, he talked about the importance of being willing to make a decision and move on. "Keep the parade moving—don't stand there and do nothing. Even if you don't know what impact the move is going to make, record it, let people know what is going to happen and march on." As he acknowledged, if it turns out that there are problems with the decision, correct them as best you can and move ahead.

I see these leaders and their organizations as reflecting an important observation of Stuart Kauffman:

> Real organizations never find the global optima of their fixed or deforming landscapes. . . . The best thing to do—indeed, the only practical thing to do—is to choose a route that is excellent, but not necessarily the very best.[56]

As noted in Chapter Six, it is like being in a drifting boat and occasionally you "stick your oar in and improve something for the better."[57] The key, it seems, is to try to do something that works, do it quickly, and keep improving it.

Prepare a Successor

Often the true test of a leader is what happens after he or she leaves the organization. Too few leaders seem willing to take the time to prepare either the successor or the organization to accept the successor.

The "changing of the guard" at Cisco and Intel seemed to go so smoothly that little public notice was taken. When in April 1998, Andy Grove announced he no longer would serve as CEO and promoted Intel's president into the job, the stock market hardly responded. *Fortune* reported that Grove and Intel's board had been planning Craig Barrett's succession "for years."[58] When John Morgridge, CEO of Cisco Systems, surprised his board by announcing his intention to retire in 1993, he recommended his replacement—John Chambers. According to the retiring CEO, "When Chambers took over, Cisco never lost a beat. That's how the company was able to stay ahead."[59]

Among leading Internet companies, both America Online and Yahoo! have already recognized the need for new leadership. The founders of both companies have been willing to relinquish control of the management, and both companies have seen their stock prices increase dramatically.

Few companies have done as well for so long as GE in preparing the next generation of leaders. Reg Jones, GE's CEO in the 1970s, made sure his successor was carefully chosen and well-prepared for the challenges he would face by giving several contenders the opportunity to run large sectors of GE just prior to his retirement.

There are reports that Welch spends more than 30 percent of his time on questions of GE management development and has his company spending approximately $800 million a year on training and leadership development—almost half of what it spends on R&D. The results are impressive. In 1997, *Business Week* identified twenty-nine U.S. executives who "could soon emerge as CEOs of major corporations." Five were GE executives.[60] In recent years Welch has described the issue of succession as "an obsession" for him. "It's on my mind constantly. Finding the right person is the most important thing I can do for the company."[61] According to a member of GE's board, "I've served on a number of boards, but GE is singular not only in its top leadership but in the institutional development of leadership. That's the outstanding attribute of the company, and it's largely a result of Jack's vision."[62] Welch even jokes about how in May 1995, GE's stock price increased when the media announced that he was in the hospital for angioplasty. When he underwent bypass surgery a few days later, the stock held steady.

At Emerson Electric, in a locked, unmarked room down the hall from CEO Chuck Knight's office, the walls reportedly are covered with passport-size photographs of Emerson's 650 top managers, each bearing a short resume of his or her current and past postings. Color-coded stickers indicate the managers' level of experience and whether he or she is ready for promotion. Knight reportedly is knowledgeable about all of them.[63]

One of the things that often seems to characterize leaders of fit organizations on rugged landscapes is that they do not choose successors in their own image. It is hard to imagine two CEOs more different in personality, style, and background than Reg Jones and Jack Welch. Intel's new CEO is described as "a laconic metallurgist" whereas Grove was described as "Mr. High-Output Management."[64] Sony's new president was a marketing executive and is viewed as more of a software person than a hardware person—the first such candidate in Sony's history to lead the company. He sees himself as "totally different" from his predecessor.[65] Strong leaders seem to choose their successor for his or her perceived ability to deal with the emerging landscape.

Act with Urgency and Energy

On a rugged landscape, leaders have to convey an almost constant sense of urgency—this usually requires a high level of energy. I was struck by an analyst's description of Jurgen Schrempp, chairman of Daimler. He is "so full of energy, you feel you should ground yourself before you touch him."[66] It is similar to descriptions I have heard applied to the leadership of leading technology companies. For example, according to *Fortune*, John Chambers of Cisco "is in overdrive all the time, on a sales call that never ends."[67] HP's new CEO, Carleton Fiorina, has been described by her predecessor as having "energy and sparkle" that cannot help but be noticed.[68]

Over and over I also have found executives of successful large companies who spoke about their organizations' future with a sense of urgency:

▲ Andy Grove of Intel talks about the importance of being "paranoid" and he acknowledges that he "never made a tough change . . . that I didn't wish I had made a year or so earlier."[69]

▲ John Chambers of Cisco talks about needing "healthy paranoia to survive."[70]

▲ Kevin Rollins of Dell talks about being "constantly paranoid."[71]

▲ Jeff Bezos of Amazon talks about telling the people around him that they should "wake up every morning petrified and afraid."[72]

▲ James Clark of Netscape talks of his fear of lost opportunity.[73]

▲ Huge McColl of BankAmerica speaks of the "fear of losing time."[74]

In my opinion, Jack Welch personifies many of the qualities that will be needed in the CEO of a large corporation in the early part of the 21st century. With all of the changes and the impressive performance that Jack Welch brought about at GE in the first few years of his tenure, when asked, with hindsight, what would he have done differently, like Grove, he emphasized speed of action—"move faster."

> [I]n hindsight, if there's a criticism [at GE], it was too evolutionary. It was perceived on the outside as revolutionary, but if you want to criticize what the hell went wrong, I didn't do it fast enough. . . . It took us a decade to do a lot of the things we had to do.[75]

Welch, too, talks about being "always scared."[76] He also talks about the importance of being "on the lunatic fringe"[77] and coming to work every day on the "razor's edge."[78] He seems to use that sense of fear to energize himself and others. He even speaks of his role as being an "energizer." He believes, "You've got to be live action all day. And you've got to be able to energize others."[79] He also wants his managers to be the same way. "They have to

have enormous energy and the incredible ability to energize others. If you can't energize others, you can't be a leader."[80]

CONCLUSION

Successful leaders of large organizations operating on rugged landscapes rarely will be the traditional lone figure, single-handedly
making the difference. Rather, they will be catalysts or facilitators
who can speed up reactions or influence the interactions of others
so that growth can occur. Leaders who play this role have, I believe, a far better chance of helping their organizations adapt to a
rapidly changing world. The ten activities discussed in this chapter are some of the most important ways that leaders of large,
complex organizations can help to shape an adaptive organization.

Postscript

J ust like in business, Richard Noble's record-setting accomplishment with his car, *Thrust SSC,* will be challenged by new competitors. In fact, new teams are already forming with the goal of breaking his record. I am sure he has no doubt that someone else eventually will do so. Such an outcome is inevitable in a competitive world.

Yet, as Richard Noble reflected on his team's success in breaking the sound barrier on land, he pondered the question that every businessperson who wants to be part of an adaptive organization should be asking after their successes and failures: "What have we learned from all this?" He answered his question with four brief lessons:

▲ If you do your research well, establish a highly professional organisation, and work tirelessly and remorselessly towards your objective, you can get there—even if the corporate establishment is not on your side.

▲ If you can establish and maintain a flat pyramid management structure based on mutual trust and real responsibility and authority, the team will outclass any organisation ten times its size. But the secret is delegation and absolute trust.

▲ If you can establish a culture of professionalism and communication, which never shirks the difficult questions and takes a great deal of convincing, this multiplies the teamwork performance very substantially.

▲ The Internet is the most powerful communication known to man—without this the project would have undoubtedly failed.[1]

As I have thought about Richard Noble's achievements, and especially how he achieved his success, the parallels to some of the practices that I have observed in successful technology companies have especially intrigued me. Like Noble's effort, these companies often have very ambitious and clear goals, highly committed and high-energy teams of people working on the achievement of those goals, a lean and flat organizational structure and leaders who know how to create the right environment. These organizations are adaptive organizations. They are what will be required of successful organizations in the high-speed and uncertain world of the 21st century. After each success, the people in these organizations will be able to look back on their experiences like Richard Noble did after the final run and say: "It's been a magic morning. It's a hell of an achievement."[2]

Notes

Preface

1. Amy Cortese, "A Way Out of the Web Maze," *Business Week*, February 24, 1997, p. 95.

Chapter 1

1. Charles Fox, "Speed War," *Automobile*, March 1996, p. 94.
2. *Ibid.*, p. 90.
3. *Ibid.*
4. *Ibid.*, p. 94.

Chapter 2

1. "Changing, But Not Happy about It," *Business Week*, September 20, 1993, p. 44.
2. *Managing Business Risk*, London: The Economist Intelligence Unit, 1995, pp. 115, 120.
3. Nikhil Deogun, "A Tough Boss Takes on Computers, with Real Trepidation," *Wall Street Journal*, July 25, 1996.
4. Andrew S. Grove, *Only the Paranoid Survive*, New York: Currency, 1996, p. 14.
5. Peter Burrows and Ira Sager, "Can Compaq Catch Up?" *Business Week*, May 3, 1999, p. 166.
6. Ira Sager and Peter Burrows, "For Compaq, a Different Kind of Y2K Problem," *Business Week*, April 26, 1999, pp. 36–38.

7. Gary McWilliams, "PC Problems May Snag Compaq Crusade," *Wall Street Journal*, April 15, 1999.

8. Joshua Cooper Ramo, "A Survivor's Tale," *Time*, December 29, 1997, pp. 57–58.

9. Eric Nee, "Compaq Computer Corp.," *Forbes*, January 12, 1998, p. 93.

10. Gary McWilliams, et al., "Compaq's Power Play," *Business Week*, February 9, 1998, p. 91.

11. Sager and Burrows, *op. cit.,* p. 36.

12. *Ibid.*

13. Dean Takahashi, "How the Competition Got Ahead of Intel in Making Cheap Chips," *Wall Street Journal*, February 12, 1998.

14. William J. Holstein, "Just Because He's Paranoid," *U.S. News & World Report*, April 6, 1998, p. 50.

15. Elizabeth Corcoran, "Reinventing Intel," *Forbes*, May 3, 1999, p. 155.

16. David Kirkpatrick, "Eckhard's Gone but the PC Rocks On," *Fortune*, May 24, 1999, pp. 153, 156.

17. *Ibid.*, p. 156.

18. *Ibid.*

19. Gary McWilliams, "Ousted CEO of Compaq Offers Defense," *Wall Street Journal*, April 22, 1999.

20. Kirkpatrick, *op. cit.*, p. 154.

21. Gary McWilliams, "Compaq Directors Mull Office of the CEO," *Wall Street Journal*, April 23, 1999.

22. Grove, *op. cit.*, pp. 16–17.

23. Gary McWilliams and Joann S. Lublin, "Compaq Could Have Averted Missteps," *Wall Street Journal*, April 20, 1999.

24. Harold Koontz, "Making Sense of Management Theory," *Harvard Business Review*, July–August 1962, p. 36.

25. Elizabeth MacDonald, "Top 50 Management Consulting Firms Break Revenue Records for Fiscal 1997," *Wall Street Journal*, June 15, 1998.

26. Keith B. Richburg, "New Hong Kong Leader's Bad Week Gets Worse," *Washington Post*, January 23, 1998.

27. Peter Burrows, "Lew Platt's Fix-It Plan for Hewlett-Packard," *Business Week*, July 13, 1998, p. 129.

28. James M. Utterback, *Mastering the Dynamics of Innovations: How Companies Can Seize Opportunities in the Face of Technological Change*, Boston: Harvard Business School Press, 1994, p. xxvii.

29. Noel M. Tichy and Stratford Sherman, "Jack Welch's Lessons for Success," *Fortune*, January 25, 1993, p. 89.

30. Charles F. Knight, "Emerson Electric: Consistent Profits, Consistently," *Harvard Business Review*, January–February 1992, p. 57.

31. Grove, *op. cit.,* p. 149.

32. Rich Karlgaard, "Present at the Creation," *Forbes*, July 7, 1997, p. 278.

33. Richard A. D'Aveni, *Hypercompetition*, New York: Free Press, p. xviii.

34. Nikhil Hutheesing, "When Haste Makes Waste," *Forbes*, April 6, 1998, p. 132.

Chapter 3

1. Sigmund Freud, *New Introductory Lectures on Psychoanalysis*, 1932, quoted in *Bartlett's Familiar Quotations*, Boston: Little Brown and Company, 1968, p. 834.

2. Albert Einstein, *Physics and Reality*, 1936, quoted in *Bartlett's Familiar Quotations*, Boston: Little Brown and Company, 1968, p. 950.

3. Joel Achenback, "The Genesis Problem," *The Washington Post Magazine*, November 2, 1997, pp. 12–17, 36.

4. H. Hartman, J. Lawless, and P. Morrison (eds.), *Search for the Universal Ancestors*, Washington, DC: NASA, SP-477, 1985, p. 1.

5. Patricia Barnes-Svarney, Editorial Director, *The New York*

Public Library's Science Desk Reference, New York: Stonesong Press, 1995, p. 91.

6. *Ibid.*

7. Peter Coveney and Roger Highfield, *Frontiers of Complexity*, London: Faber and Faber Limited, 1995, pp. 119, 121.

8. Murray Gell-Mann, *The Quark and the Jaguar*, New York: W. H. Freeman & Company, 1994, pp. 240, 246.

9. Barnes-Svarney, *op. cit.*, p. 93.

10. *Ibid.*, p. 91.

11. Fernand Braudel, *The Structures of Everyday Life, Civilization & Capitalism 15th–18th Century*, Vol. 1, New York: Harper & Row, 1979, p. 23.

12. Fernand Braudel, *The Wheels of Commerce, Civilization & Capitalism 15th–18th Century*, Vol. 2, New York: Harper & Row, 1979, p. 433.

13. Charles Darwin, *The Origin of Species*, New York: P. F. Collier & Son, 1909, p. 510.

14. Stuart A. Kauffman, *At Home in the Universe*, New York: Oxford University Press, 1995, p. 149.

15. Thomas A. Stewart, "A New Way to Think about Employees," *Fortune*, April 18, 1998, p. 170.

16. David Kirkpatrick, "Meanwhile, Back at Headquarters," *Fortune*, October 13, 1997, p. 83.

17. Braudel, *The Structures of Everyday Life*, *op. cit.*, p. 435.

18. Robert D. Hof, "PointCast: A Pioneer on Treacherous Ground," *Business Week*, February 24, 1997, p. 100.

19. Frank Maley, "Cybervisionaries," *Virginia Business*, January 1998, p. 15.

20. Elizabeth Bernstein, "Amazon.com's Amazing Allure," *Publishers Weekly*, November 4, 1996, p. 71.

21. James Lardner, "Trying to Survive the Browser Wars," *U.S. News & World Report*, April 6, 1998, p. 54.

22. Shannon Henry, "New Mission of a Young Visionary," *Washington Post*, July 12, 1999.

23. George Donnelly, "New @ttitude," *CFO*, June 1999, p. 54.

24. John Curran, "GE CAPITAL: Jack Welch's Secret Weapon," *Fortune*, November 10, 1997, p. 126.

25. Clayton M. Christensen, *The Innovator's Dilemma*, Boston: Harvard Business School Press, 1997, p. xv.

26. Peter Elstrom, et al., "The New World Order," *Business Week*, October 13, 1997, p. 27.

27. *Ibid.*

28. John Greenwald, "Bernie's Deal," *Time*, October 13, 1997, p. 62.

29. Coveney and Highfield, *op. cit.*, p. 234.

30. Kauffman, *At Home in the Universe: The Search for the Laws of Self Organization & Complexity*, 1996, pp 15, 188.

31. Adam Smith, *Wealth of Nations*, New York: Collier Press, 1909, p. 351.

32. Braudel, *The Wheels of Commerce, op. cit.*, p. 600.

33. *Ibid.*

34. Fernand Braudel, *The Perspective of the World, Civilization & Capitalism 15th–18th* Century, Vol 3, New York: Harper & Row, 1979, p. 357.

35. Kauffman, *At Home in the Universe, op. cit.*, p. 246.

36. Neil Gross, "Into the Wild Frontier," *Business Week*, June 23, 1997, pp. 72–74.

37. Zina Moukheiber, "Back to Nature," *Forbes*, October 19, 1998, p. 147.

38. Michael Schrage, "Letting Systems Run Themselves," *Across the Board*, February 1996, p. 59.

39. Neil Gross, *op. cit.* p. 77.

Chapter 4

1. Patricia Barnes-Svarney, Editorial Director, *The New York Times Public Library's Science Desk Reference*, New York: The Stonesong Press, 1995, pp. 230, 258, and 301–2.

2. Ziauddin Sardar and Iwona Abrams, *Introducing Chaos,* New York: Totem Books, 1999, p. 13.

3. Keith B. Richburg, "Stock Tumble Spreads Gloom in Hong Kong," *Washington Post,* October 28, 1997.

4. John H. Holland, *Hidden Order: How Adaptation Builds Complexity,* Reading: MA: Addison-Wesley, 1995, p. 16.

5. Robert McGarvey, "Tomorrow Land," *Entrepreneur,* February 1996, p. 136.

6. Michael Sivy, "How to Cash In on the Asia Boom," *Money,* May 1997, pp. 108–15.

7. Brett D. Fromson, "The Lionized Tigers Are Bears—Oh, My!" *Washington Post,* January 11, 1998.

8. Lee Patterson, "Future Imperfect," *Forbes ASAP,* April 6, 1998, p. 20.

9. Linda Grant, "How UPS Blew It," *Fortune,* September 29, 1997, p. 29.

10. E. C. Capen, "The Difficulty of Assessing Uncertainty," *Journal of Petroleum Technology,* August 1976, p. 843.

11. Peter L. Bernstein, *Against the Gods,* New York: John Wiley & Sons, 1996, p. 173.

12. Michael Sivy, "Now's the Time to Sell Some Stock," *Money,* August 1997, pp. 68–71.

13. Bernstein, *op. cit.,* p. 121.

14. Peter Drucker, "Planning for Uncertainty," *Wall Street Journal,* July 22, 1992.

15. Bernstein, *op. cit.,* p. 221.

16. *Ibid.,* p. 227.

17. Thomas A. Stewart, "3M Fights Back," *Fortune,* February 5, 1996, p. 99.

18. Leslie Chang, "Eating Their Lunch," *Wall Street Journal,* November 18, 1997.

19. Noel M. Tichy and Stratford Sherman, "Jack Welch's Lessons for Success," *Fortune,* January 25, 1993, p. 88.

20. Linda Grant, "Why FedEx Is Flying High," *Fortune*, November 10, 1997, p. 160.

21. Denise Caruso, "Microsoft Morphs into a Media Company," *Wired*, June 1996, p. 196.

22. *Ibid.*, p. 190.

23. The United States Marine Corps, *Warfighting*, New York: Currency, 1989, p. 12.

24. Seth Lubove, "It Ain't Broke, But Fix It Anyway," *Forbes*, August 1, 1994, p. 58.

25. Stuart Kauffman, *At Home in the Universe*, New York: Oxford University Press, 1995, p.17.

26. Stratford Sherman, "How to Prosper in the Value Decade," *Fortune*, November 30, 1992, p. 91.

27. Andy Reinhardt, et al., "Intel," *Business Week*, December 22, 1997, p. 73.

28. Julie Pitla, "Putting Out Feelers," *Forbes*, May 18, 1998, p. 207.

29. Robert McGarvey, "Tomorrow Land," *Entrepreneur*, February 1996, p. 135.

30. Steven Mufson, "Mickey Schulof and the Globalization of Sony," *Washington Post*, August 6, 1989.

31. Fred Vogelstein and William J. Holstein, "Fasten Your Seat Belts," *U.S. News & World Report*, October 26, 1998, pp. 44–45.

32. Bernstein, *op. cit.*, p. 305.

33. Tarun Khanna and David Yoffie, "Microsoft, 1995," [9-795-147] Boston: Harvard Business School Publishing, 1995, p. 14.

34. "The Bill and Warren Show," *Fortune*, July 20, 1998, p. 56.

35. Eric Nee, "Paul Saffo," *Upside*, February 1996, p. 39.

36. Fernand Braudel, *The Structures of Everyday Life, Civilization & Capitalism 15th–18th Century*, Vol. 1, New York: Harper & Row, 1979, p. 24.

37. Nicholas D. Kristof and Edward Wyatt, "Who Sank, or Swam, in Choppy Currents of a World Cash Ocean," *New York Times*, February 15, 1999.

38. Vogelstein and Holstein, *op. cit.*, pp. 44–45.

39. "Market Interconnections," *Wall Street Journal*, October 28, 1997.

40. Keith B. Richburg, "HONG KONG: A Single Risky Loan Ruined Venturesome Investment Bank," *Washington Post*, January 13, 1998.

41. William Claiborne, "Asian Monetary Crisis Sends Ripples to the US West Coast," *Washington Post*, February 10, 1998.

42. Steven Mufson, "Economic Crisis Adds New Fears," *Washington Post*, October 5, 1998.

43. William J. Holstein, et al., "One World, One Market," *U.S. News & World Report*, November 10, 1997, p. 43.

44. David Kirkpatrick, "10 Tech Trends to Bet On," *Fortune*, November 10, 1997, p. 98.

45. Henry Goldblatt and Nelson D. Schwartz, "Telecom in Play," *Fortune*, November 10, 1997, p. 84.

46. Braudel, *The Structures of Everyday Life, op. cit.*, p. 24.

Chapter 5

1. Stephen Hawkins, *A Brief History of Time*, New York: Bantam Books, 1996, p. 228.

2. Brent Schlender, "Sony's New Game," *Fortune*, April 12, 1999, p. 31.

3. Ibid, p. 152.

4. James Gleick, *Chaos*, New York: Penguin Books, 1987, p. 262.

5. Chip Bayers, "The Inner Bezos," *Wired*, March 1999, p. 118.

6. A useful companion document to the SIC Manual is the Directory of Corporate Affiliations (DCA), 1997. The DCA is published by the National Register Publishing, a division of Reed Elsevier Inc. The document is a reference tool that covers major public and private U.S. and non-U.S. businesses. The listed U.S. companies must demonstrate revenues in excess of $10 million

and a workforce in excess of 300 people. The non-U.S.-based companies must demonstrate revenues in excess of $50 million annually. The prime cross-reference index is the SIC Code. Because of the proliferation of mergers and acquisitions over the years, the parent and subcompanies are also a useful reference.

7. Kathleen Kahle and Ralph A. Walking, "The Impact of Industry Classifications on Financial Research," *Journal of Financial and Quantitative Analysis*, September 1996, p. 309.

8. Michael E. Porter, "How Competitive Forces Shape Strategy," *Harvard Business Review*, March–April 1979, pp. 137–45.

9. Frank Gibney, Jr. "A New World at Sony," *Time*, November 17, 1997, p. 57.

10. Jeffrey A. Trachtenberg, "Sony President Rules Out Buying American Network," *Wall Street Journal*, November 21, 1995.

11. Michael Moeller and Kathy Rebello, "Visionary-in-Chief," *Business Week*, May 17, 1999, p. 116.

12. Gary Hamel and C. K. Prahalad, *Competing for the Future*, Boston: Harvard Business School Press, 1994, p. 41.

13. James Moore, "The Death of Competition," *Fortune*, April 15, 1996, pp. 142–43.

14. Substitutors and complementors are terms used by Adam M. Brandenburger and Barry J. Nalebuff in their work on game theory. See "The Right Game: Use Game Theory to Shape Strategy," *Harvard Business Review*, July–August 1995, pp. 59–60.

15. Michael H. Martin, "The Next Big Thing: A Bookstore," *Fortune*, December 9, 1996, p. 170.

16. Bruce B. Auster, "It's Chaos, and It's Here to Stay," *U.S. News & World Report*, May 12, 1997, p. 34.

17. Nikhil Deogun, "A Tough Bank Boss Takes on Computers, with Real Trepidation," *Wall Street Journal*, July 25, 1996.

18. Debra Sparks, et al., "The Bitter Legacy of the AT&T Card," *Business Week*, December 22, 1997, p. 32.

19. Gary McWilliams, et al., "Power Play," *Business Week*, February 9, 1998, p. 96.

20. Andy Reinhardt and Heather Green, "It's about Capturing Eyeballs," *Business Week*, January 19, 1998, p. 37.

21. Although I have pointed out that the concept of an industry is not very useful in today's environment, I use it for the time being, since most economic data are collected using this construct.

22. Linda Himelstein, "Can IPOs Achieve Liftoff Again?" *Business Week*, September 28, 1998, p. 50.

23. John A. Byrne, "When Capital Gets Antsy," *Business Week*, September 13, 1999, p. 74.

24. Robert D. Hof, "Netspeed at NETSCAPE," *Business Week*, February 10, 1997, p. 81.

25. John Grossman, "Nowhere Men," *Inc.*, June 1996, pp. 68–69.

26. *Ibid.*

27. *Ibid.*, p. 67.

28. Rich Karlgaard, "Present at the Creation," *Forbes*, July 7, 1997, p. 276.

29. Nikhil Deogun, "A Tough Bank Boss Takes on Computers, with Real Trepidation," *op. cit.*

30. Brent Schlender, "Sony on the Brink," *Fortune*, June 12, 1995, p. 62.

31. Nikhil Deogun, "A Tough Bank Boss Takes on Computers, with Real Trepidation," *op. cit.*

32. Chip Bayers, *op. cit.*, p. 116.

33. Murray Gell-Mann, *The Quark and the Jaguar*, New York: W. H. Freeman & Company, 1994, p. 248.

34. *Ibid.*, p. 257.

35. Shawn Tully, "America's Greatest Wealth Creator," *Fortune*, November 9, 1998, pp. 194–96.

36. Adrian J. Slywotzky, *Value Migration*, Boston: Harvard Business School Press, 1996, pp. 87–88.

Chapter 6

1. John Grossman, "Nowhere Men," *Inc.*, June 1996, p. 69.

2. George Donnelly, "New @ttitude," *CFO*, June 1999, p. 44.

3. *Ibid.*, p. 53.

4. Walter Kiechel III, "Corporate Strategists under Fire," *Fortune*, December 27, 1982, p. 38.

5. "The New Breed of Strategic Planner," *Business Week*, September 17, 1984, p. 62.

6. *Ibid.*

7. Cover of *Business Week*, August 26, 1996.

8. Alfred D. Chandler, *Strategy and Structure: Chapters in the History of the Industrial Enterprise*, Boston: MIT Press, 1962, p. 13.

9. Henry Mintzberg, "Patterns in Strategy Formation," *Management Science*, Vol. 24, No. 9, May 1978, p. 935.

10. Arie P. de Geus, "Planning as Learning," *Harvard Business Review*, March–April 1988.

11. Clayton M. Christensen, *The Innovator's Dilemma: When New Technologies Cause Great Firms to Fail*, Boston: Harvard Business School Press, 1997, p. xxii.

12. *Ibid.*, p. 160.

13. "Finding an Oracle," *Wall Street Journal*, September 29, 1998.

14. Randall Lane, "Pampering the Customers, Pampering the Employees," *Forbes 400*, October 1996, p. 80.

15. L. J. Davis, "They Call Him Neutron," *Business Month*, March 1998, p. 27.

16. M. Mitchell Waldrop, *Complexity: The Emerging Science at the Edge of Order and Chaos*, New York: Touchstone Books, 1993, p. 179.

17. Peter Drucker, "Planning for Uncertainty," *Wall Street Journal*, July 22, 1992.

18. John Curran, "GE CAPITAL: Jack Welch's Secret Weapon," *Fortune*, November 10, 1997, p. 134.

19. William Green, "I Spy," *Forbes*, April 20, 1998, p. 92.

20. Brent Schlender, "The New Man Inside Intel," *Fortune*, May 11, 1998, p. 162.

21. Alan Deutschman, "The Managing Wisdom of High-Tech Superstars," *Fortune*, October 17, 1994, p. 198.

22. Robert D. Hof, "Jeff Bezos," *Business Week*, May 31, 1999, p. 140.

23. Ronald Henkoff, "Growing Your Company: Five Ways to Do It Right!" *Fortune*, November 25, 1996, p. 80.

24. Charles F. Knight, "Emerson Electric: Consistent Profits, Consistently," *Harvard Business Review*, January–February 1992, p. 70.

25. Elizabeth Corcoran, "Starting Seedlings, But Close to the Tree," *Washington Post*, July 7, 1996.

26. Noel M. Tichy and Strattford Sherman, "Jack Welch's Lessons for Success," *Fortune*, January 25, 1993, p. 86.

27. Martin, "Jack Welch Lets Fly" *Fortune*, May 29, 1995, p. 145.

28. William Taylor, "Message and Muscle: An Interview with Swatch Titan Nicolas Hayek," *Harvard Business Review*, March–April, 1993, pp. 100–101.

29. Brent Schlender, "Sony on the Brink," *Fortune*, June 12, 1995, p. 72.

30. Nanette Byrnes, et al., "Best Performers," *Business Week*, March 30, 1998, p. 77.

31. Robert D. Hof, "Finally Speaking the Same Language," *Business Week*, October 28, 1996, p. 132.

32. Nathaniel Wice, "Surfing with the Bulls," *Yahoo! Internet Life*, January 1998, pp. 72–77.

33. Eryn Brown, "Could the Very Best PC Maker Be Dell Computer?" *Fortune*, April 14, 1997, p. 26.

34. Tichy and Sherman, "Jack Welch's Lessons. . . . ," *op. cit.*, p. 86.

35. William M. Carley, "To Keep GE's Profits Rising, Welch Pushes Quality-Control Plan," *Wall Street Journal*, January 13, 1997.

36. Roger O. Crockett and Peter Elstrom, "How Motorola Lost Its Way," *Business Week*, May 4, 1998, p. 148.

37. G. Bruce Knecht, "How Wall Street Whiz Found a Niche Selling Books on the Internet," *Wall Street Journal*, May 16, 1996.

38. Andrew Pollack, "A Stunning Leap to the Top at Sony," *New York Times*, March 23, 1995.

39. Rajiv Chandrasekaran, "Traffic Cop as Internet Titan," *Washington Post*, February 2, 1997.

40. Joel Kotkin, "The Mother of All Malls," *Forbes ASAP*, April 6, 1998, p. 60.

41. See Stanley M. Davis, *Future Perfect*, Reading, MA: Addison-Wesley, 1987.

42. David Streitfeld, "Booking the Future," *Washington Post*, July 10, 1998.

43. "Jeff Bezos," *Forbes ASAP*, April 6, 1998, p. 57.

44. Amy Kover, "Never Bet against Michael Dell," *Fortune*, March 29, 1999, p. 208.

45. Toni Mack, "Wireless Warrior," *Forbes*, April 19, 1999.

46. See John Hagel III and Arthur G. Armstrong, *Net Gain*, Boston: Harvard Business School Press, 1997, pp. 41–81.

47. Julie Pitta, "Format Wars," *Forbes*, July 7, 1997, p. 263.

48. James Aley, "The Theory That Made Microsoft," *Fortune*, April 29, 1996, pp. 65–66.

49. Chandrasekaran, *op. cit.*

50. Jack Egan, "Striking It Rich on the Net," *U.S. News & World Report*, January 15, 1996, p. 51.

51. Paul Farhi, "Keeping Creativity within Site," *Washington Business*, May 26, 1997, p. 15.

52. Brent Schlender, "Computing's Next Superpower," *Fortune*, May 12, 1996, p. 101.

53. Wesley R. Iversen, "Leading the Charge to Secure Internet Payments," *Financial Services ONLINE*, January/February 1996.

54. David P. Hamilton, "Sony Heads Down Info Highway and Decides Not to Go It Alone," *Wall Street Journal*, April 14, 1995.

55. Robert D. Hof, "Netspeed at NETSCAPE," *Business Week*, February 10, 1997, p. 81.

56. Shawn Tully, "How Cisco Mastered the Net," *Fortune*, August 17, 1998, p. 210.

57. "Your Next Job," *Business Week*, October 13, 1997, p. 68.

58. *Ibid.*, p. 68.

59. See De'Ann Weimer, "3M: The Heat Is on the Boss," *Business Week*, March 15, 1998, pp. 82–84.

60. "We Push Technology as Fast as We Can," *Business Week*, December 22, 1997, p. 76.

61. Hoff, *op. cit.*, p. 84.

62. Ira Sager, "Cloning the Best of the Valley," *Business Week*, August 25, 1997, p. 147.

63. Sun Tzu, *The Art of War*, New York: Oxford University Press, 1963, p. 84.

64. Chip Bayers, "The Inner Bezos," *Wired*, March 1999, p. 187.

65. "Michael Porter on Competitive Strategy," Harvard Business School Publishing, Video 1988.

66. Heather Green, "Throw out Your Old Business Model," *Business Week E.BIZ*, March 33, 1999, EB23.

67. Edward W. Desmond, "Malone Again," *Fortune*, February 16, 1998, p. 69.

68. "America's Top Technology Companies," *Forbes ASAP*, April 5, 1999, p. 66.

69. "General Electric Company: An Interview with Jack Welch," (395–508), video, Boston: Harvard Business School Publishing, 1994.

70. Virginia I. Postrel, "Resilience vs. Anticipation," *Forbes ASAP*, August 25, 1997, pp. 57–58.

71. Andrew S. Grove, *Only the Paranoid Survive*, New York: Currency, 1996, pp. 5–6.

72. Arie de Geus, *The Living Company*, Boston: Harvard Business School Press, 1997, p. 48.

73. *Ibid.*, p. 36.

74. Joseph R. Garber, "What If . . . ?" *Forbes*, November 2, 1998, p. 76.

75. Michael Moeller, et al. "Remaking Microsoft," *Business Week*, May 17, 1999, p. 106.

76. Russell Mitchell and Judith H. Dobrzynski, "Jack Welch: How Good a Manager," *Business Week*, December 14, 1987, p. 94.

77. "General Electric: Reg Jones and Jack Welch," Boston: Harvard Business School, 1991, case # 9-391-144, p. 11.

78. Andrew S. Grove, *Only the Paranoid Survive*, New York: Currency, 1996, p. 140.

79. *Ibid.*

80. *Ibid.*

81. Youssef M. Ibrahim, "Daimler-Chrysler Merger Showed the Importance of Being Persuasive," *New York Times*, May 26, 1999.

82. Edward O. Welles, "Why Every Company Needs a Story," *INC.*, May 1996, p. 70.

83. Andy Serwer, "Michael Dell Rocks," *Fortune*, May 11, 1998, p. 70.

84. Hof, "Jeff Bezos," p. 137.

85. Gary Hamel and C. K. Prahalad, *Competing for the Future*, Boston: Harvard Business School Press, 1994, pp. 128–29.

86. Thomas A. Stewart, "3M Fights Back," *Fortune*, February 5, 1996, p. 99.

87. Melanie Warner, "How to Make the CEO Buy Your Idea," *Fortune*, December 11, 1995, p. 210.

88. Bill Birchard, "Closing the Strategy Gap," *CFO*, October 1996, p. 29.

89. Edward W. Desmond, "Intuit Online," *Fortune*, April 13, 1998, p. 152.

90. Denyse Tannenbaum, "Lost in Cyberspace," *Virginia Business*, November 1996, p. 60.

91. David W. Chen, "In Fast-Changing Silicon Alley, Companies Adapt or Abort," *New York Times*, February 7, 1997.

92. Steve Hamm, "Bill's Co-Pilot," *Business Week*, September 14, 1998, p. 77.

93. James K. Glassman, "The New Economy: Microsoft," *Washington Post*, October 7, 1997.

94. Richard J. Newman, "Renegades Finish Last," *U.S. News & World Report*, July 28, 1997, p. 35.

95. Steve Prokesch, "Unleashing the Power of Learning," *Harvard Business Review*, September–October 1994, p. 168.

Chapter 7

1. "The 200 Best Small Companies in America," *Forbes*, November 3, 1997, p. 224.

2. "America's Top Technology Companies," *Forbes ASAP*, April 5, 1999, p. 86.

3. Steven E. Prokesch, "Unleashing the Power of Learning," *Harvard Business Review*, September–October 1997, p. 148.

4. Gary McWilliams and Marcia Stepanek, "Taming the Info Monster," *Business Week*, June 22, 1998, p. 170.

5. Terrence E. Deal and Allan A. Kennedy, *Corporate Cultures*, Reading, MA: Addison-Wesley, 1982, p. 21.

6. James K. Glassman, "The New Economy: Microsoft," *Washington Post*, October 7, 1997.

7. "America's Top Technology Companies," *op. cit.*, p. 77.

8. Bill Gates, *The Road Ahead*, New York: Penguin Books, 1996 pp. 208–9.

9. Andrew S. Grove, *Only the Paranoid Survive*, New York: Currency, 1996, p. 130.

10. Julie Bick, "Running a Business . . . Microsoft Style," *Hemispheres*, September 1997, p. 46.

11. *Ibid.*

12. Arie de Geus, *The Living Company*, Boston: Harvard Business School Press, 1997, p. 135.

13. Noel Tichy and Strattford Sherman, "Jack Welch's Lessons for Success," *Fortune*, January 25, 1993, p. 89.

14. Thomas A. Stewart, "3M Fights Back," *Fortune*, February 5, 1996, p. 96.

15. Glenn Rifkin, "Nothing But Net," *Fast Company*, June–July, 1996, p. 124.

16. Tichy and Sherman, *op. cit.*, p. 88.

17. Jack Welch, "Competitiveness from Within," speech to GE employees in 1985.

18. William H. Crookston, "More Than Intuition," *USC Business*, Summer 1996, p. 51.

19. Robert McGarvey, "Tomorrow Land," *Entrepreneur*, February 1996, pp. 137–38.

20. Stuart Kauffman, *At Home in the Universe*, New York: Oxford University Press, 1995, pp. 180–81.

21. Andrew S. Grove, "Is the Internet Overhyped?" *Forbes*, September 23, 1996, p. 116.

22. Jack Egan, "Striking It Rich on the Net," *U.S. News & World Report*, January 15, 1996, p. 51.

23. *Our Story So Far*, St. Paul, MN: Minnesota Mining & Manufacturing Company, 1977, p. 70.

24. Ira Sager, "Cloning the Best of the Valley," *Business Week*, August 25, 1997, p. 146.

25. Lewis W. Lehr, "The Care and Flourishing of Entrepreneurs at 3M," *Directors and Boards*, Winter 1986, p. 20.

26. Gates, *op. cit.*, p. 70.

27. "The Mass Production of Ideas and Other Impossibilities," *The Economist*, March 18, 1995, p. 72.

28. Michelle Conlin, "The Truth," *Forbes*, February 10, 1997, p. 20.

29. "General Electric: Jack Welch's Second Wave (A)," Boston: MA, Harvard Business School, case #9-391-248, p. 11.

30. Seth Lubove, "It Ain't Broke, but Fix It Anyway," *Forbes*, August 1, 1994, p. 58.

31. John A. Byrne, "The Corporation of the Future," *Business Week*, August 31, 1998, p. 106

32. Alan M. Weber, "What's So New about the New Economy?" *Harvard Business Review*, January–February 1993, p. 41.

33. Tichy and Sherman, *op. cit.*, p. 92.

34. Robert Levering and Milton Moskowitz, *The 100 Best Companies to Work For in America*, New York: Doubleday, 1993, p. xiii.

35. Thomas A. Stewart, "Brain Power," *Fortune*, March 17, 1997, p. 110.

36. *Ibid.*

37. Andy Reinhardt, et al., "What Matters Is How Smart You Are," *Business Week*, August 25, 1997, p. 72.

38. Justin Blum and Stephanie Stoughton, "WorldCom Plans Complex on Grade Scale," *Washington Post*, April 11, 1998.

39. General Electric Company, *1998 Annual Report*, Fairfield, CT, 1999, p. 6.

Chapter 8

1. "General Electric—Jack Welch," video (886-529), Boston: Harvard Business School Publishing, 1986.

2. Regis McKenna, *Real Time*, Boston: Harvard Business School Press, 1997, p. 11.

3. Stuart Kauffman, *At Home in the Universe*, New York: Oxford University Press, 1995, p. 26 and p. 91.

4. *Ibid.* p. 223.

5. Scott Woolley, "Brain Drain," *Forbes*, July 27, 1998, p. 44.

6. Farrell Kramer, "GE's Welch: America's Most Sought-After CEO," *Investor's Business Daily*, February 18, 1993.

7. Clayton M. Christensen, *The Innovator's Dilemma: When New Technologies Cause Great Firms to Fail*, Boston: Harvard Business Review, 1997, p. 125.

8. William Drozdiak, "Germany's Media Empire," *Washington Post*, May 13, 1998.

9. Edward W. Desmond, "Intuit Online," *Fortune*, April 13, 1998, p. 152.

10. Richard Teitelbaum, "The Wal-Mart of Wall Street," *Fortune*, October 13, 1997, pp. 128–130.

11. Kauffman, *op. cit.*, p. 247.

12. Richard J. Newman, "Renegades Finish Last," *U.S. News & World Report*, July 28, 1997, p. 35.

13. Kauffman, *op. cit.*, p. 266.

14. John Curran, "GE CAPITAL: Jack Welch's Secret Weapon," *Fortune*, November 10, 1997, p. 124.

15. Michael Moeller and Kathy Rebello, "Visionary-in-Chief," *Business Week*, May 17, 1999, p. 116.

16. Melanie Warner, "How to Make the CEO Buy Your Idea," *Fortune*, December 11, 1995, p. 210.

17. "General Electric: Jack Welch's Second Wave (A)," Boston: Harvard Business School, case # 9-391-248, p. 4.

18. "SternCEOseries," *Sternbusiness*, Fall 1995, p. 22.

19. Bill Gates, *The Road Ahead*, New York: Penguin Books, 1996, p. 176.

20. David W. Chen, "In Fast-Changing Silicon Alley, Companies Adapt or Abort," *New York Times*, February 7, 1997.

21. Alan Deutschman, "The Managing Wisdom of High-Tech Superstars," *Fortune*, October 17, 1994, p. 197.

22. This account of Oticon is taken from Polly Labarre, "This Organization Is Disorganization," *Fast Company*, June–July 1996, pp. 77–83.

23. *Ibid.*

24. David H. Freedman, "Corps Values," *Inc.*, April 1988, p. 59.

25. Thomas A. Stewart, "Planning a Career in a World without Managers," *Fortune*, March 20, 1995, p. 73.

26. Diana Kunde, "For Those Riding Technology's Wave, a New Managerial Style," *Washington Post*, February 9, 1997.

27. Steve Hamm, et al., "Microsoft Refines Its Net Game," *Business Week*, September 8, 1997, p. 130.

28. Brent Schlender, "Computing's Next Superpower," *Fortune*, May 12, 1996, p. 98.

29. Brent Schlender, "The Real Road Ahead," *Fortune*, October 25, 1999, p. 139.

30. Andrew Kupfer, "The Real King of the Internet," *Fortune*, September 7, 1998, p. 86.

31. Schlender, *op. cit.*, p. 98.

32. Kupfer, *op. cit.*, p. 86.

33. Elizabeth Corcoran, "Inside Microsoft: An Edgy, Driven World," *Washington Post*, October 18, 1998.

34. Kauffman, *op. cit.*, pp. 267–68.

35. *Ibid.*

36. Gates, *op. cit.*, pp. 208–9.

37. *Ibid.*

38. *Our Story So Far*, St. Paul, MN: Minnesota Mining & Manufacturing Company, 1977, pp. 12–13.

39. *Ibid.*, p. 13.

40. Labarre, op. cit.

41. Stephen Baker, et al., "Nokia," *Business Week*, August 10, 1998, p. 57.

42. Andrew S. Grove, "Is the Internet Overhyped?" *Forbes*, September 23, 1996, p. 117.

43. "Microsoft Confirms It Will Reorganize Its Divisions," *Boston Globe*, March 14, 1999.

44. *Our Story So Far*, *op. cit.*, p. 126.

45. Arie de Geus, *The Living Company*, Boston: Harvard Business School Press, 1997, p. 145.

46. *Ibid.*, p. 147.

Chapter 9

1. Kara Swisher, "The Two Grown-Ups behind Yahoo!'s Surge," *Wall Street Journal*, April 10, 1998.

2. Rick Tetzeli, "What It's Really Like to be Marc Andreessen," *Fortune*, December 9, 1996, p. 156.

3. Frank Maley, "Cybervisionaries," *Virginia Business*, January 1998, p. 15.

4. Stuart Kauffman, *At Home in the Universe*, New York: Oxford University Press, 1995, p. 149.

5. Clayton Christensen, *The Innovator's Dilemma: When New Technologies Cause Great Firms to Fail*, Boston: Harvard Business Review, 1997. p. 211.

6. David S. Hilzenrath, "Change Is Good, They Bet," *Washington Post*, October 21, 1996.

7. Bill Gates, *The Road Ahead*, New York: Penguin Books, 1996, p. 15.

8. *Ibid.*, pp. 15–17.

9. David Kirkpatrick, "No Big Deal," *Fortune*, March 2, 1998, p. 190.

10. "A Conversation with Roberto Goizveta and Jack Welch," *Fortune*, December 11, 1995, p. 102.

11. John Curran, "GE CAPITAL: Jack Welch's Secret Weapon," *Fortune*, November 10, 1997, p. 134.

12. Elizabeth Corcoran "Reinventing Intel," *Forbes*, May 3, 1999, p. 155.

13. Andrew S. Grove, *Only the Paranoid Survive*, New York: Currency, 1996, p. 151.

14. Peter Burrows and Ira Sager, "Can Compaq Catch Up?" *Business Week*, May 3, 1999, p. 162.

15. Rich Karlgaard, "Present at the Creation," *Forbes*, July 7, 1997, p. 278.

16. Susan Greco, "Just Say No," *Inc.*, April 1996, pp. 50–55.

17. Eric Nee, "Surf's Up," *Forbes*, July 27, 1998, p. 110.

18. Kauffman, *op. cit.*, p. 269.

19. Linda Himelstein, et al., "The Great Hunt for Hot Ideas," *Business Week*, August 25, 1997, p. 107.

20. "Easy Way Out," *The Economist*, February 20, 1999, p. 22.

21. Marc Gunther, "How GE Made NBC No. 1," *Fortune*, February 3, 1997, p. 94.

22. Bill Gates, *The Road Ahead*, New York: Penguin Books, 1996, p. 48.

23. Andy Reinhardt, et al., "What Matters Is How Smart You Are," *Business Week*, August 25, 1997, p. 72.

24. Chip Bayers, "The Inner Bezos," *Wired*, March 1999, p. 174.

25. Gates, *op. cit.*, p. 48.

26. *Ibid.*, p. 45.

27. Andy Serwer, "Michael Dell Rocks," *Fortune*, May 11, 1998, p. 62.

28. Christensen, *op. cit.*, p. 159.

29. Rich Karlgaard, *op. cit.*, p. 280.

30. "The Post-It Note: An Entrepreneurial Success," *SAM Advanced Management Journal*, Summer 1987, p. 7.

31. Akio Morita, *Made in Japan: Akio Morita and Sony*, New York: Signet, 1986, p. 58.

32. Roger O. Crockett and Peter Elstrom, "How Motorola Lost Its Way," *Business Week*, May 4, 1998.

33. Paul Farhi, "Keeping Creativity within Site," *Washington Business*, May 26, 1997, p. 15.

34. Jay Akasie, "Imagine, No Inventory," *Forbes*, November 17, 1997, p. 145.

35. Kathy Rebello, "A Literary Hangout—Without the Latté," *Business Week*, September 12, 1996, p. 106.

36. "With Jeff Bezos," *Catalogue Age*, June 1996, p. 59.

37. Marcia Stepanek, "You'll Wanna Hold Their Hands," *Business Week E.BIZ*, March 33, 1999, EB30.

38. Bob Tedeschi, "Good Web Site Design Can Lead to Healthy Sales," *New York Times,* August 30, 1999.

39. Janice Maloney, "Yahoo!" *Fortune*, December 9, 1996, pp. 175–76.

40. Paul Farhi, "Keeping Creativity within Site," *Washington Business*, May 26, 1997, p. 15.

41. Elizabeth Berstein, "Amazon.com's Amazing Allure," *Publishers Weekly*, November 4, 1996, p. 26.

42. Patrick Wexler, "Amazon Pays Fee for Book Buying Referrals," *Publishers Weekly*, August 26, 1996, p. 29.

43. "An Exultation of Books," *The New Yorker*, December 23, 1996, p. 71.

44. Charles Waltner, "Bookseller Focuses on e-mail to Move Product," *Advertising Age*, June 3, 1996, p. 40.

45. William H. Cookston, "More Than Intuition," *USC Business*, Summer 1996, p. 51.

46. Jared Sandberg, "Making the Sale," *Wall Street Journal*, June 17, 1996.

47. "America's Top Technology Companies," *Forbes ASAP*, April 15, 1999, p. 86.

48. Randall Lane, "Pampering the Customers, Pampering the Employees," *Forbes 400*, October 1996, p. 80.

49. John A. Byrne, "The Corporation of the Future," *Business Week*, August 31, 1998, p. 106.

50. William H. Crookston, "More than Intuition," *USC Business*, Summer 1996, p. 53.

51. Geoff Baum, "John Chambers," *Forbes ASAP*, February 23, 1998, p. 80.

52. Sue Shellenbarger, "More Managers Find a Happy Staff Leads to Happy Customers," *Wall Street Journal*, December 23, 1998.

53. Glenn Rifkin, "Nothing but Net," *Fast Company*, June–July 1996, pp. 124–26.

54. Part of the value of game theory is to aid in thinking through options that might avoid destructive competition. See Adam M. Brandenburger and Barry J. Nalebuff, "The Right Game: Use Game Theory to Shape Strategy," *Harvard Business Review*, July–August 1995, pp. 57–71.

55. Kara Swisher, "A Web Pioneer Does a Delicate Dance with Microsoft," *Wall Street Journal*, February 12, 1998.

56. Andrew S. Grove, "Is the Internet Overhyped?" *Forbes*, September 23, 1996, pp. 116–17.

57. Elizabeth Corcoran, "Sun's Lonely Battle," *Washington Post*, February 8, 1998.

58. Larry King, "People: News & Views," *USA Today*, February 23, 1998.

59. Kauffman, *op. cit.*, p. 211.

Chapter 10

1. *Our Story So Far*, St. Paul, MN: Minnesota Mining and Manufacturing Company, 1977, p. 28.

2. Thomas A. Stewart, "3M Fights Back," *Fortune*, February 5, 1996, pp. 94–99.

3. Andrew S. Grove, *Only the Paranoid Survive*, New York: Currency, 1996, p. 162.

4. John P. Kotter, "What Effective General Managers Really Do," *Harvard Business Review*, November–December 1982, p. 161.

5. Alan Deutschman, "The Managing Wisdom of High-Tech Superstars," *Fortune*, October 17, 1994, p. 197.

6. Youssef M. Ibrahim, "Daimler-Chrysler Merger Showed the Imporance of Being Persuasive," *New York Times*, May 26, 1999.

7. *Ibid.*, p. 163.

8. Robert Lenzner and Stephen S. Johnson, "Seeing Things as They Really Are," *Forbes*, March 10, 1997, p. 125.

9. Alan Deutschman, "The Managing Wisdom," *op. cit.* p. 198.

10. Tichy and Sherman, "Jack Welch's Lessons for Success," *Fortune*, January 25, 1993, p. 93.

11. *Ibid.*, p. 160.

12. General Electric Company, *1995 Annual Report*, p. 4.

13. Thomas Martin, "Jack Welch Lets Fly" *Fortune*, May 29, 1995, p. 145.

14. General Electric Company, *1993 Annual Report*, p. 5.

15. Martin, "Jack Welch Lets Fly" *op. cit.*, p. 145.

16. Shawn Tully, "Stretch Targets," *Fortune*, November 14, 1994, p. 145.

17. See Gary Hamel, "Strategy as Revolution," *Harvard Business Review*, July–August 1996, pp. 69–82 for a discussion of how to increase a company's chances of discovering revolutionary strategies.

18. Tichy and Sherman, *op. cit.*, p. 88.

19. Marc Gunther, "The Internet Is Mr. Case's Neighborhood," *Fortune*, March 30, 1998, p. 71.

20. "The Mass Production of Ideas and Other Impossibilities," *The Economist*, March 18, 1995, p. 72.

21. Joanne Ang, "Didn't Post-it Happen by a Mistake?" *Productivity Digest*, February 1996, p. 5.

22. Marc Gunther, "How GE Made NBC No. 1," *Fortune*, February 3, 1997, p. 94.

23. Hans H. Hinterbuber and Wolfgang Popp, "Are You a Strategist or Just a Manager?" *Harvard Business Review*, January–February 1992, p. 105.

24. Thomas A. Stewart, "3M Fights Back," *Fortune*, February 5, 1996, p. 99.

25. Bob Starzynski, "Proxicom CEO Fosters 'Ambitious Spirit' among Staff," *Washington Business Journal*, July 25–31, 1997, p. 17.

26. William H. Crookston, "More Than Intuition," *USC Business*, Summer 1996, p. 52.

27. Elizabeth Corcoran, "The Trials of a High-Tech Turnaround Man," *Washington Post*, 1998.

28. John A. Byrne, "The Corporation of the Future," *Business Week*, August 31, 1998, p. 106.

29. Andrew Kupfer, "The Real King of the Internet," *Fortune*, September 7, 1998, p. 88.

30. John A. Byrne, "Strategic Planning," *Business Week*, August 26, 1996, p. 50.

31. "Fast Times at General Electric," *CFO*, June 1995, p. 33.

32. Bill Birchard, "Making IT Count," *CFO*, October 1995, p. 44.

33. "Fast Times at General Electric," *op. cit.*

34. Carrie Shook, "Leader, Not Boss," *Forbes*, December 1, 1997, p. 54.

35. Mike Brown, "We're Microsoft, We Don't Need IC," *Forbes ASAP*, April 7, 1997, p. 45.

36. *Ibid.*

37. Tichy and Sherman, *op. cit.*, pp. 88–89.

38. Stewart, *op. cit.*, p. 99.

39. Michelle Conlin, "The Truth," *Forbes*, February 10, 1997, p. 20.

40. Rick Tetzeli, "What It's Really Like to Be Marc Andreessen," *Fortune*, December 9, 1996, p. 154.

41. Hans Fantel, "Does Visionary Business Call for a Corporate Sage?" *New York Times*, June 17, 1990.

42. Russell Mitchell and Judith H. Dobrzynski, "Jack Welch: How Good a Manager," *Business Week*, December 14, 1987, p. 94.

43. Grove, *op. cit.*, p. 135.

44. Gary Hamel and C. K. Prahalad, *Competing for the Future*, Boston: Harvard Business School Press, 1994, p. 4.

45. Tichy and Sherman, *op. cit.*, p. 88.

46. Linda Grant, "Why FedEx Is Flying High," *Fortune*, November 10, 1997, p. 156.

47. "King of the Magic Kingdom," *60 Minutes*, CBS Television.

48. Tichy and Sherman, *op. cit.*, p. 88.

49. Seth Schiesel, "Marines Polish Command Skills, as the Traders Become Mentors," *New York Times*, December 16, 1996.

50. David Freedman, "Corps Values," *Inc.*, April 1998.

51. *Ibid.*

52. George Donnelly, "New @ttitude," *CFO*, June 1999, p. 45.

53. Robert D. Hof, "Netspeed at NETSCAPE," *Business Week*, February 10, 1997, p. 84.

54. Andy Reinhardt, et al., "Intel," *Business Week*, December 22, 1997, p. 73.

55. Rajiv Chandrasekaran, "Netscape's Boy Wonder Looks beyond the Browser," *Washington Post*, March 25, 1997.

56. Stuart Kauffman, *At Home in the Universe*, New York: Oxford University Press, 1995, pp. 248–49.

57. M. Mitchell Waldrop, *Complexity: The Emerging Science at the Edge of Order and Chaos*, New York: Touchstone Books, 1993, p. 331.

58. Lixandra Urresta, "The Incredible, Profitable Career of Andy Grove," *Fortune*, April 27, 1998, p. 34.

59. Geoff Baum, "John Chambers," *Forbes ASAP*, February 23, 1998, p. 80.

60. Jennifer Reingold and John A. Byrne, "The Top 20 Heads to Hunt," *Business Week*, August 11, 1997, p. 69.

61. John A. Byrne, et al., "Wanted: A Few Good CEOs," *Business Week*, August 11, 1997, p. 66.

62. Thomas A. Stewart, "Why Leadership Matters," *Fortune*, March 2, 1998, p. 80.

63. Seth Lubove, "It Ain't Broke, but Fix It Anyway," *Forbes*, August 1, 1994, p. 58.

64. Brent Schlender, "The New Man inside Intel," *Fortune*, May 11, 1998, p. 161.

65. David P. Hamilton and John Lippman, "Sony's Idea Finds Winning Path: Reject Tired Thinking," *Wall Street Journal*, May 14, 1997.

66. Alex Taylor III, "Revolution at Daimler-Benz," *Fortune*, November 10, 1997, p. 144.

67. Kupfer, *op. cit.*, p. 92.

68. Steve Lohr, "New Chief at Hewlett-Packard Prefers to Set Her Own Precedents," *New York Times,* July 23, 1999.

69. Andrew S. Grove, *Only the Paranoid Survive*, New York: Currency, 1996, p. 132.

70. Dan Debicella, "Cisco CEO Delivers Vision of 'Second Industrial Revolution,'" *The HARBUS*, February 16, 1999.

71. "America's Top Technology Companies," *Forbes ASAP*, April 5, 1999, p. 66.

72. "Revenge of the Nerds," *60 Minutes*, CBS Television.

73. Jack Egan, "Striking It Rich on the Net," *U.S. News & World Report*, January 15, 1996, p. 51.

74. Nikhil Deogun, "A Tough Bank Boss Takes on Computers, with Real Trepidation," *Wall Street Journal*, July 25, 1996.

75. "A Conversation with Roberto Goizueta and Jack Welch," *Fortune*, December 11, 1995, p. 98.

76. *Ibid.*, p. 102.

77. William M. Carley, "To Keep GE's Profits Rising, Welch Pushes Quality-Control Plan," *Wall Street Journal*, January 13, 1997.

78. Tim Smart, "GE's Welch: 'Fighting Like Hell to Be No 1,'" *Business Week*, July 8, 1996, p. 48.

79. Frank Swoboda, "Talking Management with Chairman Welch," *Washington Post*, March 23, 1997.

80. Martin, "Jack Welch Lets Fly," *op. cit.*, p. 146.

Postscript

1. "Supersonic Race: Richard Noble's November 1997 Update," Web site: www.thrustssc.com.

2. "Brits Break Sound Barrier, Set Speed Record," ESPN Sportszone, http://espn.go.com/car/news/971015/00414304.html.

Index